Atrocity Labelling

Atrocity Labelling

From Crimes Against Humanity to Genocide Studies

Markus P. Beham

BLOOMSBURY ACADEMIC
LONDON • NEW YORK • OXFORD • NEW DELHI • SYDNEY

BLOOMSBURY ACADEMIC
Bloomsbury Publishing Plc
50 Bedford Square, London, WC1B 3DP, UK
1385 Broadway, New York, NY 10018, USA
29 Earlsfort Terrace, Dublin 2, Ireland

BLOOMSBURY, BLOOMSBURY ACADEMIC and the Diana logo are trademarks of Bloomsbury Publishing Plc

First published in Great Britain 2023

Series design by Adriana Brioso

A catalogue record for this book is available from the British Library.

A catalog record for this book is available from the Library of Congress.

ISBN: HB: 978-0-7556-1753-1
ePDF: 978-0-7556-1755-5
eBook: 978-0-7556-1754-8

Typeset by Deanta Global Publishing Services, Chennai, India

In gratitude to both of my grandfathers,
Harold Bernard Harper (1926–1995)
and Alois Beham (1916–1991),
for their aspirations;
and to my parents for their encouragement to follow these.

The chapters on German South-West Africa and the Belgian Congo
I dedicate specifically to the loving memory of
Wendy Patricia Tinson (1954–2016)
for instilling in me an imagination of Africa.

Contents

List of tables ix
Preface x
Foreword xiv

1 The word 1
1.1 Genocide Studies 5
1.2 Atrocity labelling 10
1.3 This book 13

2 Conceptualizing atrocities 15
2.1 Early origins and first attempts 15
2.2 Raphaël Lemkin and genocide 20
2.3 Judgement at Nuremberg 23
2.4 The United Nations and the Genocide Convention 27
2.5 Legacy and renaissance 31
2.6 Siamese twins, separated at birth 37
2.7 War crimes, ethnic cleansing 48

3 Labelling atrocities 49
3.1 Motivations 51
3.1.1 Symbolic capital and appropriation 53
3.1.2 Activism and accusation 55
3.2 Labels 57
3.2.1 Full transplant 58
3.2.2 Adaptation 61
3.2.3 Vulgarization 66
3.3 Consequences 67
3.3.1 Dilution 68
3.3.2 Humanitarian inertia 69
3.3.3 Reimagination 71

4 Colonialism, transformation and the process of labelling 73
4.1 Belgian rubber exploitation in the Congo 80
4.1.1 Course of events 80
4.1.2 Numbers 83
4.1.3 Genocide 84
4.1.4 Holocaust 87
4.1.5 Assessment 89
4.2 The Herero and the Nama in German South-West Africa 90
4.2.1 Course of events 90
4.2.2 Numbers 93
4.2.3 Genocide 95
4.2.4 Holocaust 101
4.2.5 Assessment 105
4.3 The Armenians in Asia Minor 106
4.3.1 Course of events 106
4.3.2 Numbers 109
4.3.3 Genocide 114
4.3.4 Holocaust 124
4.3.5 Assessment 129
4.4 The famine in Ukraine between 1932 and 1933 129
4.4.1 Course of events 129
4.4.2 Numbers 133
4.4.3 Genocide 136
4.4.4 Holocaust 149
4.4.5 Assessment 152

5 Conclusion 153

Table of documents 159
Table of cases 163
Bibliography 165
Index 191

Tables

4.1 Death Toll Estimates – Leopold's Reign (from High to Low) 84
4.2 Death Toll Estimates – 1904–8 (from High to Low) 94
4.3 Death Toll Estimates – 1915 Genocide (from High to Low) 112
4.4 Death Toll Estimates – 1894–6 Massacres (from High to Low) 113
4.5 Death Toll Estimates – 1909 Massacres (from High to Low) 114
4.6 Death Toll Estimates – Holodomor (from High to Low) 135

Preface

This book is the result of a wider preoccupation with the intersection between international law and historiography. It was further encouraged by the widening – though regrettably still largely intradisciplinary[1] – interest of both disciplines in each other.

The original impetus came through a course on ethnic cleansing in the twentieth century held by Arnold Suppan – who also agreed to serve as a reviewer of the doctoral thesis that is the basis for this book – at the Department of East European History of the University of Vienna. Following the advice of my master's thesis supervisor in history, Oliver Jens Schmitt, to diversify after the previously medievalist focus of my work, I set out to explore histories of colonialism and the great transformations of the long nineteenth century reaching into the interwar years. Around that same time, I had finished my law degree and was able to secure a position at the Department of European, International and Comparative Law at the University of Vienna, which came with the need to refocus my academic trajectory on law.

Originally devised as a project for my doctoral thesis in law on international criminal law and the responsibility to protect, my interest in legal philosophy and theory tugged me further and further away from the issues of substantive law to the underlying discourse. More and more, my interest in narrative and terminology grew. I soon found myself getting lost in books of different disciplines, from history to sociology, from political science to international relations that all dealt with the same subject but from different angles: genocide, crimes against humanity, war crimes and ethnic cleansing. What had started off as an attempt to write an exposé for a legal thesis gradually developed into an unintentional discourse analysis.

[1] See Markus P. Beham, 'Bardo Fassbender and Anne Peters (Eds.), Oxford Handbook of the History of International Law (Oxford University Press 2012)' (2013) 18 Austrian Review of International and European Law 392.

Taking recourse to the syllabus and bibliography of Arnold Suppan's course, I started to look into how historians had been using legal terminology and whether it was really the legal parameters that made them pass 'judgement' on events. First suspicions and assumptions slowly fell into abstract patterns and allowed for the creation of a methodology to explore their validity. Comparative legal methodology helped to shape the main question.

However, a generous grant by the University of Vienna for the completion of a doctoral degree in law required me to set aside this first sketch before picking it up again after penning down a doctoral thesis in law.[2] Hopefully, perspective and scope were benefitted by this imposed abstinence from the historian's work.

In this regard, I would like to greatly thank my supervisor, Christoph Augustynowicz, for his patience and encouragement to continue the project of a doctoral thesis in history. He continuously, wholeheartedly and understandingly supported each and every step of my career, gently calling deadlines, all the way critically commenting and countering my methodology. His unique down-to-earth, out-of-the-box approach to teaching history and historiography analysis has greatly shaped my research agenda way beyond this book.

Even throughout my historian's hiatus, I was able to explore and expand on the ideas feeding into the research presented here at conferences and workshops. Most importantly, on the very kind invitation by Marija Wakounig of the University of Vienna, discrete parts of the underlying doctoral thesis were presented at the annual meetings of the Centres for Austrian Studies (the 'Austrian Centres') in Vienna (2012) and Leiden (2013) before publication in the respective conference volumes.[3] Both Arnold Suppan and Ruth Fine of the Hebrew University of Jerusalem provided valuable comments. Without the critical remarks by Gary Cohen of the

2 Markus P Beham, *State Interest and the Sources of International Law. Doctrine, Morality, and Non-Treaty Law* (Routledge 2018).

3 See Markus P. Beham, '"Borrowed" Concepts: The Pitfalls of "Atrocity Labelling" in Contemporary Historiography' in Markus P. Beham and Marija Wakounig (eds), *Transgressing Boundaries: Humanities in Flux* (Lit Verlag 2013); Markus P. Beham, 'Genocide and Crimes Against Humanity: Siamese Twins or Separated at Birth?' in Markus P. Beham and Marija Wakounig (eds), *Mind and Memory in Discourse: Critical Concepts and Constructions* (Lit Verlag 2014).

University of Minnesota, the case study on the 'Holodomor' would also not exist in its present form.

Aspects related to collective memory were presented at the XVII International Conference of Young Scholars at the University of Economics in Prague in May 2013 and published in the corresponding conference volume.[4] The ideas of the main research question were further discussed at the workshop 'Genocide Studies: Sound, Image, Archive' organized by Ian Biddle and Beate Müller at the University of Newcastle in November 2013. Finally, an advanced version of the thesis was presented at the Doctoral Colloquium, supervised by Marija Wakounig at the University of Vienna in June 2016.

An invitation by the editors of the *Austrian Review of International and European Law* to publish an article on the occasion of the seventieth anniversary of the Genocide Convention allowed for consolidation and revision of parts of the doctoral thesis.[5] A symposium on 'The UN Convention on the Prevention and Punishment of the Crime of Genocide (1948)' at the Charles University, Prague, on 15 October 2020 allowed for discussion of the process of atrocity labelling and awaits publication in a conference volume.

The basis of this book is my doctoral thesis in history at the Department of East European History of the University of Vienna. All chapters have been subject to – in some sections quite extensive – revision during the completion of the manuscript for publication, allowing for the inclusion of additional literature and source material. Thanks go to the three anonymous peer-reviewers and the reviewer of the final manuscript for their time and valuable suggestions.

As always, there is an infinite list of colleagues and friends, and more often both, that I must thank for intellectual exchanges, advice, and support. An enumerative list would prove impossible. The invaluable help of Alina Alma, Cecilie Reckhorn and Katharina Schötta in reviewing the tables of documents and cases as well as the bibliography is greatly appreciated, as is the assistance of Manuel Merz in compiling the index. Marie-Lidvine and Janet Beham kindly offered a fresh pair of eyes during the different stages of proofreading.

4 Markus P. Beham, 'Genocide and Collective Memory in International Relations' in Nicolas Maslowski (ed.), *Collective Memory and International Relations. Conference Proceedings* (TROAS 2013).

5 Markus P Beham, 'The 1948 Genocide Convention: Origins, Impact, Legacy' (2018) 23 Austrian Review of International and European Law 85.

At Bloomsbury, working with Nayiri Kendir and Atifa Jiwa proved a thoroughly constructive and pleasant experience that deserves recognition beyond the obligatory words of gratitude usually given to the publishers in a preface. Thanks must finally go to Vishnu Prasad for his diligent work and responsiveness throughout the copy editing process.

Once more, I thank Lidi for all her patience and attentiveness.

Foreword

This book is both a necessary and welcome addition for two reasons: first, there is an inflationary use of the term 'genocide' in contemporary writing, transferring the term to areas of life that have nothing at all to do with the intentional mass killing of human beings. Second, in comparing the many atrocities of the twentieth century – from the Ottoman genocide of the Armenians to the mass crimes committed by the Serbian military against Bosnian Muslim men in Srebrenica in 1995 – it is imperative to sharpen terminology.

Beham portrays both the relevant 'Genocide Studies' and the development of the term 'genocide' via the Treaty of Versailles (1919) and the 'Charter of the International Military Tribunal' of August 1945 that defined exactly what the International Military Tribunal in Nuremberg should consider 'Crimes against Humanity'. Similar provisions were made a year later for the Military Tribunal in Tokyo. The International Criminal Tribunals for the former Yugoslavia and for Rwanda in the 1990s provided further clarification. These definitions under international law were based on the fundamental studies of the Polish international legal scholar Raphaël Lemkin, who published his seminal work 'Axis Rule in Occupied Europe' in Washington, DC, in 1944. Lemkin's suggestions were eventually incorporated into the United Nations Genocide Convention, adopted by the General Assembly in 1948.

In Chapter 4, Beham uses four case studies as examples to illustrate the difficulty of retrospectively applying the term 'genocide':

To the exploitation of rubber in the Belgian Congo, which in just a few decades cost the lives of several million people;

To the 'extermination order' issued by German Lieutenant General Trotha against the Herero people in 1904, which cost the lives of tens of thousands of Herero and Nama;

To the Ottoman leadership's deportation order in the spring of 1915 against the Armenians in Eastern Anatolia, which resulted in the violent deaths of over a million men, women and children;

And to the catastrophic famine orchestrated by Stalin ('Holodomor') in Ukraine and Southern Russia in 1932–3 with several million deaths, described by Lemkin himself as 'the classic example of Soviet genocide'.

The reader may easily compare the four case studies following the uniform structure of each section: 'Course of events', 'Numbers', 'Genocide', 'Holocaust' and 'Assessment'. Beham depicts the different appraisals by international historiography and through his analysis emphasizes the importance of Article II of the Genocide Convention, which unequivocally speaks of 'the intent to destroy, in whole or in part, a national, ethnic, racial, or religious group'.

Beham's research will surely invite further comparative studies into the history of human violence.

Em. Univ. Prof. Dr.phil. Arnold Suppan
Vice president of the Austrian Academy of Sciences

1

The word

'Genocide'. A word laying bare the horrors of industrialized killing, loss of home and division of families.[1] It is 'the darkest word in the human language'.[2] A word that targets its perpetrators across jurisdictions.[3] It is 'a word that evokes immediate moral outrage'.[4] A word so powerful that it may trigger the use of force by states.[5] It is 'the "gold standard" of humanitarian emergencies'.[6] A word that stands as a substitute since 1945 for a 'crime without a name',[7]

1 Cf Berel Lang, 'The Concept of Genocide' in A. Dirk Moses (ed), *Genocide. Critical Concepts in Historical Studies. Volume I. The Discipline of Genocide Studies* (Routledge 2010) 115.

2 Gijs M. de Vries, 'Genocide: An Agenda for Action' in Richard G. Hovannisian (ed), *Looking Backward, Moving Forward. Confronting the Armenian Genocide* (Transaction Publishers 2003) 9.

3 For example, § 64(1)(6) Austrian Criminal Code.

4 Alexander Laban Hinton, 'Introduction. Genocide and Anthropology' in Alexander Laban Hinton (ed), *Genocide. An Anthropological Reader* (Blackwell 2002) 2.

5 See United Nations General Assembly Resolution 60/1, '2005 World Summit Outcome', 24 October 2005, A/RES/60/1, 138–9.

6 A. Dirk Moses, 'Raphael Lemkin, Culture, and the Concept of Genocide' in Donald Bloxham and A. Dirk Moses (eds), *The Oxford Handbook of Genocide Studies* (Oxford University Press 2010) 41.

7 Taken from a speech by Winston Churchill of 24 August 1941, the expression a 'crime without a name' has entered the discourse on the genesis of the origin of the term. In the speech, however, while he was emphasizing the extent and brutality of the 'aggressor', any ordinary reading of his speech shows that what Churchill was referring to in this particular passage were war crimes of an extensive scale, committed against combatants rather than the deportation and systematic killing of civilians. Churchill was referring specifically to the killing of Soviet soldiers: 'The Russian Armies and all the peoples of the Russian Republic have rallied to the defence of their hearths and homes. For the first time Nazi blood has flowed in a fearful flood. Certainly a million and a half, perhaps two millions of Nazi cannon-fodder, have bitten the dust of the endless plains of Russia. The tremendous battle rages along nearly two thousand miles of front. The Russians fight with magnificent devotion. Not only that, our generals who have visited the Russian front line report with admiration the efficiency of their military organization and the excellence of their equipment. The aggressor is surprised, startled, staggered. For the first time in his experience mass murder has become unprofitable. He retaliates by the most frightful cruelties. As his armies advance, whole districts are being exterminated. Scores of thousands, literally scores of thousands of executions in cold blood are being perpetrated by the German police troops upon the Russian patriots who defend their native soil. Since the Mongol invasions of Europe in the sixteenth century there has never been methodical, merciless butchery on such a scale or approaching such a scale. And this is but the beginning. Famine and pestilence have yet to follow in the bloody ruts of Hitler's tanks. We are in the presence of a crime without a name.' See Prime Minister Winston Churchill's Broadcast to the World About the Meeting With President Roosevelt, 24 August 1941, <http://www.ibiblio.org/pha/policy/1941/410824a.html>.

for '[i]n the beginning, there was no word'.[8] It has since been recognized as the 'most heinous'[9] and the 'crime of crimes'.[10] A word carrying a maximum prison term of a decade if denied.[11] A word that instils fear of reparations and restitution in revisionist governments and profiteers of past sorrow.[12]

These impacts and effects of the word 'genocide' are not accidental. As Samantha Power recounts in her best-seller *A Problem from Hell*, in 'one of his surviving notebooks, Lemkin' – the lawyer behind the composite neologism 'genocide' – 'scribbled and circled "THE WORD" and drew a line connecting the circle to the phrase, penned firmly, "MORAL JUDGMENT"'.[13]

Inherent in its origins is the political, a trajectory surpassed by the subsequent impact of the word. Devised as a legal concept against the background of the Second World War, the word has become synonymous with the destruction of the European Jews.[14] It carries the full weight of the Holocaust engraved in collective memory as the 'genocide of genocides'.[15]

The term 'genocide' was first included outside the ring of scholarly debate on and off during the Nuremberg trials,[16] then in a United Nations General Assembly resolution[17] and, finally, a multilateral treaty between states,[18] as the international community was still under the impression of 'the shadow

8 Helen Fein, *Accounting for Genocide. National Responses and Jewish Victimization during the Holocaust* (Free Press 1979) 3.

9 Cf the CNN documentary and report by Christiane Amanpour et al., 'Scream Bloody Murder. The World's Most Heinous Crime', 12 January 2009 <http://edition.cnn.com/2008/WORLD/europe/11/20/sbm.overview/index.html#cnnSTCText>.

10 See for an early use of this description Pieter N. Drost, *The Crime of State. Penal Protection for Fundamental Freedoms of Persons and Peoples. Book II. Genocide. United Nations Legislation on International Criminal Law* (AW Sythoff 1959) ii. The phrase was popularized by the ICTR in *Prosecutor v. Jean Kambanda*, Judgement and Sentence of 4 September 1998, Case No. ICTR-97-23-S, para 16.

11 For example, § 3h Austrian Prohibition Act 1947.

12 Cf the recent Polish legislation introducing a statute of limitations for compensation claims related to seized property. See 'Israel Furious as Poland's President Signs Bill to Limit Property Claims' *Reuters* (14 August 2021) <https://www.reuters.com/world/europe/polands-president-signs-bill-limit-ww2-property-restitution-claims-2021-08-14/>.

13 Samantha Power, *A Problem from Hell. America and the Age of Genocide* (Basic Books 2013) 42.

14 See Stig Förster and Gerhard Hirschfeld, 'Einleitung' in Stig Förster and Gerhard Hirschfeld (eds), *Genozid in der modernen Geschichte* (Lit Verlag 1999) 5; Jürgen Zimmerer, 'Kolonialer Genozid? Vom Nutzen und Nachteil einer historischen Kategorie für eine Globalgeschichte des Völkermordes' in Vivianne Berg and others (eds), *Enteignet – Vertrieben – Ermordet. Beiträge zur Genozidforschung* (Chronos 2004) 110. Cf also A. Dirk Moses, 'Genocide and Settler Society in Australian History' in A. Dirk Moses (ed.), *Genocide and Settler Society. Frontier Violence and Stolen Indigenous Children in Australian History* (Berghahn Books 2004) 23.

15 Mark Levene, *Genocide in the Age of the Nation-State. Volume I: The Meaning of Genocide* (I.B. Tauris 2005) 1.

16 See p. 27.

17 See p. 31.

18 See p. 31.

of Auschwitz'[19] and 'the shadow of the Holocaust',[20] making the term 'at once universally known and widely invoked'[21] as an expression of 'collective memory'.[22] The experience is 'nothing less than a discursive explosion'.[23] The knowledge of the event allows for an understanding of the term.[24]

In the greater scheme of things, the term is still quite new. But considering that the organized destruction of civilian population has been suggested as one of the identifying phenomena of the twentieth century,[25] its quick rise to 'success' may not seem surprising. States, peoples, indigenous populations, minorities, groups, politicians, NGOs, activists and scholars have all come to recognize its power in the public discourse.[26] It creates 'a new site of collective identification that recounts the historical relationship between injury, state power, and group identity'.[27] Yet, it does not constitute the only word or phrase created to grasp or conceptualize mass atrocities: crimes against humanity, war crimes, ethnic cleansing, pogrom, massacre, extermination and annihilation. But none of these alternatives offer the same immediate representation, as does the term 'genocide'.

19 Robert Gellately and Ben Kiernan, 'The Study of Mass Murder and Genocide' in Robert Gellately and Ben Kiernan (eds), *The Specter of Genocide. Mass Murder in Historical Perspective* (Cambridge University Press 2003) 6. See *verbatim* also Johan Dietsch, 'Holodomor: The 1932–1933 Ukrainian Famine-Genocide: Argumentum Ex Silentio' in Lubomyr Y. Luciuk (ed), *Holodomor: Reflections on the Great Famine of 1932–1933 in Soviet Ukraine* (Kashtan Press 2008) 181.

20 Payam Akhavan, 'Preventing Genocide: Measuring Success by What Does Not Happen' (2011) 22 *Criminal Law Forum* 1, 2.

21 Donald Bloxham and A. Dirk Moses, 'Editor's Introduction: Changing Themes in the Study of Genocide' in Donald Bloxham and A. Dirk Moses (eds), *The Oxford Handbook of Genocide Studies* (Oxford University Press 2010) 1.

22 See Beham, 'Genocide and Collective Memory in International Relations' (preface, n 4).

23 Benjamin Meiches, *The Politics of Annihilation. A Genealogy of Genocide* (University of Minnesota Press 2019) 21.

24 Cf Dietrich Busse, 'Architekturen des Wissens. Zum Verhältnis von Semantik und Epistemologie' in Ernst Müller (ed), *Begriffsgeschichte im Umbruch?* (Felix Meiner Verlag 2004) 46–8; Oliver Harry Gerson, 'Wahrnehmungslenkende Funktion der Sprache im Strafprozess – Verfahrensbalance durch kommunikative Autonomie' in Günter Köhnken and Rüdiger Deckers (eds), *Die Erhebung und Bewertung von Zeugenaussagen im Strafprozess. Juristische, aussagepsychologische und psychiatrische Aspekte. 3. Band* (Berliner Wissenschafts-Verlag 2018) 156.

25 See Jacques Sémelin, *Säubern und Vernichten. Die politische Dimension von Massakern und Völkermorden* (Hamburger Edition 2007) 13, 124–5, and 336. Cf also Leo Kuper, 'Types of Genocide and Mass Murder' in Israel W Charny (ed), *Toward the Understanding and Prevention of Genocide. Proceedings of the International Conference on the Holocaust and Genocide* (Westview Press 1984) 36: 'The twentieth century is sometimes viewed as initiating a new process in genocide.'

26 Cf Irving Louis Horowitz, *Taking Lives. Genocide and State Power* (5th edn, Transaction Publishers 2002) 35 and 320; Kevin Lewis O'Neill, 'Anthropology and Genocide' in Donald Bloxham and A. Dirk Moses (eds), *The Oxford Handbook of Genocide Studies* (Oxford University Press 2010) 195.

27 Meiches, *The Politics of Annihilation. A Genealogy of Genocide* (ch 1, n 23) 19.

What does it take then for past or present atrocities to be considered under the one or other word or phrase? Is it an analysis of legal requirements, the elements of the crime, or is the benchmark something else, memories of the Holocaust invoked – think of the picture of the emaciated men behind barbed wire in the Trnopolje internment camp on the cover of *Time* magazine during the Bosnian War[28] – or simply a rhetorical whim?

Whoever delves into the darker places of human history where individuals have been discriminated against, tortured or murdered – most often not committed by thugs in the night but by a state apparatus carrying the support of 'civil society' and the legal profession – for essentially being at the wrong time in the wrong place will experience a deep, soul-wrenching feeling of incredulity at such events.

Any attempt at differentiation, relativization or typology – for example, seeking to 'distinguish between massacre and pogrom and partial genocide'[29] – must seem utterly off point at this moment in which the victims' fate reveals itself to anyone capable of the slightest empathy and compassion. Yet this is the primary activity of a scholarly field aimed at the study, comprehension and, ultimately, prevention of the atrocities in question.[30]

28 *Time* (17 August 1992).

29 Robert Melson, 'Problems in the Comparison of the Armenian Genocide and the Holocaust: Definitions, Typologies, Theories, and Fallacies' in Stig Förster and Gerhard Hirschfeld (eds), *Genozid in der modernen Geschichte* (Lit Verlag 1999) 27.

30 See on the latter point, particularly, Israel W. Charny, 'Editor's Preface' in Israel W. Charny (ed), *Toward the Understanding and Prevention of Genocide. Proceedings of the International Conference on the Holocaust and Genocide* (Westview Press 1984) xvii. Moses sees the trend towards activism arising, in particular, in the 1990s against the background of inaction in the Balkans and Rwanda. See A. Dirk Moses, 'Introduction: The Field of Genocide Studies' in A. Dirk Moses (ed), *Genocide. Critical Concepts in Historical Studies. Volume I. The Discipline of Genocide Studies* (Routledge 2010) 4–5. See on this idea, generally, also Sémelin, *Säubern und Vernichten. Die politische Dimension von Massakern und Völkermorden* (ch 1, n 25) 397–412. For an earlier appraisal of such preventive measures, see Israel Charny, 'Intervention and Prevention of Genocide' in Israel Charny (ed), *Genocide. A Critical Bibliographical Review* (Facts on File Publications 1988) 20–30. See also the concluding chapters in Donald Bloxham and A. Dirk Moses (eds), *The Oxford Handbook of Genocide Studies* (Oxford University Press 2010). Yehuda Bauer even sees the issue of defining genocide as a 'necessary step to taking preventive measures'. See Yehuda Bauer, 'Comparison of Genocides' in Levon Chorbajian and George Shirinian (eds), *Studies in Comparative Genocide* (Palgrave Macmillan/St Martin's Press 1999) 31.

1.1 Genocide Studies

From the earliest efforts to legally conceptualize and deal with mass atrocities has sprung a field of scholarship of its own. The loose interdisciplinary *chapeau* of 'Genocide Studies' comprises scholars dealing with atrocities on a broad scale, most often at the comparative level and not necessarily with genocide itself. Predominantly a sociological endeavour[31] on the search for the causes of mass atrocities within a society,[32] the field leads a semi-symbiotic life alongside lawyers engaged in international criminal law, proponents of humanitarian intervention and the more specific yet related 'Holocaust Studies'.[33]

The comparative study of genocides gained momentum in the 1970s through a number of seminal articles and books on the subject.[34] Many more, in particular political scientists and sociologists,[35] followed suit.[36] Its earliest shapes were given by scholars whose biographies include the Holocaust as personal experience or part of their wider family history.[37] It cannot seem

[31] See Vivienne Jabri, *Discourses on Violence. Conflict Analysis Reconsidered* (Manchester University Press 1996) 3–4.

[32] See Förster and Hirschfeld, 'Einleitung' (ch 1, n 14) 6–7; Gellately and Kiernan, 'The Study of Mass Murder and Genocide' (ch 1, n 19) 8.

[33] See Moses, 'Introduction: The Field of Genocide Studies' (ch 1, n 30) 3. Donald Bloxham and A. Dirk Moses also refer to Genocide Studies as 'part offspring of, part uneasy junior partner to, the longer standing discipline Holocaust studies'. See Bloxham and Moses, 'Editor's Introduction: Changing Themes in the Study of Genocide' (ch 1, n 21) 3.

[34] For example, Vahakn N. Dadrian, 'A Typology of Genocide' (1975) 5 *International Review of Modern Sociology* 201; Leo Kuper, *Genocide. Its Political Use in the Twentieth Century* (Yale University Press 1982). See also Frank Chalk and Kurt Jonassohn, 'Conceptualizations of Genocide and Ethnocide' in Bohdan Krawchenko and Roman Serbyn (eds), *Famine in Ukraine 1932–1933* (University of Toronto Press 1986) 182–6; Adam Jones, *Genocide. A Comprehensive Introduction* (3rd edn, Routledge 2017) 17 and 22; Dominik J. Schaller, 'Genozidforschung: Begriffe und Debatten. Einleitung' in Vivianne Berg and others (eds), *Enteignet – Vertrieben – Ermordet. Beiträge zur Genozidforschung* (Chronos 2004) 9. Cf, however, Eric D. Weitz, *A Century of Genocide. Utopias of Race and Nation* (Princeton University Press 2003) x, who sees the emergence in the 1990s with the International Association of Genocide Scholars and Samantha Power's book. See Power, *A Problem from Hell. America and the Age of Genocide* (ch 1, n 13).

[35] See Barbara Harff, 'No Lessons Learned from the Holocaust? Assessing Risks of Genocide and Political Mass Murder since 1955' (2003) 97 *American Political Science Review* 57; Moses, 'Introduction: The Field of Genocide Studies' (ch 1, n 30) 1; Dan Stone, 'Introduction' in Dan Stone (ed), *The Historiography of Genocide* (Palgrave Macmillan 2008) 3. See on the debate also Moses, 'Introduction: The Field of Genocide Studies' (ch 1, n 30) 5–6.

[36] For a short overview, see Robert Gellately and Ben Kiernan, 'Investigating Genocide' in Robert Gellately and Ben Kiernan (eds), *The Specter of Genocide. Mass Murder in Historical Perspective* (Cambridge University Press 2003) 375; Jones, *Genocide. A Comprehensive Introduction* (ch 1, n 34) 22; Martin Shaw, *What Is Genocide?* (2nd edn, Polity Press 2015) 4; Yves Ternon, *L'État Criminel. Les Génocides au XXe Siècle* (Seuil 1995) 62–4. See also David Kader, 'Progress and Limitations in Basic Genocide Law' in Israel W. Charny (ed), *Genocide. A Critical Bibliographical Review. Volume Two* (Facts on File Publications 1991) 142–3 with regard to legal literature on genocide.

[37] See Moses, 'Introduction: The Field of Genocide Studies' (ch 1, n 30) 2.

surprising then that the crime of genocide became the lens through which other events were also viewed.

The field of Genocide Studies is concerned with labelling and comparing atrocities, oftentimes leaving it to the reader to sort through the bulk and tie events together or to draw their individual conclusions. In reviewing the literature, one cannot help but identify a Linnaean urge to collect and sort.[38] Many publications in the area of Genocide Studies start with a historical appraisal of mass atrocities, reviewing the period since adoption of the Genocide Convention[39] or trying to go as far back in history as possible to find the earliest instance of the crime[40] (perhaps as far back as the Neanderthals)[41] – an effort that Raphaël Lemkin, the 'inventor'[42] of the word, had already pursued in attempting to compile a complete history of genocide that to this day remains unpublished.[43] Lemkin has been deemed 'the founding father of genocide studies' for that very reason.[44]

On a sidenote, there also seems to be a general trend, particularly in relatively 'young' fields of international law – such as international criminal

38 Since eighteenth-century Swedish botanist and zoologist Carl von Linné may stand here as a representative of formal categorizations with his championing of a binomial nomenclature to identify the species of the world.

39 For example, Harff, 'No Lessons Learned from the Holocaust? Assessing Risks of Genocide and Political Mass Murder since 1955' (ch 1, n 35) 60.

40 For example, Frank Chalk and Kurt Jonassohn, 'The History and Sociology of Genocidal Killings' in Israel W. Charny (ed), *Genocide. A Critical Bibliographical Review* (Facts on File Publications 1988) 41–4; Frank Chalk and Kurt Jonassohn, *The History and Sociology of Genocide. Analyses and Case Studies* (Yale University Press 1990) 32–40; Jones, *Genocide. A Comprehensive Introduction* (ch 1, n 34) *passim*; Ben Kiernan, *Blood and Soil. A World History of Genocide and Extermination from Sparta to Darfur* (Yale University Press 2007); Kuper, *Genocide. Its Political Use in the Twentieth Century* (ch 1, n 34) 11–4; Norman M. Naimark, *Genocide. A World History* (Oxford University Press 2017); William D. Rubinstein, *Genocide: A History* (Pearson Longman 2004); Ternon, *L'État Criminel. Les Génocides au XXe Siècle* (ch 1, n 36) 267–357. See also Sémelin, *Säubern und Vernichten. Die politische Dimension von Massakern und Völkermorden* (ch 1, n 25) 336.

41 See Jones, *Genocide. A Comprehensive Introduction* (ch 1, n 34) 4–5.

42 Cf Raphaël Lemkin, 'Genocide. A Modern Crime' (1945) 4 *Free World* 39.

43 See John Cooper, *Raphael Lemkin and the Struggle for the Genocide Convention* (Palgrave Macmillan 2015) 57; Ann Curthoys and John Docker, 'Defining Genocide' in Dan Stone (ed), *The Historiography of Genocide* (Palgrave Macmillan 2008) 12; Norman M Naimark, 'How the Holodomor Can Be Integrated into Our Understanding of Genocide' in Andrij Makuch and Frank E Sysyn (eds), *Contextualising the Holodomor. The Impact of Thirty Years of Ukrainian Famine Studies* (Canadian Institute of Ukrainian Studies Press 2015) 113; Power, *A Problem from Hell. America and the Age of Genocide* (ch 1, n 13) 54–5. See already Raphaël Lemkin, *Axis Rule in Occupied Europe. Laws of Occupation, Analysis of Government, Proposals for Redress* (Carnegie Endowment for International Peace 1944) 80.

44 Naimark, 'How the Holodomor Can Be Integrated into Our Understanding of Genocide' (ch 1, n 43) 113. See also Cooper, *Raphael Lemkin and the Struggle for the Genocide Convention* (ch 1, n 43) 242; Schaller, 'Genozidforschung: Begriffe und Debatten. Einleitung' (ch 1, n 34) 13.

law – to establish a linear narrative across time and space,[45] as 'pedigree'.[46] Thereby, a red thread can be spun from the International Criminal Court back to the trial of Peter von Hagenbach of 1474, who was tried before an 'international tribunal' for 'war crimes'.[47] Today, the creation of the two ad hoc tribunals that triggered the renaissance of international criminal law,[48] the International Criminal Tribunal for Rwanda (ICTR) and the International Criminal Tribunal for the former Yugoslavia (ICTY), is embedded in the 'Meistererzählung' of human rights.[49]

The reason might rest in the legal value of 'pedigree' as proof of customary international law. Evidence of longstanding practice and the conviction of states that this practice is based on a sense of legal obligation adds authority to the proposition, particularly in light of the legal principle that no crime or punishment may be handed out retroactively (expressed through the Latin phrases 'nullum crimen' or 'nulla poena sine lege', 'no crime' or 'no punishment without law').[50] Tracing the search for justice and the fight against impunity as far back as possible becomes a matter not only of historical interest but also of normative policy.

At the beginning of the twenty-first century, the bookshelf presence of Genocide Studies has reached a high point[51] and it is considered 'one of the

[45] Cf Alfred P. Rubin, *Ethics and Authority in International Law* (Cambridge University Press 1997) xiii–xiv; William A. Schabas, *Unimaginable Atrocities. Justice, Politics, and Rights at the War Crimes Tribunals* (Oxford University Press 2012) 6.

[46] Gerry Simpson, 'History of Histories' in Kevin Jon Heller and Gerry Simpson (eds), *The Hidden Histories of War Crimes Trials* (Oxford University Press 2013) 5–6.

[47] Cf Gregory S. Gordon, 'The Trial of Peter von Hagenbach: Reconciling History, Historiography and International Criminal Law' in Kevin Jon Heller and Gerry Simpson (eds), *The Hidden Histories of War Crimes Trials* (Oxford University Press 2013).

[48] See Christian J. Tams, Lars Berster and Björn Schiffbauer, 'General Introduction' in Christian J. Tams, Lars Berster and Björn Schiffbauer (eds), *Convention on the Prevention and Punishment of the Crime of Genocide: A commentary* (CH Beck/Hart/Nomos 2014) 21. Cf Samuel Moyn, *The Last Utopia. Human Rights in History* (Belknap Press of Harvard University Press 2010) 176.

[49] Dietmar Müller, 'Zu den Anfängen des Völkerstrafrechts. Vespasian Pella und Raphael Lemkin' in Dietmar Müller and Adamantios Skordos (eds), *Leipziger Zugänge zur rechtlichen, politischen und kulturellen Verflechtungsgeschichte Ostmitteleuropas* (Leipziger Universitätsverlag 2015) 29. See also Bartholomé Clavero, *Genocide or Ethnocide 1933–2007. How to Make, Unmake, and Remake Law With Words* (Giuffrè Editore 2008) 172.

[50] See Mark Osiel, *Mass Atrocity, Collective Memory, and the Law* (Transaction Publishers 1997) 61–5. Cf Louis René Beres, 'Reason and Realpolitik: International Law and the Prevention of Genocide' in Israel W. Charny (ed), *Toward the Understanding and Prevention of Genocide. Proceedings of the International Conference on the Holocaust and Genocide* (Westview Press 1984) 309.

[51] See Jakob Tanner, 'Der Historiker und der Richter. Der Genozid an den Armeniern und die Genozidforschung aus rechtlicher und geschichtswissenschaftlicher Sicht' in Hans-Lukas Kieser and Elmar Plozza (eds), *Der Völkermord an den Armeniern, die Türkei und Europa / The Armenian Genocide, Turkey and Europe* (Chronos 2006) 177.

fastest-growing disciplines in the humanities and social sciences'.[52] It is almost impossible for any scholar to be acquainted with this rich field of academic literature beyond bibliographical sketches[53] and select case studies.[54] There exists today an 'International Association of Genocide Scholars'[55] with its journal *Genocide Studies and Prevention*[56] and an 'International Network of Genocide Scholars'[57] with a *Journal of Genocide Research*.[58] Oxford University Press also has its own journal, *Holocaust and Genocide Studies*.[59] Yale University tends to its own 'Genocide Studies Program';[60] the International Institute for Genocide and Human Rights Studies of the Zoryan Institute in Toronto[61] organizes an annual two-week summer university; the University of Amsterdam even offers an MA in history in 'Holocaust and Genocide Studies';[62] the University of Uppsala has its own 'Master Programme in Holocaust and Genocide Studies';[63] and a sheer number of centres and institutes are devoted to Holocaust and Genocide Studies worldwide. This list goes on.

Evidently, Genocide Studies has come a long way since the 1970s and 1980s. Assessments vary from the field having 'now attained a level of intellectual sobriety, academic credibility and official recognition that was inconceivable

52 Stone, 'Introduction' (ch 1, n 35) 1.

53 Any attempt at a comprehensive or even exemplary list of historiographical literature dealing with genocide would surely prove an arduous undertaking, considering the vast amount of literature on the Holocaust alone. For example, the literature listed within the following research guides: Georgetown Law Library, War Crimes Research Guide <http://guides.ll.georgetown.edu/c.php?g=365751&p=2471267>; Monash University, Holocaust and Genocide Studies, <http://guides.lib.monash.edu/c.php?g=219731&p=1452958>; Rutgers, Genocide Studies <http://libguides.rutgers.edu/genocide>; United States Holocaust Memorial Museum, Bibliographies <https://www.ushmm.org/research/research-in-collections/search-the-collections/bibliography>; Yale University, Genocide Studies Program, <http://gsp.yale.edu/>. Cf also Dan Stone (ed), *Historiography of Genocide* (Palgrave Macmillan 2010).

54 For a very accessible introduction to the field, see Jones, *Genocide. A Comprehensive Introduction* (ch 1, n 34).

55 See International Association of Genocide Scholars <http://www.genocidescholars.org/>.

56 See UTP Journals, Genocide Studies and Prevention <https://www.utpjournals.press/loi/gsp/>.

57 See International Network of Genocide Scholars <http://www.inogs.com/>.

58 See International Network of Genocide Scholars, Journal of Genocide Research <http://inogs.com/journal-of-genocide-research/>.

59 See Oxford Academic, Holocaust and Genocide Studies <https://academic.oup.com/hgs/>.

60 See Yale University, Genocide Studies Program <https://gsp.yale.edu/>.

61 See International Institute for Genocide and Human Rights Studies <http://www.genocidestudies.org>.

62 See University of Amsterdam, Holocaust and Genocide Studies (History) <https://www.uva.nl/en/programmes/masters/holocaust-and-genocide-studies-history/holocaust-and-genocide-studies.html>.

63 See Uppsala Universitet, Syllabus for Master Programme in Holocaust and Genocide Studies <https://www.uu.se/en/admissions/master/selma/utbplan/?pKod=HFF2M&lasar=13/14>.

forty years ago'[64] to less positive reviews: 'Today, genocide studies is a field torn between historians,[65] legal scholars and social scientists, between two generations, between interventionists and advocates of analytical scholarship, and between "liberal" and "post-liberals."'[66] Or even less positive reviews:

> The field of comparative genocide studies has grown beyond recognition over the past two decades, though more quantitatively than qualitatively. [. . .] The amount of genocide literature (of varying quality) has reached a point beyond which we may start talking about the emergence of a 'genocide industry'. The field is in crisis, which has never been acknowledged within the larger scholarly community.[67]

But perhaps this 'lack of clarity in the field can also [. . .] be an indication of great potential'.[68] After all, it means that the research agenda is not yet closed. Others have identified two different branches within the discipline: scholars and activists.[69] Some will consider themselves to be both.[70]

Yet, diversity and interdisciplinarity must not necessarily be detrimental to the study of a field; its subject matter may even necessitate it.[71] Mass atrocities are events subject to historical and political analysis, sociological and psychological comprehension, as well as prevention and legal redress. These different angles should not block the view towards the fact that Genocide Studies is glued together by a number of common questions occupying all disciplines:

> What is genocide? Is it limited to mass killing or does group culture also play a central role for group survival? How and why has it occurred in the past? Are certain kinds of societies particularly susceptible? Are particular periods of world history structurally vulnerable to mass violence? Why do people –

64 Moses, 'Introduction: The Field of Genocide Studies' (ch 1, n 30) 1. For a detailed account of the development of Genocide Studies see ibid 3–13, although largely written as a critique of the International Association of Genocide Scholars.

65 Cf on the more limited role of historians in the field, however, Bloxham and Moses, 'Editor's Introduction: Changing Themes in the Study of Genocide' (ch 1, n 21) 6.

66 Christian Gerlach, 'Extremely Violent Societies. An Alternative to the Concept of Genocide' in A. Dirk Moses (ed), *Genocide. Critical Concepts in Historical Studies. Volume I. The Discipline of Genocide Studies* (Routledge 2010) 455.

67 Anton Weiss-Wendt, 'Problems in Comparative Genocide Scholarship' in Dan Stone (ed), *The Historiography of Genocide* (Palgrave Macmillan 2008) 42.

68 Stone, 'Introduction' (ch 1, n 35) 2.

69 See Moses, 'Introduction: The Field of Genocide Studies' (ch 1, n 30) 9–11.

70 For an introspection, see Samuel Totten (ed), *Advancing Genocide Studies. Personal Accounts and Insights from Scholars in the Field* (Transaction Publishers 2015).

71 See Ternon, *L'État Criminel. Les Génocides au XXe Siècle* (ch 1, n 36) 11–2.

> elites and non-elites – plan or participate in it? How can it be prevented? How are post-genocidal societies reconstructed, let alone "reconciled"? [72]

In engaging with these issues, Genocide Studies always begins with the simple – or as this book might show, perhaps not so simple – process of atrocity labelling.

1.2 Atrocity labelling

As the title suggests, this book deals with the phenomenon of how, why and to which effect scholars attach certain labels – such as 'genocide', 'crimes against humanity' or 'war crimes' – to mass atrocities. The subtitle offers a progressive tale 'from crimes against humanity to Genocide Studies' that finds reflection in the historical narrative of conceptualizing mass atrocities.[73]

Today, more than ever, 'genocide' is but one term among many. But it is certainly the central one towards which any process of atrocity labelling gravitates.[74] In none of the case studies discussed throughout this book does anyone really raise the question whether the label 'crimes against humanity' or 'war crimes' might be (more) appropriate.[75]

At first glance, 'labelling' simply implies the process of attaching a certain term (in the present case, 'genocide', 'crimes against humanity', 'war crimes', 'ethnic cleansing' or other) to a certain event in space and time (here, an atrocity). Yet, in this process, events become inextricably linked with all of the ascribed term's connotations, its collective memory and implications, the need for action, the entire 'conceptual baggage'.[76] By attaching such a term, the discourse forms, in the words of Émile Durkheim, 'a quality of its own' or 'a new form of existence' ('une nature *sui generis*' or 'une nouvelle forme

[72] Moses, 'Introduction: The Field of Genocide Studies' (ch 1, n 30) 13.

[73] See Chapter 2.

[74] Cf Michael J. Kelly, 'Genocide – The Power of a Label' (2007) 40 *Case Western Reserve Journal of International Law* 147, 148: 'Is this genocide? Does it matter? Why?' And Mahmood Mamdani, 'The Politics of Naming. Genocide, Civil War, Insurgency' in A. Dirk Moses (ed), *Genocide. Critical Concepts in Historical Studies. Volume I. The Discipline of Genocide Studies* (Routledge 2010) 353: 'Why the difference? Who does the naming? Who is being named? What difference does it make?'

[75] Although some do use crimes against humanity as the default baseline for atrocities. For example, Michael Ellman, 'Stalin and the Soviet Famine of 1932–33 Revisited' (2007) 59 *Europe-Asia Studies* 663, 690.

[76] See Sally McConnell-Ginet, 'Words in the World: How and Why Meanings Can Matter' (2008) 84 *Language* 497, 512.

d'existence'),[77] forming a separate, perhaps now even primary social reality.[78] Equally, the opposite may be the case, in that the 'interpretive process [. . .] also generates competing systems of knowledge'.[79] The many disciplines and voices of Genocide Studies are either welded together by a common label or separated by competing narratives.

Atrocity labelling sees knowledge, language and power intertwined at multiple levels.[80] The 'power of the discourse' serves as 'symbolic capital',[81] subject to abuse and with the potential of profound effects upon reality. This power is wielded by anyone attaching a particular term to an event. Depending on the choice of label, language itself becomes action.[82] Russia's narrative of genocide in Ukraine[83] and, in turn, Ukraine's use of this proposition to bring the conflict within the jurisdiction of the International Court of Justice[84] are blatant examples. Yet this book is less about those one must be wary of for creating political narrative or banishing memories of the past than about the humanities – first and foremost history – and the political and social sciences whose scholars – at least that should be the default position – seek to make earnest enquiries.

By 'prosecuting' historical facts and labelling atrocities, it is historians particularly who participate in a quasi-legal process, juxtaposing the prerogative of law over international crimes.[85] Thereby, 'it is the scholarly community that defines and explains events, not governments and public officials or even the

77 See Émile Durkheim, *Les Règles de La Méthode Sociologique* (Ancienne Librairie Germer Baillière et Cie 1895) 151.

78 See Hannelore Bublitz, *Diskurs* (Transcript 2003) 10.

79 Paul R. Brass, 'Introduction: Discourses of Ethnicity, Communalism, and Violence' in Paul R. Brass (ed), *Riots and Pogroms* (Macmillan 1996) 1, who analyses this process – as the title suggests – with regard to riots and pogroms.

80 See Bublitz, *Diskurs* (ch 1, n 78) 6. Cf the seminal work by Michel Foucault, *L'Archéologie Du Savoir* (Éditions Gallimard 1969).

81 David E. Apter, 'Political Violence in Analytical Perspective' in David E. Apter (ed), *The Legitimization of Violence* (Macmillan 1997) 13.

82 See Achim Landwehr, *Geschichte Des Sagbaren. Einführung in Die Historische Diskursanalyse* (2nd edn, Edition Diskord 2004) 10.

83 See Permanent Mission of the Russian Federation to the United Nations, Statement by Permanent Representative Vassily Nebenzia at the Eleventh Emergency Special Session of the General Assembly, 28 February 2022 <https://russiaun.ru/en/news/ga_ess2802>.

84 See International Court of Justice, *Allegations of Genocide under the Convention on the Prevention and Punishment of the Crime of Genocide* (Ukraine *v.* Russian Federation), Application for the Institution of Proceedings of 26 February 2022.

85 Cf Michael Stolleis, 'Der Historiker als Richter – der Richter als Historiker' in Norbert Frei, Dirk van Laak and Michael Stolleis (eds), *Geschichte vor Gericht. Historiker, Richter und die Suche nach Gerechtigkeit* (CH Beck 2000) 175–6.

United Nations.'[86] The proposition that such definitions and explanations remain without consequence[87] becomes invalid as historical determinants, in turn, shape the response to political or legal questions.[88] For example, in the discussion of a 'responsibility to protect' – commonly abbreviated as 'RtoP' or 'R2P' – under international law, 'genocide, war crimes, ethnic cleansing and crimes against humanity' serve as triggers for intervention.[89]

But when historians seek to 'indict', the crimes may be different from those prosecuted by international criminal lawyers or those investigated by UN fact-finding missions: 'A lot of current literature on genocide, however true, would not stand up before the law.'[90] Scholars do not necessarily restrict themselves to an application of legal terminology in accordance with the underlying concepts. They may create their own definitions, relevant for the text alone or with the hope of future exploration, or simply not give much thought to the precise meaning at all.[91]

Intentional or not, it is all of these considerations against which the discipline of Genocide Studies must be held accountable. The book is, in one sense, descriptive of a process. At the same time, in highlighting and bringing to attention the phenomenon of atrocity labelling and its formative impact on the discourse, it carries a normative agenda. As 'genocide' has come to dominate all other labels available for conveying the gravity of atrocities, this book is as much about atrocity labelling as it is about the 'crime of crimes'. The discussion ultimately revolves around the applicability or inapplicability of the term 'genocide' – and leaves the question: 'Could such a polemically-loaded term be operationalised for serious academic investigation?'[92]

[86] David R. Marples, 'Ethnic Issues in the Famine of 1932–1933 in Ukraine' in Vincent Comerford, Lindsay Janssen and Christian Noack (eds), *Holodomor and Gorta Mór. Histories, Memories and Representations of Famine in Ukraine and Ireland* (Anthem Press 2012) 40.

[87] See Stolleis, 'Der Historiker als Richter – der Richter als Historiker' (ch 1, n 85) 178–9.

[88] See Dirk van Laak, 'Widerstand gegen die Geschichtsgewalt. Zur Kritik an der "Vergangenheitsbewältigung"' in Norbert Frei, Dirk van Laak and Michael Stolleis (eds), *Geschichte vor Gericht. Historiker, Richter und die Suche nach Gerechtigkeit* (CH Beck 2000) 11.

[89] See United Nations General Assembly Resolution 60/1, '2005 World Summit Outcome', 24 October 2005, A/RES/60/1, 138–9.

[90] Clavero, *Genocide or Ethnocide 1933–2007. How to Make, Unmake, and Remake Law With Words* (ch 1, n 49) 93.

[91] See Chapter 3.

[92] Moses, 'Introduction: The Field of Genocide Studies' (ch 1, n 30) 1.

1.3 This book

Scholars of Genocide Studies have themselves given ample thought to the process of labelling, the underlying mechanisms and their implications. The feeling that 'genocide studies need a new phase of conceptual discussion to overcome the present state of contestation and confusion'[93] is not new:

> While many case studies, historical and contemporary, adopt conflicting definitions according to the circumstances of particular cases, and others either implicitly or explicitly use the Holocaust as a standard (although one case could never act as an adequate definition of the general concept), there is a strong need for greater conceptual clarity.[94]

Here is now an attempt at drawing together all of these suspicions, assumptions, empirical evidence and proposals to create a better understanding or at least set the stage for further discussion of the phenomenon. It should be useful for anyone engaged in Genocide Studies as it is for any lawyer or even policy-maker wondering how atrocities ultimately become known as genocide, crimes against humanity or war crimes.

Four historical case studies have been chosen to explore the phenomenon of atrocity labelling: the Belgian rubber exploitation in the Congo under King Leopold II; the campaign to subjugate the Herero and Nama peoples in German South-West Africa at the outset of the twentieth century; the expulsion of the Armenians from Asia Minor during the First World War; the famine in Ukraine of 1932 and 1933, known commonly as the Holodomor.

Focussing on terminology applied to those events in historiography and, more broadly, Genocide Studies, this book tracks paths firmly trodden by historical semantics.[95] It goes beyond the mere analysis of language as a code, trying to pierce the discourse by exposing part of its machinery and the societal construction of reality.[96] Seeking to discover 'meaning and representation' and the 'regularities in the construction and function of linguistic resources'[97]

[93] Martin Shaw, 'Sociology and Genocide' in Donald Bloxham and A. Dirk Moses (eds), *The Oxford Handbook of Genocide Studies* (Oxford University Press 2010) 158.

[94] Ibid. See also Shaw, *What Is Genocide?* (ch 1, n 36) 5.

[95] For example, Dietrich Busse, *Historische Semantik. Analyse eines Programms* (Klett-Cotta 1987).

[96] See ibid 38–9 and 105–7; Siegfried Jäger, *Kritische Diskursanalyse. Eine Einführung* (6th edn, UNRAST-Verlag 2012) 15–6; Achim Landwehr, *Historische Diskursanalyse* (Campus 2009) 14 and 18–9.

[97] Jabri, *Discourses on Violence. Conflict Analysis Reconsidered* (ch 1, n 31) 94.

throughout the four case studies, patterns and tendencies in atrocity labelling may be identified from the common denominators distilled.

The analysis moves forward in three parts. Following this introduction, Chapter 2 traces the history of conceptualizing mass atrocities in international criminal law to provide context for the legal concepts at play. Considering its fundamental role in the discussion, the concept of genocide takes centre stage and is contrasted with the related development of a concept recently proposed to surpass or engulf it: crimes against humanity. Anyone already familiar with the history and development of international criminal law, the biography of Raphaël Lemkin, or the genesis of the Genocide Convention may wish to skip this chapter and go directly to the discussion of atrocity labelling.

Chapter 3 discusses the phenomenon of atrocity labelling itself, following a line of three questions: Which label is chosen? Why is it chosen? What are the consequences? Chapter 4 then engages in discourse analysis of the four case studies to illustrate the process of atrocity labelling. The book ends with an evaluation and a number of conclusions drawn from these four case studies that may be put into contrast with the legal parameters one might expect to determine the application of concepts of international law and, more specifically, international criminal law as labels.

2

Conceptualizing atrocities

'The word is new, the crime is ancient.'[1] What may be true for genocide is equally true for all other labels, from 'crimes against humanity', to 'war crimes', to 'ethnic cleansing'. The humanitarian and scholarly effort to conceptualize mass atrocities to prevent or punish arose about one and a half centuries ago and is closely connected to a number of normative projects, from humanitarian to international criminal law.

Equally, it is entwined with a number of biographies, most prominently the 'inventor' of the word 'genocide', Raphaël Lemkin, but also Henry Dunant, Friedrich Fromhold Martens, Arnold Toynbee, Vespasian Pella and Hersch Lauterpacht, to name a few. On the other side stand the perpetrators of genocide whose names have become entangled with the collective memory of mass atrocities or even synonymous with them, from Belgian King Leopold II, to German General Lothar von Trotha, to Talaat Pasha, to Josef Stalin, to Adolf Eichmann and the whole Nazi cast.

2.1 Early origins and first attempts

Throughout the long nineteenth century, the first cornerstones of international humanitarian law were laid with codes of conduct during armed conflict.[2] When Henry Dunant eternalized the horrors of the battlefield in *Un souvenir de Solférino* in 1862,[3] he gave the impetus for the creation of the International

1 Kuper, *Genocide. Its Political Use in the Twentieth Century* (ch 1, n 34) 11. See again Leo Kuper, 'The Turkish Genocide of Armenians, 1915–1917' in Richard G. Hovannisian (ed), *The Armenian Genocide in Perspective* (Transaction Books 1986) 43.

2 For example, the 1863 Lieber Code.

3 Henry Dunant, *Un Souvenir de Solférino* (Imprimerie Jules-Guillaume Fick 1862).

Committee of the Red Cross. The now-famous 'Martens clause' in the preamble of the 1899/1907 Hague Convention on the Laws and Customs of War on Land found that '[u]ntil a more complete code of the laws of war is issued, [. . .], populations and belligerents remain under the protection and empire of the principles of international law, as they result from the usages established between civilized nations, from the laws of humanity and the requirements of the public conscience'.[4]

The term 'war crimes' was, supposedly, first used in a legal sense in a publication of 1872.[5] As opposed to the later neologism 'genocide', its German equivalent 'Völkermord' had already found application in the first half of the nineteenth century[6] to refer to the destruction of nations.[7] 'Crimes against humanity' has been traced even further back, well into the eighteenth century[8] and came into use during 'abolition and the related practice of enforcing it [. . .] in the course of the long nineteenth century' whereby 'it developed from a moral category to an accepted norm in international politics and finally in international law'.[9] The lawyer and diplomat Henry Wheaton used the phrase in connection with the slave trade in a legal treatise as early as 1842.[10] But its origins have also been sought in the reference to the already mentioned 'laws of humanity' of the Martens clause[11] and, much later, the 'debates within the United Nations War Crimes Commission (UNWCC), founded in 1943, which

4 For a comparative reproduction of the slightly different wording of both treaties, see James Brown Scott (ed), *The Hague Conventions and Declarations of 1899 and 1907, Accompanied by Tables of Signatures, Ratifications and Adhesions of the Various Powers, and Texts of Reservations* (Oxford University Press 1915) 100–32.

5 See Myriam Gessler and Daniel Marc Segesser, 'Raphael Lemkin and the International Debate on the Punishment of War Crimes (1919–1948)' in A. Dirk Moses (ed), *Genocide. Critical Concepts in Historical Studies. Volume I. The Discipline of Genocide Studies* (Routledge 2010) 27; Daniel Marc Segesser, *Recht statt Rache oder Rache durch Recht? Die Ahndung von Kriegsverbrechen in der internationalen wissenschaftlichen Debatte 1872–1945* (Ferdinand Schöningh 2010) 50.

6 See Kurt Böttcher and others, *Geflügelte Worte. Zitate, Sentenzen und Begriffe in ihrem geschichtlichen Zusammenhang* (VEB Bibliographisches Institut Leipzig 1981) 466, para 3059.

7 See Matthias Heine, 'Völkermord – Eine deutsche Erfindung' *Welt* (22 April 2015) <https://www.welt.de/kultur/article139894880/Voelkermord-eine-deutsche-Erfindung.html>.

8 See Schabas, *Unimaginable Atrocities. Justice, Politics, and Rights at the War Crimes Tribunals* (ch 1, n 45) 53.

9 Fabian Klose, '"A War of Justice and Humanity": Abolition and Establishing Humanity as an International Norm' in Fabian Klose and Mirjam Thulin (eds), *Humanity a History of European Concepts in Practice From the Sixteenth Century to the Present* (Vandenhoeck & Ruprecht 2016) 171.

10 See ibid 184.

11 See M. Cherif Bassiouni, 'Revisiting the Architecture of Crimes Against Humanity. Almost a Century in the Making, with Gaps and Ambiguities Remaining – the Need for a Specialized Convention' in Leila Nadya Sadat (ed), *Forging a Convention for Crimes Against Humanity* (Cambridge University Press 2011) 44. See also Beth Van Schaack, 'The Definition of Crimes against Humanity: Resolving the Incoherence' (1999) 37 *Columbia Journal of Transnational Law* 787, 795–6.

had been concerned with formulating a minimum standard in dealing with mass atrocities whilst the war still raged on'.[12]

In a Joint Declaration of 15 May 1915, the Entente powers France, Great Britain and Russia referred to the atrocities committed against the Armenian population of the Ottoman Empire as 'new crimes of Turkey against humanity and civilization' and 'massacres':

> In view of those new crimes of Turkey against humanity and civilization, the Allied governments announce publicly to the Sublime-Porte that they will hold personally responsible [for] these crimes all members of the Ottoman government and those of their agents who are implicated in such massacres.[13]

The Declaration has been described as the birthdate of 'one of the most potent concepts of human rights and, eventually, of international law',[14] although the term was already 'very familiar and in common usage' by that time.[15] Not only did it reflect the idea of (ethnic and religious) minority protection through which much of the involvement of the European powers in the affairs of the Ottoman Empire was justified throughout the 'Eastern Question' – the wording of a draft propagated by Russia had been 'crimes [. . .] against Christianity and civilization'[16] – but also the contemporaneous understanding of international law as a closed community of 'civilised nations'.[17]

The contemporary voice on the atrocities committed against the Armenian population of Asia Minor, British historian Arnold Toynbee famously spoke of the 'murder of a nation',[18] placing the events under the modern understanding of genocide. Reports of the atrocities and their aftermath feature as part of Lemkin's biographical 'revelation' leading to the creation of the term 'genocide' – particularly the case of Soghomon Tehlirian shooting and killing former Ottoman Minister of the Interior and Grand Vizier Mehmed Talaat

12 Kerstin von Lingen, 'Fulfilling the Martens Clause: Debating "Crimes Against Humanity", 1899–1945' in Fabian Klose and Mirjam Thulin (eds), *Humanity. A History of European Concepts in Practice From the Sixteenth Century to the Present* (Vandenhoeck & Ruprecht 2016) 187–8.

13 See Joint Declaration of France, Great Britain and Russia, 24 May 1915 <http://www.armenian-genocide.org/Affirmation.160/current_category.7/affirmation_detail.html>.

14 Jones, *Genocide. A Comprehensive Introduction* (ch 1, n 34) 710.

15 Schabas, *Unimaginable Atrocities. Justice, Politics, and Rights at the War Crimes Tribunals* (ch 1, n 45) 53.

16 See Jones, *Genocide. A Comprehensive Introduction* (ch 1, n 34) 710; Adam Jones, *Crimes Against Humanity: A Beginner's Guide* (Oneworld 2008) 1–2.

17 Cf James Sloan, 'Civilized Nations', *Max Planck Encyclopedia of Public International Law* <http://opil.ouplaw.com/home/EPIL>.

18 Arnold J. Toynbee, *Armenian Atrocities. The Murder of a Nation* (Hodder & Stoughton 1915).

Pasha, who had been sentenced to death but continued to live out his life in Germany, on the streets of Berlin in 1921.[19]

A new phase of conceptualization came with the Paris Peace Conference following the First World War. Part VIII of the Treaty of Versailles sought penalties for the former German emperor Wilhelm II of Hohenzollern and 'persons accused of having committed acts in violation of the laws and customs of war', as well as those 'guilty of criminal acts against the nationals of one of the Allied and Associated Powers'.[20] It resulted in several trials before the German Reichsgericht in Leipzig in 1921, the so-called Leipzig trials.[21]

Similarly, the Treaty of Sèvres would have included such provisions on criminal responsibility for persons 'responsible for the massacres committed during the continuance of the state of war on territory which formed part of

[19] For example, Michael Bazyler, *Holocaust, Genocide, and the Law. A Quest for Justice in a Post-Holocaust World* (Oxford University Press 2016) 33; Cooper, *Raphael Lemkin and the Struggle for the Genocide Convention* (ch 1, n 43) 15; Gessler and Segesser, 'Raphael Lemkin and the International Debate on the Punishment of War Crimes (1919–1948)' (ch 2, n 5) 28; Douglas Irvin-Erickson, *Raphaël Lemkin and the Concept of Genocide* (University of Pennsylvania Press 2017) 36; Jones, *Genocide. A Comprehensive Introduction* (ch 1, n 34) 14; Meiches, *The Politics of Annihilation. A Genealogy of Genocide* (ch 1, n 23) 239–40; Power, *A Problem from Hell. America and the Age of Genocide* (ch 1, n 13) 17–9; Henry C. Theriault and Samuel Totten, *The United Nations Genocide Convention. An Introduction* (University of Toronto Press 2020) 4.

[20] See Articles 227–9 of the Treaty of Versailles, 28 June 1919: 'ARTICLE 227. The Allied and Associated Powers publicly arraign William II of Hohenzollern, formerly German Emperor, for a supreme offence against international morality and the sanctity of treaties. A special tribunal will be constituted to try the accused, thereby assuring him the guarantees essential to the right of defence. It will be composed of five judges, one appointed by each of the following Powers: namely, the United States of America, Great Britain, France, Italy and Japan. In its decision the tribunal will be guided by the highest motives of international policy, with a view to vindicating the solemn obligations of international undertakings and the validity of international morality. It will be its duty to fix the punishment which it considers should be imposed. The Allied and Associated Powers will address a request to the Government of the Netherlands for the surrender to them of the ex-Emperor in order that he may be put on trial. ARTICLE 228. The German Government recognises the right of the Allied and Associated Powers to bring before military tribunals persons accused of having committed acts in violation of the laws and customs of war. Such persons shall, if found guilty, be sentenced to punishments laid down by law. This provision will apply notwithstanding any proceedings or prosecution before a tribunal in Germany or in the territory of her allies. The German Government shall hand over to the Allied and Associated Powers, or to such one of them as shall so request, all persons accused of having committed an act in violation of the laws and customs of war, who are specified either by name or by the rank, office or employment which they held under the German authorities. ARTICLE 229. Persons guilty of criminal acts against the nationals of one of the Allied and Associated Powers will be brought before the military tribunals of that Power. Persons guilty of criminal acts against the nationals of more than one of the Allied and Associated Powers will be brought before military tribunals composed of members of the military tribunals of the Powers concerned. In every case the accused will be entitled to name his own counsel. ARTICLE 230. The German Government undertakes to furnish all documents and information of every kind, the production of which may be considered necessary to ensure the full knowledge of the incriminating acts, the discovery of offenders and the just appreciation of responsibility.'

[21] See Gerd Hankel, *The Leipzig Trials: German War Crimes and Their Legal Consequences after World War I* (Republic of Letters 2014).

the Turkish Empire on August 1, 1914'.[22] The provision was dropped from the subsequent Treaty of Lausanne of 1923.[23]

Much of the intellectual groundwork for the idea of international criminal law was laid during the interwar period and discussions surrounding the term 'war crimes'.[24] The creation of an International Criminal Court was debated in the context of the League of Nations, a set of atrocity crimes was proposed by the International Law Association and a number of additional suggestions were made within the framework of the Association Internationale de Droit Pénal, the International Association of Criminal Law.[25]

But it was not until a Polish lawyer and 'norm entrepreneur'[26] by the name of Raphaël Lemkin,[27] under the impression of the horrors of the Second World

[22] See Article 230 of the Treaty of Sèvres, 10 August 1920: 'The Turkish Government undertakes to hand over to the Allied Powers the persons whose surrender may be required by the latter as being responsible for the massacres committed during the continuance of the state of war on territory which formed part of the Turkish Empire on August 1, 1914. The Allied Powers reserve to themselves the right to designate the tribunal which shall try the persons so accused, and the Turkish Government undertakes to recognise such tribunal. In the event of the League of Nations having created in sufficient time a tribunal competent to deal with the said massacres, the Allied Powers reserve to themselves the right to bring the accused persons mentioned above before such tribunal, and the Turkish Government undertakes equally to recognise such tribunal.'

[23] See Jennifer Balint, 'The Ottoman State Special Military Tribunal for the Genocide of the Armenians: "Doing Government Business"' in Kevin Jon Heller and Gerry Simpson (eds), *The Hidden Histories of War Crimes Trials* (Oxford University Press 2013) 84; Bassiouni, 'Revisiting the Architecture of Crimes Against Humanity. Almost a Century in the Making, with Gaps and Ambiguities Remaining – the Need for a Specialized Convention' (ch 2, n 11) 49.

[24] See Gessler and Segesser, 'Raphael Lemkin and the International Debate on the Punishment of War Crimes (1919–1948)' (ch 2, n 5) 28–30; Segesser, *Recht statt Rache oder Rache durch Recht? Die Ahndung von Kriegsverbrechen in der internationalen wissenschaftlichen Debatte 1872–1945* (ch 2, n 5) 212–31.

[25] See on this Cooper, *Raphael Lemkin and the Struggle for the Genocide Convention* (ch 1, n 43) 18 and 24; Gessler and Segesser, 'Raphael Lemkin and the International Debate on the Punishment of War Crimes (1919–1948)' (ch 2, n 5) 30; Irvin-Erickson, *Raphaël Lemkin and the Concept of Genocide* (ch 2, n 19) 40–2; Claudia Kraft, 'Nationalisierende Transnationalisierung. (Inter) nationale Strafrechtswissenschaft in der Zwischenkriegszeit' in Dietmar Müller and Adamantios Skordos (eds), *Leipziger Zugänge zur rechtlichen, politischen und kulturellen Verflechtungsgeschichte Ostmitteleuropas* (Leipziger Universitätsverlag 2015) 23–4; Müller, 'Zu den Anfängen des Völkerstrafrechts. Vespasian Pella und Raphael Lemkin' (ch 1, n 49) 33–4; Segesser, *Recht statt Rache oder Rache durch Recht? Die Ahndung von Kriegsverbrechen in der internationalen wissenschaftlichen Debatte 1872–1945* (ch 2, n 5) 232–302 and the following chapter; Ternon, *L'État Criminel. Les Génocides au XXe Siècle* (ch 1, n 36) 24–7.

[26] Jones, *Genocide. A Comprehensive Introduction* (ch 1, n 34) 12. Cf also ibid 17.

[27] Lemkin has recently been the centre of attention in a number of publications, including biographies, a theatrical play and a work of popular non-fiction, see Philippe Sands, *East West Street. On the Origins of Genocide and Crimes Against Humanity* (Weidenfeld & Nicolson 2017); Harmen G. van der Wilt and others (eds), *The Genocide Convention: The Legacy of 60 Years* (Martinus Nijhoff 2012). For an overview of publications until 2012, see Jeroen Vervliet, 'Raphael Lemkin (1900–1959) and the Genocide Convention of 1948. Brief Biographical and Bibliographical Notes' in Harmen van der Wilt and others (eds), *The Genocide Convention: The Legacy of 60 Years* (Martinus Nijhoff 2012) xi.

War, came to create a word that rings louder today than any other possible atrocity label:[28] 'genocide'.

2.2 Raphaël Lemkin and genocide

Born in Bezwodne in 1900, in what was then still the Russian Empire (now Belarus),[29] Lemkin studied law in Lemberg, where news of the treatment of perpetrators of the Armenian genocide and the already mentioned trial of the vigilante Tehlirian supposedly left a great impression upon the young student.[30] After completing his studies, he went on to serve first as a court secretary and then as a public prosecutor in Warsaw, where he also began teaching law.[31]

A first milestone in conceptualizing the idea of 'genocide' is usually seen in a presentation given in Madrid in 1933 – though not by the author himself, having been denied a visa to travel there[32] – on two novel crimes: 'barbarity' and 'vandalism'.[33] The underlying idea was to break with the barrier of state sovereignty and overcome the resulting impunity of individuals for acts of atrocity.[34]

At the outbreak of the Second World War, Lemkin fled first via Lithuania to Sweden and then via the Soviet Union and Japan to the United States, where he managed to secure a professorship at Duke University.[35] In 1944, Lemkin's

[28] Cf William A. Schabas, *Genocide in International Law. The Crime of Crimes* (2nd edn, Cambridge University Press 2009) 14.

[29] See Cooper, *Raphael Lemkin and the Struggle for the Genocide Convention* (ch 1, n 43) 6; Irvin-Erickson, *Raphaël Lemkin and the Concept of Genocide* (ch 2, n 19) 17.

[30] See Chapter 2, n 19.

[31] See Cooper, *Raphael Lemkin and the Struggle for the Genocide Convention* (ch 1, n 43) 17; Gessler and Segesser, 'Raphael Lemkin and the International Debate on the Punishment of War Crimes (1919–1948)' (ch 2, n 5) 30; Irvin-Erickson, *Raphaël Lemkin and the Concept of Genocide* (ch 2, n 19) 39.

[32] See Cooper, *Raphael Lemkin and the Struggle for the Genocide Convention* (ch 1, n 43) 20–1; Irvin-Erickson, *Raphaël Lemkin and the Concept of Genocide* (ch 2, n 19) 49–50; Jones, *Genocide. A Comprehensive Introduction* (ch 1, n 34) 14; Power, *A Problem from Hell. America and the Age of Genocide* (ch 1, n 13) 22; Theriault and Totten, *The United Nations Genocide Convention. An Introduction* (ch 2, n 19) 6. Cf, based on Lemkin's own recollection of events, Müller, 'Zu den Anfängen des Völkerstrafrechts. Vespasian Pella und Raphael Lemkin' (ch 1, n 49) 37.

[33] See Cooper, *Raphael Lemkin and the Struggle for the Genocide Convention* (ch 1, n 43) 18–9; Irvin-Erickson, *Raphaël Lemkin and the Concept of Genocide* (ch 2, n 19) 45–50; Lang, 'The Concept of Genocide' (ch 1, n 1) 116; Shaw, *What Is Genocide?* (ch 1, n 36) 14–5 with a table of definitions; Ternon, *L'État Criminel. Les Génocides au XXe Siècle* (ch 1, n 36) 26.

[34] See Jones, *Genocide. A Comprehensive Introduction* (ch 1, n 34) 14.

[35] See Cooper, *Raphael Lemkin and the Struggle for the Genocide Convention* (ch 1, n 43) 25–42; Gessler and Segesser, 'Raphael Lemkin and the International Debate on the Punishment of War Crimes (1919–1948)' (ch 2, n 5) 33; Irvin-Erickson, *Raphaël Lemkin and the Concept of Genocide* (ch 2, n 19) 70–81; Jones, *Genocide. A Comprehensive Introduction* (ch 1, n 34) 15; Power, *A Problem from Hell. America and the Age of Genocide* (ch 1, n 13) 23–6.

study on the laws and decrees of the territories occupied by Nazi Germany, which he had started to gather in Sweden,[36] was published through the Carnegie Endowment of International Peace: *Axis Rule in Occupied Europe*.[37]

Finding little political support for his concepts of 'barbarism' and 'vandalism'[38] – and apparently inspired by Churchill's famous 1941 radio address on the 'crime without a name'[39] and the artificial fantasy name 'Kodak' selected for being short, simple and unique[40] – Lemkin had come up with a neologism that was both 'concise and memorable':[41] 'genocide'.

An entire chapter of his book is devoted to this new category of international crime. Drawing upon several earlier proposals, including his own of 1933,[42] the term 'genocide' was to 'convey the racial and national motivation of the crime', as opposed to 'mass-murder' or 'mass-extermination'.[43] It is Lemkin's frequently quoted introduction to the concept, in which he not only meticulously explains the composition of the term but also outlines its scope of application:

> New conceptions require new terms. By 'genocide' we mean the destruction of a nation or of an ethnic group. This new word, coined by the author to denote an old practice in its modern development, is made from the ancient Greek word *genos* (race, tribe) and the Latin *cide* (killing), thus corresponding in its formation to such words as tyrannicide, homocide [*sic*], infanticide, etc. Generally speaking, genocide does not necessarily mean the immediate destruction of a nation, except when accomplished by mass killings of all members of a nation. It is intended rather to signify a coordinated plan of different actions aiming at the destruction of essential foundations of the life of national groups, with the aim of annihilating the groups themselves. The objectives of such a plan would be disintegration of

36 See Power, *A Problem from Hell. America and the Age of Genocide* (ch 1, n 13) 39.

37 Lemkin, *Axis Rule in Occupied Europe. Laws of Occupation, Analysis of Government, Proposals for Redress* (ch 1, n 43).

38 See Irvin-Erickson, *Raphaël Lemkin and the Concept of Genocide* (ch 2, n 19) 138–9; Power, *A Problem from Hell. America and the Age of Genocide* (ch 1, n 13) 27–9.

39 See Power, *A Problem from Hell. America and the Age of Genocide* (ch 1, n 13) 40.

40 See Jones, *Genocide. A Comprehensive Introduction* (ch 1, n 34) 15; Power, *A Problem from Hell. America and the Age of Genocide* (ch 1, n 13) 41–2.

41 Jones, *Genocide. A Comprehensive Introduction* (ch 1, n 34) 15.

42 See Gessler and Segesser, 'Raphael Lemkin and the International Debate on the Punishment of War Crimes (1919–1948)' (ch 2, n 5) 36.

43 Memorandum from Raphaël Lemkin to R. Kempner, 5 June 1946, United States Holocaust Memorial Museum, R. Kempner Papers (RS 71.001), quoted from Moses, 'Raphael Lemkin, Culture, and the Concept of Genocide' (ch 1, n 6) 28. In this context it is not clear why Cathie Carmichael writes that Lemkin 'was creating a neologism rather than simply forging a juridical concept', see Cathie Carmichael, *Genocide before the Holocaust* (Yale University Press 2009) 9.

> the political and social institutions, of culture, language, national feelings, religion, and the economic existence of national groups, and the destruction of the personal security, liberty, health, dignity, and even the lives of the individuals belonging to such groups. Genocide is directed against the national group as an entity, and the actions involved are directed against individuals, not in their individual capacity, but as members of the national group.[44]

Alternatively, he proposed a second term, 'ethnocide'[45] (which came to be adapted later by Genocide Studies to describe the phenomenon of cultural genocide[46]).

In the context of his study of laws and decrees of the territories occupied by Nazi Germany, Lemkin conceived genocide also as a policy of occupation, as a kind of 'biological' or 'genetical' warfare:[47]

> Because the imposition of this policy of genocide is more destructive for a people than injuries suffered in actual fighting, the German people will be stronger than the subjugated peoples after the war even if the German army is defeated. In this respect genocide is a new technique of occupation aimed at winning the peace even though the war itself is lost.[48]

The chapter goes on to list various examples of Nazi Germany's means of implementing this policy of genocide[49] and recommendations for its future prohibition, calling for a 'review' of international law and minority protection, amendment of the Hague Regulations, the creation of an international multilateral treaty and monitoring of occupational practices.[50]

Lemkin immediately went on to promote his concept, trying to secure favourable book reviews for his publication.[51] Reactions were not all praise,[52]

[44] Lemkin, *Axis Rule in Occupied Europe. Laws of Occupation, Analysis of Government, Proposals for Redress* (ch 1, n 43) 79.

[45] Ibid 79 fn 1.

[46] See Dadrian, 'A Typology of Genocide' (ch 1, n 34) 205; Jones, *Genocide. A Comprehensive Introduction* (ch 1, n 34) 35.

[47] See Lemkin, *Axis Rule in Occupied Europe. Laws of Occupation, Analysis of Government, Proposals for Redress* (ch 1, n 43) 80–1.

[48] Ibid 81.

[49] See ibid 82–90.

[50] See ibid 90–5.

[51] See Cooper, *Raphael Lemkin and the Struggle for the Genocide Convention* (ch 1, n 43) 62–4 and 67.

[52] Cf Irvin-Erickson, *Raphaël Lemkin and the Concept of Genocide* (ch 2, n 19) 150.

but the book became a talking point.[53] The epistemic context of the Holocaust was still fresh and, thus, the term easily stuck as a label to these unspeakable events. Lemkin sought to draw further attention through a number of articles[54] published in *Free World*,[55] the *American Scholar*[56] and the *American Journal of International Law*.[57]

2.3 Judgement at Nuremberg

But when the opportunity for prosecution came in the trials before the International Military Tribunal in Nuremberg, genocide did not take centre stage as might perhaps have been expected. What had been included in the Charter of the International Military Tribunal – the 'Nuremberg Charter' – upon suggestion of Hersch Lauterpacht[58] were crimes against humanity:

> CRIMES AGAINST HUMANITY: namely, murder, extermination, enslavement, deportation, and other inhumane acts committed against any civilian population, before or during the war; or persecutions on political, racial or religious grounds in execution of or in connection with any crime within the jurisdiction of the Tribunal, whether or not in violation of the domestic law of the country where perpetrated.[59]

[53] See Cooper, *Raphael Lemkin and the Struggle for the Genocide Convention* (ch 1, n 43) 70; Irvin-Erickson, *Raphaël Lemkin and the Concept of Genocide* (ch 2, n 19) 140.

[54] See Segesser, *Recht statt Rache oder Rache durch Recht? Die Ahndung von Kriegsverbrechen in der internationalen wissenschaftlichen Debatte 1872–1945* (ch 2, n 5) 387; Vervliet, 'Raphael Lemkin (1900–1959) and the Genocide Convention of 1948. Brief Biographical and Bibliographical Notes' (ch 2, n 27) xiii–xiv.

[55] Lemkin, 'Genocide. A Modern Crime' (ch 1, n 42).

[56] Raphaël Lemkin, 'Genocide' (1946) XV *American Scholar* 227

[57] Raphaël Lemkin, 'Genocide as a Crime under International Law' (1947) 41 *American Journal of International Law* 145.

[58] See Cooper, *Raphael Lemkin and the Struggle for the Genocide Convention* (ch 1, n 43) 66. On the influence of other lawyers such as Bohuslav Ecer, Egon Schwelb and Antonin Trainin, see von Lingen, 'Fulfilling the Martens Clause: Debating "Crimes Against Humanity", 1899–1945' (ch 2, n 12) 198–205. On the relations between the two, recently contrasted in popular non-fiction by Philippe Sands, see Stefan Troebst, 'Eastern Europes Imprint on Modern International Law' in Annalisa Ciampi (ed), *History and International Law* (Edward Elgar Publishing 2019); Ana Filipa Vrdoljak, 'Human Rights and Genocide: The Work of Lauterpacht and Lemkin in Modern International Law' (2009) 20 *European Journal of International Law* 1163.

[59] Charter of the International Military Tribunal, Annex to the Agreement by the Government of the United Kingdom of Great Britain and Northern Ireland, the Government of the United States of America, the Provisional Government of the French Republic and the Government of the Union of Soviet Socialist Republics for the Prosecution and Punishment of the Major War Criminals of the European Axis, 8 August 1945, 82 United Nations Treaty Series 280, Article 6(c). For an early appraisal, see the seminal article by Egon Schwelb, 'Crimes Against Humanity' (1946) 178 *British Year Book of International Law* 178.

When the two United Nations *ad hoc* tribunals deliberated extensively upon the historical development of crimes against humanity and its scope, both concluded that it was here, in Article 6(c) of the Nuremberg Charter, that the legal concept first crystallized[60] (the same wording was also used in the Charter of the International Military Tribunal for the Far East).[61] But the definition came far short of providing a general conceptualization of mass atrocities.

At first glance, Article 6(c) of the Nuremberg Charter is broad enough. The subordinate clause 'whether or not in violation of the domestic law of the country where perpetrated' was included due to the fact that as far as such crimes committed vis-à-vis German nationals went, they were to a large extent even provided for by German domestic laws at the time of their commission.[62] The general principle that criminal law could not apply retroactively – *nullum crimen* or *nulla poena sine lege*, 'no crime' or 'no punishment without law' – might otherwise have stood in contrast with the punishment of perpetrators acting in accordance with the racist and unjust laws of Nazi Germany (as the German legal philosopher and criminal lawyer Gustav Radbruch would later express, justice must prevail over 'unbearably unjust' law).[63]

However, the prior subordinate clause of Article 6(c) of the Nuremberg Charter 'in execution of or in connection with any crime within the jurisdiction of the Tribunal' – that is 'crimes against peace' and 'war crimes'[64] – was interpreted by the judges at Nuremberg as requiring a nexus between crimes

60 See *Prosecutor v. Duško Tadić aka 'Dule'*, Judgement of 7 May 1997, Case No. No. IT-94-1-T, para 618 and *Prosecutor v. Jean-Paul Akayesu*, Judgement of 2 September 1998, Case No. ICTR-96-4-T, para 563.

61 Charter of the International Military Tribunal for the Far East, 19 January 1946, as amended on 26 April 1946, 27 Treaties and Other International Acts Series 1589, Article 5(c): 'Crimes against Humanity: Namely, murder, extermination, enslavement, deportation, and other inhumane acts committed against any civilian population, before or during the war, or persecutions on political or racial grounds in execution of or in connection with any crime within the jurisdiction of the Tribunal, whether or not in violation of the domestic law of the country where perpetrated. Leaders, organizers, instigators and accomplices participating in the formulation or execution of a common plan or conspiracy to commit any of the foregoing crimes are responsible for all acts performed by any person in execution of such plan.'

62 See William A. Schabas, 'Crimes Against Humanity' in Dinah L. Shelton (ed), *Encyclopedia of Genocide and Crimes Against Humanity. Vol. 1 [A-H]* (Thomson Gale 2005) 212.

63 The so-called Radbruch formula. See Gustav Radbruch, 'Gesetzliches Unrecht und übergesetzliches Recht' (1946) 1 *Süddeutsche Juristenzeitung* 105.

64 See Charter of the International Military Tribunal, Annex to the Agreement by the Government of the United Kingdom of Great Britain and Northern Ireland, the Government of the United States of America, the Provisional Government of the French Republic and the Government of the Union of Soviet Socialist Republics for the Prosecution and Punishment of the Major War Criminals of the European Axis, 8 August 1945, 82 United Nations Treaty Series 280, Article 6.

against humanity and war, irrespective of the perhaps suggestive semi-colon.[65] Atrocities during peacetime were excluded from the scope of crimes against humanity as understood under the Nuremberg Charter. The reason for this interpretation supposedly lay in the concern of the victorious Allies that they might themselves be confronted with issues regarding the treatment of minorities within their own territories and jurisdiction.[66] This nexus requirement added salt to the thirst for an alternative, inclusive concept:

> Had Nuremberg affirmed the reach of international criminal law into peacetime atrocities, the Genocide Convention might never have been adopted. The term 'genocide' might then have remained a popular or colloquial label used by journalists, historians, and social scientists but absent from legal discourse.[67]

Though Lemkin was unsuccessful in getting genocide included among the list of crimes in the Charter of the International Military Tribunal, he had achieved a small victory with the inclusion of the term for the first time in an official legal document under 'Count Three' of the indictment of the major Nazi war criminals before the International Military Tribunal,[68] probably 'the first formal recognition of the crime of genocide'.[69] The indictment reads:

> They conducted deliberate and systematic genocide, viz., the extermination of racial and national groups, against the civilian populations of certain occupied territories in order to destroy particular races and classes of people and national, racial, or religious groups, particularly Jews, Poles, and Gypsies and others.[70]

[65] See Schabas, 'Crimes Against Humanity' (ch 2, n 62) 211–12.

[66] See ibid 212. On the discussions at the London Conference, see Schabas, *Genocide in International Law* (ch 2, n 28) 38–42; Schabas, *Unimaginable Atrocities. Justice, Politics, and Rights at the War Crimes Tribunals* (ch 1, n 45) 108.

[67] Schabas, *Genocide in International Law* (ch 2, n 28) 128. See also Schabas, *Unimaginable Atrocities. Justice, Politics, and Rights at the War Crimes Tribunals* (ch 1, n 45) 110; Schabas, 'Crimes Against Humanity' (ch 2, n 62) 212.

[68] 'International Military Tribunal, Indictment, The United States of America et al. against Herman Wilhelm Göring et al.' reprinted in John C. Watkins and John Paul Weber (eds), *War Crimes and War Crime Trials: From Leipzig to the ICC and Beyond. Cases, Materials and Comments* (Carolina Academic Press 2006) 127–43.

[69] Kuper, *Genocide. Its Political Use in the Twentieth Century* (ch 1, n 34) 22.

[70] Reproduced in Watkins and Weber, *War Crimes and War Crime Trials: From Leipzig to the ICC and Beyond. Cases, Materials and Comments* (ch 2, n 68) 138.

Lemkin had himself travelled to Nuremberg to lobby the use of his neologism by the prosecution,[71] even becoming part of the US team there,[72] although he has been characterized as only 'a marginal figure' at the trials.[73] Although there were no consecutive references to Lemkin's neologism by the International Military Tribunal itself,[74] the concept did take on a subliminal role,[75] picked up in subsequent trials.[76]

Having perhaps caused irritation by 'trying to push international law into a field where it did not belong',[77] Lemkin was consternated by the restriction of Article 6(c) of the Nuremberg Charter to crimes committed during wartime.[78] The apocryphal story goes that he heard on a Paris hospital radio of the newly established United Nations General Assembly setting up its agenda.[79] Lemkin came up with the first draft of what would later become General Assembly Resolution 96 (I) on 'The Crime of Genocide' – the first formal recognition of the concept by the United Nations – on the plane to New York.[80]

[71] See John Q. Barrett, 'Raphael Lemkin and "Genocide" at Nuremberg, 1945–1946' in Eckart Conze and Christoph Safferling (eds), *The Genocide Convention Sixty Years After Its Adoption* (TMC Asser Press 2010) 47–9; Irvin-Erickson, *Raphaël Lemkin and the Concept of Genocide* (ch 2, n 19) 143; Power, *A Problem from Hell. America and the Age of Genocide* (ch 1, n 13) 48.

[72] See Barrett, 'Raphael Lemkin and "Genocide" at Nuremberg, 1945–1946' (ch 2, n 71) 41–51; Gessler and Segesser, 'Raphael Lemkin and the International Debate on the Punishment of War Crimes (1919–1948)' (ch 2, n 5) 38; Irvin-Erickson, *Raphaël Lemkin and the Concept of Genocide* (ch 2, n 19) 140.

[73] Cooper, *Raphael Lemkin and the Struggle for the Genocide Convention* (ch 1, n 43) vii. See also Irvin-Erickson, *Raphaël Lemkin and the Concept of Genocide* (ch 2, n 19) 150. Cf, however, ibid 143.

[74] See Kuper, *Genocide. Its Political Use in the Twentieth Century* (ch 1, n 34) 22.

[75] Cf the table provided by Moyn Samuel, 'From Aggression to Atrocity: Rethinking the History of International Criminal Law' in Kevin Jon Heller and others (eds), *The Oxford Handbook of International Criminal Law* (Oxford University Press 2020) 351.

[76] See Barrett, 'Raphael Lemkin and "Genocide" at Nuremberg, 1945–1946' (ch 2, n 71) 38–49; Bazyler, *Holocaust, Genocide, and the Law. A Quest for Justice in a Post-Holocaust World* (ch 2, n 19) 35; Cooper, *Raphael Lemkin and the Struggle for the Genocide Convention* (ch 1, n 43) vii and 75; Irvin-Erickson, *Raphaël Lemkin and the Concept of Genocide* (ch 2, n 19) 143–4; Ternon, *L'État Criminel. Les Génocides au XXe Siècle* (ch 1, n 36) 39.

[77] Power, *A Problem from Hell. America and the Age of Genocide* (ch 1, n 13) 50.

[78] See Cooper, *Raphael Lemkin and the Struggle for the Genocide Convention* (ch 1, n 43) 73 and 77–8; Irvin-Erickson, *Raphaël Lemkin and the Concept of Genocide* (ch 2, n 19) 148; William A. Schabas, 'Genocide in International Law and International Relations Prior to 1948' in Eckart Conze and Christoph Safferling (eds), *The Genocide Convention Sixty Years After Its Adoption* (TMC Asser Press 2010) 19; Schabas, *Unimaginable Atrocities. Justice, Politics, and Rights at the War Crimes Tribunals* (ch 1, n 45) 109.

[79] See Cooper, *Raphael Lemkin and the Struggle for the Genocide Convention* (ch 1, n 43) 74–5 and 78; Power, *A Problem from Hell. America and the Age of Genocide* (ch 1, n 13) 50.

[80] See Power, *A Problem from Hell. America and the Age of Genocide* (ch 1, n 13) 50. Cf, however, the narratives created by Cooper, *Raphael Lemkin and the Struggle for the Genocide Convention* (ch 1, n 43) 79; Irvin-Erickson, *Raphaël Lemkin and the Concept of Genocide* (ch 2, n 19) 152.

2.4 The United Nations and the Genocide Convention

Raphaël Lemkin relentlessly lobbied his concept at the United Nations and, finally, managed to get a select number of delegates to support, put forward and discuss his idea.[81] It did not take long for the newly established United Nations to put atrocity prevention on its agenda. On 11 December 1946, the General Assembly first passed a resolution reaffirming 'the principles of international law recognized by the Charter of the Nürnberg Tribunal and the judgment of the Tribunal' and directed:

> the Committee on the codification of international law established by the resolution of the General Assembly of 11 December 1946, to treat as a matter of primary importance plans for the formulation of offences against the peace and security of mankind, or of an International Criminal Code, of the principles recognized in the Charter of the Nürnberg Tribunal and in the judgment of the Tribunal.[82]

On 2 November 1946, the delegations of Cuba, India and Panama had already submitted a draft resolution on genocide to be adopted by the General Assembly.[83] It included the commitment that it

> draws the attention of the Social and Economic Council to the crime of genocide and invites the Council to study this problem and to prepare a report on the possibilities of declaring genocide an International Crime and assuring international co-operation for its prevention and punishment and also recommending among others that genocide and related offenses should be dealt with by National Legislations in the same way as other international crimes such as piracy, trade in women, children and slaves, and others.

[81] See Cooper, *Raphael Lemkin and the Struggle for the Genocide Convention* (ch 1, n 43) 79–110, 132–229, and 160–271; Irvin-Erickson, *Raphaël Lemkin and the Concept of Genocide* (ch 2, n 19) 152–96; Power, *A Problem from Hell. America and the Age of Genocide* (ch 1, n 13) 51–64; Schabas, *Unimaginable Atrocities. Justice, Politics, and Rights at the War Crimes Tribunals* (ch 1, n 45) 105; Theriault and Totten, *The United Nations Genocide Convention. An Introduction* (ch 2, n 19) 7–8.

[82] United Nations General Assembly Resolution 95 (I), 'Affirmation of the Principles of International Law Recognized by the Charter of the Nürnberg Tribunal', 11 December 1946, UN Doc. A/64/Add. 1.

[83] United Nations General Assembly, 'The Crime of Genocide (Request from the Delegations for Cuba, India and Panama for the Inclusion of an Additional Item in the Agenda)', 2 November 1946, A/BUR/50. On the process at the United Nations, see Drost, *The Crime of State. Penal Protection for Fundamental Freedoms of Persons and Peoples. Book II. Genocide. United Nations Legislation on International Criminal Law* (ch 1, n 10). With a focus on Lemkin's involvement, see also Cooper, *Raphael Lemkin and the Struggle for the Genocide Convention* (ch 1, n 43) 79–80; Irvin-Erickson, *Raphaël Lemkin and the Concept of Genocide* (ch 2, n 19) 153.

The resolution on the Nuremberg principles of 11 December 1946 was immediately followed by the unanimous adoption of Resolution 96(I) on 'The Crime of Genocide'.[84] It went further than the original draft by instructing the Economic and Social Council of the United Nations to draw up 'a draft convention on the crime of genocide to be submitted to the next regular session of the General Assembly'.[85]

On 9 December 1948, four years after Lemkin's original treatise had been published, the General Assembly of the United Nations approved the text of the Genocide Convention in Paris.[86] Lemkin himself had travelled to Geneva, where the future Genocide Convention was being discussed, and to Paris, where it was adopted – often to the detriment of his own health.[87]

Personal drama has repeatedly been woven into the adoption of the Genocide Convention by attesting Lemkin 'a literally one-man obsession to have the League of Nations and, latterly, the United Nations take up the issue'.[88] With contemporary voices such as the *Washington Post* speaking of a 'personal crusade'[89] was born the image of 'a one-man crusade for a genocide convention',[90] and 'if ever there was a "prophet without honour", Lemkin was this man',[91] for a long time largely forgotten in the history of his home country of Poland.[92] To add to the narrative of selfless commitment, he is often portrayed along the impressions of Henry King as he had observed him in Nuremberg: 'he was unshaven, his clothing was in tatters and he looked dishevelled';[93] 'but

84 United Nations General Assembly Resolution 96 (I), 'The Crime of Genocide', 11 December 1946, UN Doc A/64/Add 1.

85 United Nations General Assembly Resolution 96 (I), 'The Crime of Genocide', 11 December 1946, UN Doc A/64/Add 1.

86 See United Nations Treaty Collection, Depositary, Chapter IV: Human Rights, 1. Convention on the Prevention and Punishment of the Crime of Genocide <https://treaties.un.org/pages/ViewDetails.aspx?src=TREATY&mtdsg_no=IV-1&chapter=4&lang=en>.

87 See Cooper, *Raphael Lemkin and the Struggle for the Genocide Convention* (ch 1, n 43) 79–110, 132–229, and 160–271; Irvin-Erickson, *Raphaël Lemkin and the Concept of Genocide* (ch 2, n 19) 152–96; Power, *A Problem from Hell. America and the Age of Genocide* (ch 1, n 13) 51–64; Schabas, *Unimaginable Atrocities. Justice, Politics, and Rights at the War Crimes Tribunals* (ch 1, n 45) 105.

88 Levene, *Genocide in the Age of the Nation-State. Volume I: The Meaning of Genocide* (ch 1, n 15) 43.

89 'U.N. Assembly Vote Outlaws Genocide' *Washington Post* (10 December 1948).

90 Kuper, *Genocide. Its Political Use in the Twentieth Century* (ch 1, n 34) 22. For a more differentiated view of Lemkin within the context of his contemporaries, cf Mira L. Siegelberg, 'Unofficial Men, Efficient Civil Servants: Raphael Lemkin in the History of International Law' (2013) 15 *Journal of Genocide Research* 297.

91 Rubinstein, *Genocide: A History* (ch 1, n 40) 308. Cf, however, Irvin-Erickson, *Raphaël Lemkin and the Concept of Genocide* (ch 2, n 19) 163.

92 See Ryszard Szawłowski, 'Raphael Lemkin (1900–1959). The Polish Lawyer Who Created the Concept of "Genocide"' (2005) 2 *The Polish Quarterly of International Affairs* 98, 100–1.

93 Henry T. King Jr., 'Genocide and Nuremberg' in Paul Behrens and Ralph Henham (eds), *The Criminal Law of Genocide. International, Comparative and Contextual Aspects* (Ashgate 2007) 29.

he possessed a soul which had a steely determination to correct national and international wrong and the world is better for it today'.[94]

Be that as it may, the 'crusade' was a success. 'A remarkably short time' had passed[95] between the 'invention' of the word 'genocide' in 1944 and its inclusion in the decision of an international organization just two years later. An equally short time had passed from Lemkin's original definition to the confusion over what should fall within the scope of this new crime.

The preambular paragraphs of Resolution 96(I) frames genocide as 'a denial of the right of existence of entire human groups, as homicide is the denial of the right to live of individual human beings' and goes on to find that '[m]any instances of such crimes of genocide have occurred when racial, religious, political and other groups have been destroyed, entirely or in part' (Lemkin's history of genocides resonates between the lines).[96] The resolution goes on to affirm in its operative paragraphs

> that genocide is a crime under international law which the civilized world condemns and for the commission of which principals and accomplices – whether private individuals, public officials or statesmen, and whether the crime is committed on religious, racial, political or any other ground – are punishable.

In contrast to the later Genocide Convention it includes political groups within its scope.[97]

Although the Preamble of the Genocide Convention makes reference to Resolution 96(I),[98] its definition differs in a slight but very important detail.[99] While one of the original drafts had simply referred to 'a group of human beings',[100] political groups were now eliminated from the scope of the definition

[94] Ibid 34.

[95] Yuval Shany, 'The Road to the Genocide Convention and Beyond' in Paola Gaeta (ed), *The UN Genocide Convention: A Commentary* (Oxford University Press 2009) 3.

[96] See Chapter 1, n 43–4.

[97] See already Drost, *The Crime of State. Penal Protection for Fundamental Freedoms of Persons and Peoples. Book II. Genocide. United Nations Legislation on International Criminal Law* (ch 1, n 10) 29–30 and 60–3.

[98] Convention for the Prevention and Punishment of the Crime of Genocide, 9 December 1948, 78 United Nations Treaty Series 277, Preamble.

[99] Cf Drost, *The Crime of State. Penal Protection for Fundamental Freedoms of Persons and Peoples. Book II. Genocide. United Nations Legislation on International Criminal Law* (ch 1, n 10) 29–30 and 60–3.

[100] See Jones, *Genocide. A Comprehensive Introduction* (ch 1, n 34) 21.

and the term 'ethnical' was added as context 'to make it clearer that the word "national" did not refer to and was not related to the term "political"':[101]

> Article II
> In the present Convention, genocide means any of the following acts committed with intent to destroy, in whole or in part, a national, ethnical, racial or religious group, as such:
>
> (a) Killing members of the group;
> (b) Causing serious bodily or mental harm to members of the group;
> (c) Deliberately inflicting on the group conditions of life calculated to bring about its physical destruction in whole or in part;
> (d) Imposing measures intended to prevent births within the group;
> (e) Forcibly transferring children of the group to another group.

It has been often restated that during the drafting of the Genocide Convention, the Soviet Union was the main advocate for omitting political groups.[102] Opposition to their inclusion was, however, more widespread.[103] Other members of the Communist bloc and a couple of Latin American states shared concerns with regard to the suppression of internal revolts.[104] The United States, on the other hand, saw the problem of overbearing intrusion into state sovereignty[105] – an issue that persisted irrespective of the inclusion of political groups.[106] As Timothy Snyder points out, 'this particular murder statute was co-drafted by some of the murderers'.[107]

Lemkin himself had eventually opposed including political groups, apparently favouring a speedy adoption.[108] He feared failure in the negotiations,

[101] Drost, *The Crime of State. Penal Protection for Fundamental Freedoms of Persons and Peoples. Book II. Genocide. United Nations Legislation on International Criminal Law* (ch 1, n 10) 61.

[102] For example, United Nations Economic and Social Council, Commission on Human Rights, Sub-Commission on Prevention of Discrimination and Protection of Minorities, 'Revised and Updated Report on the Question of the Prevention and Punishment of the Crime of Genocide', 2 July 1985, UN Doc E/CN.4/Sub.2/1985/6, at 18, para 35.

[103] See in detail Schabas, *Genocide in International Law* (ch 2, n 28) 153–60; Schabas, *Unimaginable Atrocities. Justice, Politics, and Rights at the War Crimes Tribunals* (ch 1, n 45) 111.

[104] See Power, *A Problem from Hell. America and the Age of Genocide* (ch 1, n 13) 68–9.

[105] See ibid 69.

[106] Cf Lawrence LeBlanc, 'The United States and the Genocide Convention: The Sovereignty Package in Perspective' in Harmen G. van der Wilt and others (eds), *The Genocide Convention: The Legacy of 60 Years* (Martinus Nijhoff 2012).

[107] Timothy Snyder, *Bloodlands. Europe Between Hitler and Stalin* (The Bodley Head 2010) 413.

[108] See Just Dülffer, 'The United Nations and the Origins of the Genocide Convention 1946–1948' in Eckart Conze and Christoph Safferling (eds), *The Genocide Convention Sixty Years After Its Adoption* (TMC Asser Press 2010) 61; Irvin-Erickson, *Raphaël Lemkin and the Concept of Genocide* (ch 2,

hoping to later add on an additional protocol.[109] Needless to say, no such protocol was ever adopted.

Another aspect, cultural genocide, although still envisioned in the preliminary discussion and drafts of the Genocide Convention,[110] was equally excluded,[111] although the act of 'forcibly transferring children of the group to another group' remained upon the insistence of Greece that had experienced such abductions – albeit within a political context – during its Civil War that raged from 1946 to 1949.[112]

2.5 Legacy and renaissance

While December 1948 also saw the adoption of the 'Universal Declaration of Human Rights' by the General Assembly, the Genocide Convention was 'the first human rights treaty of the modern system'.[113] The International Court of Justice (ICJ) attested the Genocide Convention a 'humanitarian and civilizing purpose'.[114] It reminds the international community of the ultimate consequences of the *domaine reservé*, that treatment of a state's own nationals would rest at its discretion.

The Genocide Convention entered into force just over two years later on 12 January 1951, and its Article II is still state of the art today as the 'most

n 19) 152–96; Schabas, *Genocide in International Law* (ch 2, n 28) 154; William A. Schabas, 'The Law and Genocide' in Donald Bloxham and A. Dirk Moses (eds), *The Oxford Handbook of Genocide Studies* (Oxford University Press 2010) 133.

[109] See Power, *A Problem from Hell. America and the Age of Genocide* (ch 1, n 13) 69 and 531, fn 14. Additionally, Jewish interest groups, partly on pressure from Lemkin himself, opposed the inclusion. See Cooper, *Raphael Lemkin and the Struggle for the Genocide Convention* (ch 1, n 43) 96–7 and 165–70; Schabas, *Genocide in International Law* (ch 2, n 28) 154.

[110] See Drost, *The Crime of State. Penal Protection for Fundamental Freedoms of Persons and Peoples. Book II. Genocide. United Nations Legislation on International Criminal Law* (ch 1, n 10) 10–11, 23, 31–3, 41–3, and 58–60; Irvin-Erickson, *Raphaël Lemkin and the Concept of Genocide* (ch 2, n 19) 183.

[111] See Irvin-Erickson, *Raphaël Lemkin and the Concept of Genocide* (ch 2, n 19) 182–8.

[112] See Payam Akhavan, 'Cultural Genocide: Legal Label of Mourning Metaphor?' (2016) 61 *McGill Law Journal / Revue de droit de McGill* 243, 261–2; Drost, *The Crime of State. Penal Protection for Fundamental Freedoms of Persons and Peoples. Book II. Genocide. United Nations Legislation on International Criminal Law* (ch 1, n 10) 59 and 81. See also ibid 81.

[113] William A. Schabas, 'Genocide and Crimes against Humanity: Clarifying the Relationship' in Harmen G. van der Wilt and others (eds), *The Genocide Convention: The Legacy of 60 Years* (Martinus Nijhoff 2012) 3.

[114] *Reservations to the Convention on the Prevention and Punishment of the Crime of Genocide*, Advisory Opinion of 28 May 1951, (1951) ICJ Reports 15, 23.

widely accepted'[115] definition of genocide under international law, included in numerous national legislations.[116] Lemkin had managed to define a phenomenon of intersocietal atrocity in the form of a technical legal provision that nowadays stands in the criminal codes of nations and expresses a moral gravity way beyond that of murder or any of its specifications. He must surely be deemed a 'norm entrepreneur'.[117]

Lemkin had created a word with such impact that very few other neologisms can match today. The very same year that *Axis Rule in Occupied Europe* was published, 'genocide' entered *Webster's International Dictionary*.[118] The Genocide Convention not only introduced to the level of international law a word comprising an entire legal concept, it also helped popularize and make it understood across the world today. It is surely unique in that it has probably had the most interdisciplinary and popular impact of any idea of international law.

Yet, immediately following the adoption of the Genocide Convention, 'the Nuremberg precedent was something of a dead letter' when it came to the prosecution of individuals for the commission of atrocities.[119] With the exception of singular instances in domestic trials,[120] the first ten years have little to show for, a factor to which 'postwar geopolitics contributed the most'.[121] It was mainly used as a rhetorical accusation between Western states and the Communist bloc throughout the 1950s.[122] In fact, it took the Genocide Convention almost half a century to bloom and the United States did not ratify

[115] Chalk and Jonassohn, *The History and Sociology of Genocide. Analyses and Case Studies* (ch 1, n 40) 3. See also John Quigley, *The Genocide Convention. An International Law Analysis* (Ashgate 2006) 10.

[116] See Schabas, *Genocide in International Law* (ch 2, n 28) 6.

[117] See Chapter 2, n 26.

[118] See Augustine Brannigan, *Beyond the Banality of Evil: Criminology and Genocide* (Oxford University Press 2013) 50.

[119] Gellately and Kiernan, 'The Study of Mass Murder and Genocide' (ch 1, n 19) 4. See also Eckart Conze and Christoph Safferling (eds), *The Genocide Convention Sixty Years After Its Adoption* (TMC Asser Press 2010) 3; Dülffer, 'The United Nations and the Origins of the Genocide Convention 1946–1948' (ch 2, n 108) 67.

[120] See Matthew Lippman, 'The Convention on the Prevention and Punishment of the Crime of Genocide: Fifty Years Later' (1998) 15 *Arizona Journal of International and Comparative Law* 415, 446–8; Vrdoljak, 'Human Rights and Genocide: The Work of Lauterpacht and Lemkin in Modern International Law' (ch 2, n 58) 1192–3.

[121] Anton Weiss-Wendt, 'The Soviet Perspective on the Drafting of the UN Genocide Convention' in Harmen G. van der Wilt and others (eds), *The Genocide Convention: The Legacy of 60 Years* (Martinus Nijhoff 2012) 188.

[122] See Moses, 'Introduction: The Field of Genocide Studies' (ch 1, n 30) 1 with further references; Weiss-Wendt, 'The Soviet Perspective on the Drafting of the UN Genocide Convention' (ch 2, n 121) 191; Anton Weiss-Wendt, *A Rhetorical Crime. Genocide in the Geopolitical Discourse of the Cold War* (Rutgers University Press 2018).

it until 1988 for fears of restricting its sovereignty as a state (in fact, it made reservations to the extent of limiting the consequences in case of a violation).[123]

The establishment of the two ad hoc tribunals by the United Nations Security Council for Yugoslavia and Rwanda in the 1990s brought about a '*renaissance* of international criminal law'.[124] The prosecution of perpetrators of these two conflicts made the crime of genocide relevant to practice and gave it centre stage of the international judicial discourse. The definition of the Genocide Convention was included *verbatim* in the statutes of both the ICTY and the ICTR[125] and later in the Rome Statute of the International Criminal Court (the ICC).[126] When the Rome Statute was adopted in 1998, only Cuba argued for the adaptation of the definition and inclusion of political groups.[127]

Apart from the issue of political groups, Article II of the Genocide Convention 'like most legal definitions its language is subject to various interpretations'.[128] It has been elaborated on and expanded in the jurisprudence and by the 'Elements of Crimes' provided by the ICC as an addition to Article 6 of its Statute, which also calls into question the 'monolithical' legal definition by adding a large number of specific acts falling within the scope of the crime.[129] Domestic statutes see the implementation of the Convention with

[123] For the reservations and interpretative declarations of the United States, see United Nations Office of Legal Affairs, Treaty Section, Depositary Notification, Convention on the Prevention and Punishment of the Crime of Genocide, Ratification by the United States of America, 29 December 1988, C.N.281.1988.TREATIES-2.

[124] Tams, Berster and Schiffbauer, 'General Introduction' (ch 1, n 48) 21. Cf Moyn, *The Last Utopia. Human Rights in History* (ch 1, n 48) 176.

[125] See Updated Statute of the International Criminal Tribunal for the former Yugoslavia as of September 2009, Article 4(2) <http://www.icty.org/x/file/Legal%20Library/Statute/statute_sept09_en.pdf>; Statute of the International Criminal Tribunal for Rwanda as of 31 January 2010, Article 2(2), <http://www.unictr.org/Portals/0/English%5CLegal%5CStatute%5C2010.pdf>. Cf, however, Schabas, *Genocide in International Law* (ch 2, n 28) 151–3.

[126] See Rome Statute of the International Criminal Court, 17 July 1998, 2187 United Nations Treaty Series 3, Article 6. See also Hans-Peter Kaul, 'The International Criminal Court and the Crime of Genocide' in Eckart Conze and Christoph Safferling (eds), *The Genocide Convention Sixty Years After Its Adoption* (TMC Asser Press 2010) 197 and 210.

[127] See Summary Records of the Meetings of the Committee of the Whole, 3rd Meeting of the Committee of the Whole, 17 June 1998, A/CONF.183/C.1/SR.3, in United Nations Diplomatic Conference of Plenipotentiaries on the Establishment of an International Criminal Court, Rome, 15 June–17 July 1998, Volume 2, A/CONF.183/13 (Vol. II), at 151: 'Ms. Cueto Milián (Cuba), while agreeing that the provisions on genocide in the draft Statute were generally acceptable, thought that they could be expanded by the inclusion of social and political groupings and a reference to intentional conduct.' See also Schabas, *Genocide in International Law* (ch 2, n 28) 106 and 130–1.

[128] Schabas, *Unimaginable Atrocities. Justice, Politics, and Rights at the War Crimes Tribunals* (ch 1, n 45) 104.

[129] International Criminal Court, Elements of Crimes, ICC-ASP/1/3(part II-B), 9 September 2002 <https://www.icc-cpi.int/NR/rdonlyres/336923D8-A6AD-40EC-AD7B-45BF9DE73D56/0/ElementsOfCrimesEng.pdf>:

'Article 6(a) Genocide by killing – Elements 1. The perpetrator killed one or more persons. 2. Such person or persons belonged to a particular national, ethnical, racial or religious group. 3. The

varying definitions and scope as to groups or acts covered.[130] Some have indeed expanded the scope[131] and scholarship continues to call for a broadening of the Genocide Convention definition.[132]

In accordance with legal doctrine and jurisprudence, the prohibition of genocide finds its legal basis not only in the Genocide Convention but also in customary international law,[133] signifying widespread recognition in state

perpetrator intended to destroy, in whole or in part, that national, ethnical, racial or religious group, as such. 4. The conduct took place in the context of a manifest pattern of similar conduct directed against that group or was conduct that could itself effect such destruction.

Article 6(b) Genocide by causing serious bodily or mental harm – Elements 1. The perpetrator caused serious bodily or mental harm to one or more persons. 2. Such person or persons belonged to a particular national, ethnical, racial or religious group. 3. The perpetrator intended to destroy, in whole or in part, that national, ethnical, racial or religious group, as such. 4. The conduct took place in the context of a manifest pattern of similar conduct directed against that group or was conduct that could itself effect such destruction.

Article 6(c) Genocide by deliberately inflicting conditions of life calculated to bring about physical destruction – Elements 1. The perpetrator inflicted certain conditions of life upon one or more persons. 2. Such person or persons belonged to a particular national, ethnical, racial or religious group. 3. The perpetrator intended to destroy, in whole or in part, that national, ethnical, racial or religious group, as such. 4. The conditions of life were calculated to bring about the physical destruction of that group, in whole or in part. 5. The conduct took place in the context of a manifest pattern of similar conduct directed against that group or was conduct that could itself effect such destruction.

Article 6(d) Genocide by imposing measures intended to prevent births – Elements 1. The perpetrator imposed certain measures upon one or more persons. 2. Such person or persons belonged to a particular national, ethnical, racial or religious group. 3. The perpetrator intended to destroy, in whole or in part, that national, ethnical, racial or religious group, as such. 4. The measures imposed were intended to prevent births within that group. 5. The conduct took place in the context of a manifest pattern of similar conduct directed against that group or was conduct that could itself effect such destruction.

Article 6(e) Genocide by forcibly transferring children – Elements 1. The perpetrator forcibly transferred one or more persons. 2. Such person or persons belonged to a particular national, ethnical, racial or religious group. 3. The perpetrator intended to destroy, in whole or in part, that national, ethnical, racial or religious group, as such. 4. The transfer was from that group to another group. 5. The person or persons were under the age of 18 years. 6. The perpetrator knew, or should have known, that the person or persons were under the age of 18 years. 7. The conduct took place in the context of a manifest pattern of similar conduct directed against that group or was conduct that could itself effect such destruction.'

130 See Tamás Hoffmann, 'The Crime of Genocide in Its (Nearly) Infinite Domestic Variety' in Marco Odello and Piotr Łubiński (eds), *The Concept of Genocide in International Criminal Law – Developments after Lemkin* (Routledge 2020); Ben Saul, 'The Implementation of the Genocide Convention at the National Level' in Paola Gaeta (ed), *The UN Genocide Convention: A Commentary* (Oxford University Press 2009) 64–6.

131 For an overview, see Quigley, *The Genocide Convention. An International Law Analysis* (ch 2, n 115) 15–20. On the French implementation of the Genocide Convention, see Schabas, *Genocide in International Law* (ch 2, n 28) 6 and 131. On the Canadian implementation of the Rome Statute, see ibid 6 and 151. For further examples, including Bangladesh, Costa Rica, Lithuania, Panama, Peru and Slovenia, see ibid 161–2. Cf also ibid 123–4.

132 For example, already Drost, *The Crime of State. Penal Protection for Fundamental Freedoms of Persons and Peoples. Book II. Genocide. United Nations Legislation on International Criminal Law* (ch 1, n 10) 122–4. See also Schabas, *Genocide in International Law* (ch 2, n 28) 161 with further references.

133 See Schabas, *Genocide in International Law* (ch 2, n 28) 6 and 648; Andreas L. Paulus and Bruno Simma, 'The Responsibility of Individuals for Human Rights Abuses in Internal Conflicts: A Positivist View' (1999) 93 *American Journal of International Law* 302, 308–9, in particular also fns 36–9. For a detailed discussion, see Quigley, *The Genocide Convention. An International Law*

practice and a corresponding conviction that this practice follows a legal obligation.[134]

It is further attested the prohibition of genocide the status of a *ius cogens* norm,[135] far atop of the hierarchical pyramid of manifestations of international law and as a normative barrier against which all conflicting international law, is deflected as null and void. In fact, when the concept of *ius cogens* first formally appeared in an international treaty, the drafters were also thinking of genocide.[136] In the *Barcelona Traction* case, the ICJ suggested a catalogue of norms of *erga omnes* character, meaning those norms owed to the entire international community, naturally including the prohibition of genocide.[137] As a peremptory norm,[138] any violation of the prohibition, be it under the Convention or under customary international law, must lead to cooperation by the international community 'to bring to an end through lawful means' the breach.[139]

The two ad hoc tribunals, the ICTY and the ICTR, have prosecuted and convicted individuals for the commission of genocide and, thereby, shaped the concept through practical application.[140] Their work finds continuation in the International Residual Mechanism for Criminal Tribunals. Further examples of the prosecution of individuals by hybrid tribunals[141] include the Extraordinary Chambers in the Courts of Cambodia[142] or the Special Court for Sierra Leone.[143]

Analysis (ch 2, n 115) 80–4. Cf with regard to a possible expansion of the definition under customary international law David Shea Bettwy, 'The Genocide Convention and Unprotected Groups: Is the Scope of Protection Expanding under Customary International Law?' (2011) 2 *Notre Dame Journal of International & Comparative Law*.

134 Cf Statute of the International Court of Justice, 26 June 1945, Article 38(1)(b).

135 See in particular the judgement by the ICJ in *Armed Activities on the Territory of the Congo (New Application: 2002)* (Democratic Republic of the Congo *v.* Rwanda), Judgement of 3 February 2006 (Jurisdiction and Admissibility), (2006) ICJ Reports 6, 32, para 64.

136 See Yearbook of the International Law Commission, 1966, Vol. II, 248, para 3.

137 See *Barcelona Traction, Light and Power Company, Limited (New Application: 1962)* (Belgium *v* Spain), Judgment of 5 February 1970, (1970) ICJ Reports 3, 32 para 34.

138 See *Armed Activities on the Territory of the Congo* (New Application: 2002; Democratic Republic of the Congo *v* Rwanda), Judgement of 3 February 2006 on Jurisdiction of the Court and Admissibility of the Application, (2006) ICJ Reports 6, 32, para 64

139 See Article 41 (1) ASR.

140 For a concise overview of the creation of these tribunals together with some of their landmark cases regarding genocide, see Amabelle C. Asuncion, 'Pulling the Stops on Genocide: The State or the Individual?' (2009) 20 *European Journal of International Law* 1195, 1197–202.

141 The label is somewhat misleading in that the act of creation of such tribunals is either international or domestic. The 'hybrid' nature stems rather from the usual reference to both international and domestic crimes, as well as the appointment of international and domestic judges.

142 See Extraordinary Chambers in the Courts of Cambodia <https://www.eccc.gov.kh/en>.

143 See Special Court for Sierra Leone <http://rscsl.org/>.

The International Court of Justice has applied the Genocide Convention in finding that Serbia and Montenegro had failed to prevent, prosecute and punish perpetrators of genocide in Srebrenica.[144] Following the appointment of Special Rapporteurs on Genocide in the former Sub-Commission on Prevention of Discrimination and Protection of Minorities of the Commission on Human Rights that had produced two prominent reports on the prohibition of genocide,[145] the United Nations created the office of Special Advisor on the Prevention of Genocide in 2004.[146] In 2009, the ICC indicted then president of Sudan, Omar al-Bashir, for genocide.[147]

As of 2021, the Genocide Convention counts a total of 152 parties, of which 41 are original signatories.[148] Although this number of states parties has been described as 'comparatively low',[149] the Genocide Convention has become an iconic pillar of international law. Originally a legal term, 'genocide' has come to be used by scholars of history, political science and sociology, to name but a few,[150] entering popular culture[151] as 'part of our normal linguistic currency and, indeed, an important facet of our sense of the world and what happens in it'.[152]

144 *Application of the Convention on the Prevention and Punishment of the Crime of Genocide* (Bosnia and Herzegovina *v* Serbia and Montenegro), Judgment of 26 February 2007, (2007) ICJ Reports 43. For a critical assessment of the case, see Asuncion, 'Pulling the Stops on Genocide: The State or the Individual?' (ch 2, n 140).

145 The 1978 Ruhashyankiko Report and the 1985 Whitaker Report. See United Nations Economic and Social Council, Commission on Human Rights, Sub-Commission on Prevention of Discrimination and Protection of Minorities, 'Study of the Question of the Prevention and Punishment of the Crime of Genocide', 4 July 1978, E/CN.4/Sub.2/416; United Nations Economic and Social Council, Commission on Human Rights, Sub-Commission on Prevention of Discrimination and Protection of Minorities, 'Revised and Updated Report on the Question of the Prevention and Punishment of the Crime of Genocide', 2 July 1985, E/CN.4/Sub.2/1985/6.

146 See United Nations Office on Genocide Prevention and the Responsibility to Protect, Mandate <https://www.un.org/en/genocideprevention/office-mandate.shtml>.

147 ICC, Pre-Trial Chamber I, Warrant of Arrest for Omar Hassan Ahmad al-Bashir of 4 March 2009, ICC-02/05-01/09-1.

148 At time of writing, forty-two – primarily African, American and Asian – states had not yet acceded: Angola, Bhutan, Botswana, Brunei Darussalam, Cameroon, Central, African Republic, Chad, Congo, Djibouti, Dominican Republic, Equatorial Guinea, Eritrea, Grenada, Guyana, Indonesia, Japan, Kenya, Kiribati, Madagascar, Marshall Islands, Mauritania, Micronesia, Nauru, Niger, Oman, Palau, Qatar, Saint Lucia, Saint Kitts and Nevis, Samoa, Sao Tome and Principe, Sierra Leone, Solomon Islands, Somalia, South Sudan, Suriname, Swaziland, Thailand, Timor-Leste, Tuvalu, Vanuatu and Zambia. Of these, the Dominican Republic is an original signatory. All European states have ratified. Palestine acceded in 2014. See United Nations Treaty Collection, Depositary, Chapter IV: Human Rights 1. Convention on the Prevention and Punishment of the Crime of Genocide <https://treaties.un.org/Pages/ViewDetails.aspx?src=IND&mtdsg_no=IV-1&chapter=4&clang=_en>.

149 Schabas, 'Genocide and Crimes against Humanity: Clarifying the Relationship' (ch 2, n 113) 3.

150 See also already Chapter 1 Section A.

151 See Horowitz, *Taking Lives. Genocide and State Power* (ch 1, n 26) 319.

152 Levene, *Genocide in the Age of the Nation-State. Volume I: The Meaning of Genocide* (ch 1, n 15) 37.

2.6 Siamese twins, separated at birth

If Lemkin failed at having the term 'genocide' introduced into the Nuremberg Charter, this was in no way predictive of the long-term impact of his ideas over the 'first-mover advantage' of 'crimes against humanity'. This is easily demonstrated by a simple Google search bringing up around 113,000,000 hits for 'genocide' and 'only' approximately 12,300,000 hits for 'crimes against humanity'.[153] There is no such thing as 'Crimes against Humanity Studies' and the somewhat awkward abbreviation 'CAH' has not managed to gain broader acceptance.

Yet, it is impossible to understand the legacy of Lemkin's 'invention' without looking at its 'rival sibling' in Nuremberg: 'The development and history of genocide as a legal concept cannot be properly understood without considering the parallel existence of crimes against humanity.'[154] Though both are distinct offences under international criminal law today, their rival yet synonymous character at Nuremberg gives these two criminal offences the character of 'Siamese twins', though separated at birth.

What perhaps tainted crimes against humanity as a human rights concept was that the Nuremberg precedent affirmed that they must be committed in times of war, the so-called nexus requirement. It did not cover atrocities committed during peacetime. Efforts at emancipation from this nexus can already be found in the ensuing domestic piece of legislation introducing crimes against humanity into domestic German law, Control Council Law No. 10.[155] Its Article II(c) reads:

> Crimes against Humanity. Atrocities and offenses, including but not limited to murder, extermination, enslavement, deportation, imprisonment, torture, rape, or other inhumane acts committed against any civilian population, or persecutions on political, racial or religious grounds whether or not in violation of the domestic laws of the country where perpetrated.[156]

[153] Last search conducted on 15 October 2021. Of course, the number of results is volatile, but it does give a sense of proportion.

[154] Schabas, *Unimaginable Atrocities. Justice, Politics, and Rights at the War Crimes Tribunals* (ch 1, n 45) 106.

[155] Cf Van Schaack, 'The Definition of Crimes against Humanity: Resolving the Incoherence' (ch 2, n 11) 807–18.

[156] Control Council Law No. 10. Punishment of Persons Guilty of War Crimes, Crimes Against Peace and Against Humanity, 20 December 1945 <http://avalon.law.yale.edu/imt/imt10.asp>.

Neither does the wording require any connection to other crimes within the jurisdiction of the tribunal as did Article 6(c) of the Nuremberg Charter.[157] Although there are further instances of the concept evolving beyond its original scope[158] and the United Nations General Assembly passed a number of resolutions on the need to prosecute war crimes and crimes against humanity,[159] the precedent of the Nuremberg Charter was reconfirmed as late as 1993 in the (since unamended) Statute of the ICTY:

> The International Tribunal shall have the power to prosecute persons responsible for the following crimes *when committed in armed conflict*, whether international or internal in character, and directed against any civilian population: (a) murder; (b) extermination; (c) enslavement; (d) deportation; (e) imprisonment; (f) torture; (g) rape; (h) persecutions on political, racial and religious grounds; (i) other inhumane acts.[160]

But this understanding of crimes against humanity has since evolved. In open contradiction to the Statute of the ICTY, the United Nations Secretary-General's Report on the establishment of the tribunal had stated that '[c]rimes against humanity are aimed at any civilian population and are prohibited *regardless of whether they are committed in an armed conflict*, international or internal in character'(emphasis in original).[161] This turned out to be a self-fulfilling prophecy, as the ICTY overcame the nexus requirement simply by relying on customary international law.[162]

[157] See Richard S. Clark, 'History of Efforts to Codify Crimes Against Humanity. From the Charter of Nuremberg to the Statute of Rome' in Leila Nadya Sadat (ed), *Forging a Convention for Crimes Against Humanity* (Cambridge University Press 2011) 12–13.

[158] See Schabas, 'Crimes Against Humanity' (ch 2, n 62) 212, referring to the use of the term within the following treaties: Convention on the Non-Applicability of Statutory Limitations to War Crimes and Crimes Against Humanity, 26 November 1968, 754 United Nations Treaty Series 73 and the International Convention on the Suppression and Punishment of the Crime of Apartheid, 30 November 1973, 1015 United Nations Treaty Series 243.

[159] See Payam Akhavan, 'The Universal Repression of Crimes Against Humanity before National Jurisdictions: The Need for a Treaty-Based Obligation to Prosecute' in Leila Nadya Sadat (ed), *Forging a Convention for Crimes Against Humanity* (Cambridge University Press 2011) 38–40.

[160] Updated Statute of the International Criminal Tribunal for the former Yugoslavia as of September 2009, Article 4(2) <http://www.icty.org/x/file/Legal%20Library/Statute/statute_sept09_en.pdf>, emphasis added.

[161] Report of the Secretary General Pursuant to Paragraph 2 of Security Council Resolution 808 (1993), 3 May 1993, S/25704, 13, para 47, emphasis added. Cf Paulus and Simma, 'The Responsibility of Individuals for Human Rights Abuses in Internal Conflicts: A Positivist View' (ch 2, n 133) 310.

[162] *Prosecutor v. Duško Tadić aka 'Dule'*, Case No. IT-94-1-AR72, Decision on the Defence Motion for Interlocutory Appeal on Jurisdiction of 2 October 1995, para 141. See also Irvin-Erickson, *Raphaël Lemkin and the Concept of Genocide* (ch 2, n 19) 236; Paulus and Simma, 'The Responsibility of Individuals for Human Rights Abuses in Internal Conflicts: A Positivist View' (ch 2, n 133) 310.

The Statute of the ICTR, in turn, was already rid of the nexus requirement in its text:[163]

> The International Tribunal for Rwanda shall have the power to prosecute persons responsible for the following crimes when committed as part of a widespread or systematic attack against any civilian population on national, political, ethnic, racial or religious grounds: (a) Murder; (b) Extermination; (c) Enslavement; (d) Deportation; (e) Imprisonment; (f) Torture; (g) Rape; (h) Persecutions on political, racial and religious grounds; (i) Other inhumane acts.[164]

However, it blurs the relationship between the crime of genocide and crimes against humanity by adding a subjective element requiring that the attack occur 'on national, political, ethnic, racial or religious grounds', a notion equally dating back to the Nuremberg Charter. This also influenced the definition of crimes against humanity applied by the Extraordinary Chambers in the Courts of Cambodia,[165] a tribunal tasked with prosecuting the atrocities committed by the Khmer Rouge during their reign of dystopian horror.

The definition of the Statue of the ICTR also included what has since been referred to as the 'contextual elements',[166] the requirement that crimes, to qualify as crimes against humanity, must take place 'as part of a widespread or systematic attack'. This approach was later adopted in the Rome Statute of the ICC in 1998, a consensus 'developed by multilateral negotiations among 160 states'[167] and now constituting 'the gold standard in terms of definitions of crimes against humanity':[168]

[163] Cf Paulus and Simma, 'The Responsibility of Individuals for Human Rights Abuses in Internal Conflicts: A Positivist View' (ch 2, n 133) 310.

[164] Statute of the International Criminal Tribunal for Rwanda as of 31 January 2010, Article 3, <http://www.unictr.org/Portals/0/English%5CLegal%5CStatute%5C2010.pdf>.

[165] Law on the Establishment of the Extraordinary Chambers, with inclusion of amendments as promulgated on 27 October 2004 (NS/RKM/1004/006) <http://www.eccc.gov.kh/sites/default/files/legal-documents/KR_Law_as_amended_27_Oct_2004_Eng.pdf>.

[166] See Schabas, 'Crimes Against Humanity' (ch 2, n 62) 212.

[167] Darryl Robinson, 'Defining "Crimes Against Humanity" at the Rome Conference' (1999) 93 *American Journal of International Law* 43, 56.

[168] Schabas, *Unimaginable Atrocities. Justice, Politics, and Rights at the War Crimes Tribunals* (ch 1, n 45) 140. See also Clark, 'History of Efforts to Codify Crimes Against Humanity. From the Charter of Nuremberg to the Statute of Rome' (ch 2, n 157) 22: 'It is probably possible to forge a consensus, at the least, around the proposition that the customary law definition of crimes against humanity was crystallized with the adoption of the Rome Statute on July 17, 1998.'

> Article 7
> Crimes against humanity
> 1. For the purpose of this Statute, 'crime against humanity' means any of the following acts when committed as part of a widespread or systematic attack directed against any civilian population, with knowledge of the attack:
> (a) Murder; (b) Extermination; (c) Enslavement; (d) Deportation or forcible transfer of population; (e) Imprisonment or other severe deprivation of physical liberty in violation of fundamental rules of international law; (f) Torture; (g) Rape, sexual slavery, enforced prostitution, forced pregnancy, enforced sterilization, or any other form of sexual violence of comparable gravity; (h) Persecution against any identifiable group or collectivity on political, racial, national, ethnic, cultural, religious, gender as defined in paragraph 3, or other grounds that are universally recognized as impermissible under international law, in connection with any act referred to in this paragraph or any crime within the jurisdiction of the Court; (i) Enforced disappearance of persons; (j) The crime of apartheid; (k) Other inhumane acts of a similar character intentionally causing great suffering, or serious injury to body or to mental or physical health.[169]

The provision in the Rome Statute goes further in narrowing down the scope through contextual elements by clarifying in its second paragraph that an '"[a]ttack directed against any civilian population" means a course of conduct involving the multiple commission of acts referred to in paragraph 1 against any civilian population, pursuant to or in furtherance of a State or organizational policy to commit such attack'.[170] Therefore, not only is it necessary for there to be 'a widespread or systematic attack' – of which the state is aware – but also that such an attack must be part 'of a State or organizational policy'.

However, the Rome Statute does away fully with the requirement of a discriminatory motive as included in the definition of the Statue of the ICTR.[171] While this opens the scope and distinguishes its legal elements from those of genocide, the contextual elements of crimes against humanity have conversely impacted the understanding of what constitutes genocide.

[169] Rome Statute of the International Criminal Court, 17 July 1998, 2187 United Nations Treaty Series 3, Article 7(1).

[170] Rome Statute of the International Criminal Court, 17 July 1998, 2187 United Nations Treaty Series 3, Article 7(2).

[171] See Robinson, 'Defining "Crimes Against Humanity" at the Rome Conference' (ch 2, n 167) 46–7.

There is a historical run-up to this understanding: when genocide appeared for the first time in an official legal document under 'Count Three' of the indictment of the major Nazi war criminals before the International Military Tribunal, it was accompanied by the description as 'deliberate and systematic'. A contribution in the *Washington Post* in 1946 described the Nazi crimes that this new crime of genocide should cover as 'systematic and purposeful': 'The gas chambers and furnaces were not improvisations; they were scientifically designed instruments for the extermination of an entire ethnic group.'[172]

Oftentimes now, instead of the legal definition of the Genocide Convention, the contextual elements of crimes against humanity are seen as indicative of genocide.[173] Boris Barth, in his history of twentieth-century genocides, writes that criteria of genocide are 'neither the number of victims, nor the degree of cruelty, but intent, organization, and identity of the victims' ('weder Zahl der Opfer noch der Grad der Grausamkeit, sondern Vorsatz, Planmäßigkeit und die Identität der Opfer').[174]

However, the international crime of genocide does not include any such requirement of organization, even if the commission of genocide often goes hand in hand with such an overarching state policy and its implementation.[175] But legally, any such reference is off point:

> The limitations of this ontological or phenomenological construction are evident: it is not based on the proper interpretation of the relevant international rules, but rather on the inherent features of what is considered to be genocide as a historical occurrence.[176]

It might be that the charge of 'deliberate and systematic genocide' under 'Count Three' of the indictment of the major Nazi war criminals before the

[172] 'Genocide' *Washington Post* (3 December 1944) 4.

[173] For a number of proponents of this view under international law, see Antonio Cassese, 'The Policy Element in Genocide: When Is It Required by International Rules?' in Eckart Conze and Christoph Safferling (eds), *The Genocide Convention Sixty Years After Its Adoption* (TMC Asser Press 2010) 135, fn 3.

[174] See Boris Barth, *Genozid. Völkermord Im 20. Jahrhundert. Geschichte, Theorien, Kontroversen* (Beck 2006) 19.

[175] See Cassese, 'The Policy Element in Genocide: When Is It Required by International Rules?' (ch 2, n 173) 136–9, with an analysis of the jurisprudence of the International Criminal Tribunal for the Former Yugoslavia and the International Criminal Tribunal for Rwanda. Cf, however Stefan Kirsch, 'The Two Notions of Genocide: Distinguishing Macro Phenomena and Individual Misconduct' in Eckart Conze and Christoph Safferling (eds), *The Genocide Convention Sixty Years After its Adoption* (TMC Asser Press 2010) 145–8.

[176] Kirsch, 'The Two Notions of Genocide: Distinguishing Macro Phenomena and Individual Misconduct' (ch 2, n 175) 135.

International Military Tribunal has contributed to this understanding of genocide requiring the contextual elements of crimes against humanity. During the preparations and in the indictments for the Nuremberg trials, after all, both the terms were used as if synonymous.[177] But genocide had not yet found a clear legal definition then.

This close connection in the conception of both criminal provisions has led to proposals of relying on the broadened definition of crimes against humanity as the more suitable concept, that the definition of crimes against humanity in the Rome Statute is 'really no more than the "expanded" definition of genocide that many have argued for over the years'[178] and 'has evolved to such an extent that it can certainly now cover acts of ethnic cleansing and cultural genocide, even when committed in peacetime'.[179]

Seeing as the nexus requirement between crimes against humanity and armed conflict is 'no longer of any relevance',[180] genocide becomes a subset of crimes against humanity,[181] 'usefully viewed as the most extreme form'.[182] The ICTY has referred to genocide as one of the 'most egregious manifestations' of crimes against humanity,[183] echoing how scholars had previously framed the crime.[184] James Mace, director of the US Commission into the study of the Ukrainian famine, suggested that, of course, genocide was 'a crime against humanity as such because it is an attempt to destroy an irreplaceable component of humanity'.[185] But when France had propagated describing

[177] See Schabas, *Unimaginable Atrocities. Justice, Politics, and Rights at the War Crimes Tribunals* (ch 1, n 45) 125.

[178] Schabas, *Genocide in International Law* (ch 2, n 28) 12.

[179] Schabas, *Unimaginable Atrocities. Justice, Politics, and Rights at the War Crimes Tribunals* (ch 1, n 45).

[180] Ibid 123. See also Schabas, 'Crimes Against Humanity' (ch 2, n 62) 216.

[181] See Schabas, *Genocide in International Law* (ch 2, n 28) 14–15; Schabas, *Unimaginable Atrocities. Justice, Politics, and Rights at the War Crimes Tribunals* (ch 1, n 45) 123; Schabas, 'Crimes Against Humanity' (ch 2, n 62) 216; Ternon, *L'État Criminel. Les Génocides au XXe Siècle* (ch 1, n 36) 111. See also already Drost, *The Crime of State. Penal Protection for Fundamental Freedoms of Persons and Peoples. Book II. Genocide. United Nations Legislation on International Criminal Law* (ch 1, n 10) 196.

[182] Schabas, 'Crimes Against Humanity' (ch 2, n 62) 216.

[183] *Prosecutor v. Duško Tadić aka 'Dule'*, Case No. No. IT-94-1-T, Judgement of 7 May 1997, at para 622.

[184] For example, Levon Chorbajian, 'Introduction' in Levon Chorbajian and George Shirinian (eds), *Studies in Comparative Genocide* (Palgrave Macmillan/St Martin's Press 1999) xv; Drost, *The Crime of State. Penal Protection for Fundamental Freedoms of Persons and Peoples. Book II. Genocide. United Nations Legislation on International Criminal Law* (ch 1, n 10) 196; Ternon, *L'État Criminel. Les Génocides au XXe Siècle* (ch 1, n 36) 111.

[185] James E. Mace, 'Genocide in the U.S.S.R.' in Israel W. Charny (ed), *Genocide. A Critical Bibliographical Review* (Facts on File Publications 1988) 117.

genocide as a 'crime against humanity' during the drafting process of the Genocide Convention, this was rejected.[186]

This attempt at finding convergence might also overcome one of the early criticisms of the concept of genocide. While the United Nations pushed the focus of international law towards the individual as expressed in the Universal Declaration of Human Rights of 1948, the definition of genocide in the Genocide Convention of that very same year did the exact opposite: it reinforced the idea of the collective and of group categorization.[187] This has been most recently emphasized in both scholarship[188] and popular non-fiction,[189] contrasting the contributions of Hersch Lauterpacht and Raphaël Lemkin to international law.

Paradoxically, under the respective definition, the crime of genocide may apply to the killing of a single individual,[190] whereas crimes against humanity may not. While genocide is oftentimes understood as the greater crime in terms of scale and magnitude, this is not reflected in its legal definition. Crimes against humanity, under today's state of the art definition under the Rome Statute, require 'a widespread or systematic attack' including 'the multiple commission of acts'. Article II of the Genocide Convention simply requires '[k]illing members of the group', albeit with the 'intent to destroy, in whole or in part, a national, ethnical, racial or religious group, as such'. At maximum, this can be interpreted to require the killing of more than one individual.[191] While 'a genocide conviction would not reflect the large number killed', 'a conviction for a crime against humanity alone would not reflect the intent to destroy the group of which the victims were members'.[192] This also stands in the way of viewing genocide as a specific emanation of crimes against humanity, as the ICTR has pointed out:

[186] See Schabas, *Genocide in International Law* (ch 2, n 28) 73.

[187] See Tanner, 'Der Historiker und der Richter. Der Genozid an den Armeniern und die Genozidforschung aus rechtlicher und geschichtswissenschaftlicher Sicht' (ch 1, n 51) 179 and 192; Vrdoljak, 'Human Rights and Genocide: The Work of Lauterpacht and Lemkin in Modern International Law' (ch 2, n 58).

[188] See Vrdoljak, 'Human Rights and Genocide: The Work of Lauterpacht and Lemkin in Modern International Law' (ch 2, n 58) 1163.

[189] See Sands, *East West Street. On the Origins of Genocide and Crimes Against Humanity* (ch 2, n 27).

[190] Cf Bazyler, *Holocaust, Genocide, and the Law. A Quest for Justice in a Post-Holocaust World* (ch 2, n 19) 43–4.

[191] Cf, however, on the requirement that the intent comprises a certain threshold number of eventual victims, Quigley, *The Genocide Convention. An International Law Analysis* (ch 2, n 115) 141–2.

[192] Ibid 13.

> The definition of the crime of genocide was based upon that of crimes against humanity, that is, a combination of 'extermination and persecutions on political, racial or religious grounds' and it was intended to cover '*the intentional destruction of groups in whole or in substantial part*' (emphasis added). The crime of genocide is a type of crime against humanity. Genocide, however, is different from other crimes against humanity. The essential difference is that genocide requires the aforementioned specific intent to exterminate a protected group (in whole or in part) while crimes against humanity require the civilian population to be targeted as part of a widespread or systematic attack. There are instances where the discriminatory grounds coincide and overlap. [193]

Still, genocide stands on firmer legal ground in comparison to its 'first-born sibling', even though this might appear astonishing. While it may be true that the existence of multiple definitions reflects the underdeveloped state of

[193] *Prosecutor v. Clément Kayishema and Obed Ruzindana*, Case No. ICTR-95-1, Judgement of 21 May 1999, para 89. See also *Prosecutor v. Clément Kayishema and Obed Ruzindana*, Separate and Dissenting Opinion of Judge Tafazzal Hossain Khan Regarding the Verdicts Under the Charges of Crimes Against Humanity/Murder and Crimes Against Humanity/Extermination of 21 May 1999, Case No. ICTR-95-1-T, paras 8-13: '8. The Defence submitted that the Trial Chamber should not *convict* for both genocide and crimes against humanity because there is *a concur d'infractions*. The Defence for Ruzindana submitted that "Crimes Against Humanity have been largely absorbed by the Genocide Convention" and that there was a *partial* overlap in the protected social interest of the two Articles of the Statute. 9. The Prosecution, on the other hand, contended that it is permissible to convict the accused for all the established counts for which the accused persons were responsible and to impose multiple sentences. By issuing multiple sentences, the Prosecution submitted, the Chamber would adequately address the gravity of each crime, the role of the accused, and the totality of their culpable conduct. The Prosecution further submitted that "multiple sentencing will not prejudice the convicted person. The Chamber may remedy any prejudicial effect by imposing concurrent sentences for offences which arise from the same factual circumstances." 10. I find that the substance of the Prosecution's submission is in line with the applicable jurisprudence from the International Criminal Tribunals. [. . .] 11. The jurisprudence from national courts and the views of legal commentators on the issue of concurrence is mixed. Some argue that it is wrong to *convict* for two or more crimes that suffer from concurrence while others argue that an accused can be convicted for all the established crimes but, in order to avoid prejudice, *punished* for the established crimes concurrently (generally by imposing the sentence for the gravest crime). 12. Notwithstanding this general lack of uniformity, the international criminal jurisprudence most relevant to this Tribunal has been consistent in its approach from the very first case at the ICTY – *Prosecutor v. Dusko Tadic*. The ICTY and ICTR have consistently opined that the issue of cumulative charges should be addressed at the stage of penalty – by sentencing the accused concurrently for the established crimes that are supported by the same culpable conduct. 13. In dealing with the issue of concurrence, it appears that the ICTY Chambers have limited their analysis to the overlap of the accused's culpable conduct. They have placed less emphasis on the overlapping elements of the cumulative crimes. I agree with this approach. What must be punished is culpable conduct; this principle applies to situations where the conduct offends two or more crimes, whether or not the factual situation also satisfies the distinct elements of the two or more crimes, as proven.' See further *Prosecutor v. Georges Anderson Nderubumwe Rutaganda*, Judgement of 6 December 1999, Case No. ICTR-96-3-T, para 115.

crimes against humanity in the 1990s,[194] it appears bizarre to question its status as customary international law, a reflection of practice and recognition of the prohibition as a universal standard by states. After all, the acts prohibited are equally horrific, and it appears obscene that any such acts against a civilian population should be permissible. This view is increasingly accepted – or at least not challenged – today.[195]

But even if it is argued that 'the obligations upon States found in the Genocide Convention now apply *mutatis mutandis*, on a customary basis, in the case of crimes against humanity',[196] the Genocide Convention allows for the jurisdiction of the International Court of Justice.[197] There is no such provision with regard to crimes against humanity.[198]

In 2008, an expert group calling itself the 'Crimes Against Humanity Initiative' of the Whitney R. Harris World Law Institute at the Washington University in St. Louis School of Law was established to propagate the creation of a treaty similar to the Genocide Convention that would provide not only for individual international responsibility.[199] Article 1 of its 2010 'Proposed International Convention on the Prevention and Punishment of Crimes Against Humanity' reads:

> Crimes against humanity, whether committed in time of armed conflict or in time of peace, constitute crimes under international law for which there is individual criminal responsibility. In addition, States may be held responsible for crimes against humanity pursuant to principles of State responsibility for internationally wrongful acts.[200]

[194] See Leila Nadya Sadat, 'Preface and Acknowledgments' in Leila Nadya Sadat (ed), *Forging a Convention for Crimes Against Humanity* (Cambridge University Press 2011) xxii.

[195] Cf Göran Sluiter, '"Chapeau Elements" of Crimes Against Humanity in the Jurisprudence of the UN Ad Hoc Tribunals' in Leila Nadya Sadat (ed), *Forging a Convention for Crimes Against Humanity* (Cambridge University Press 2011) 111–13; Vervliet, 'Raphael Lemkin (1900–1959) and the Genocide Convention of 1948. Brief Biographical and Bibliographical Notes' (ch 2, n 27) 111–13.

[196] Schabas, *Genocide in International Law* (ch 2, n 28) 14.

[197] Convention for the Prevention and Punishment of the Crime of Genocide, 9 December 1948, 78 United Nations Treaty Series 277, Article IX.

[198] See Schabas, 'Crimes Against Humanity' (ch 2, n 62) 216.

[199] See Crimes Against Humanity Initiative <http://crimesagainsthumanity.wustl.edu/>. See also Leila Nadya Sadat, *Forging a Convention for Crimes Against Humanity* (Cambridge University Press 2011). Here, particularly the chapter Leila Nadya Sadat, 'A Comprehensive History of the Proposed International Convention on the Prevention and Punishment of Crimes Against Humanity' in Leila Nadya Sadat (ed), *Forging a Convention for Crimes Against Humanity* (Cambridge University Press 2011) 449–501.

[200] Whitney R. Harris World Law Institute, Washington University School of Law, Crimes Against Humanity Initiative, Proposed International Convention on the Prevention and Punishment of

The further definition basically follows that of the Rome Statute.[201] In 2013, following the efforts of Sean Murphy of George Washington University, the International Law Commission of the United Nations included the agenda in its long-term work programme at its Sixty-Fifth Session.[202]

For now, under international law, one may still distinguish between a customary law crime, crimes against humanity and a treaty-based crime, genocide.[203] Until further progress is made, public opinion will continue to perceive crimes against humanity as something less severe, not calling for the same resolute kind of action required in such instances by the international community.[204] In its 2005 report, the International Commission of Inquiry on Darfur to the United Nations Secretary-General still felt the need to emphasize the terrible equivalence of crimes against humanity with genocide:

> The conclusion that no genocidal policy has been pursued and implemented in Darfur by the Government authorities, directly or through the militias under their control, should not be taken in any way as detracting from the gravity of the crimes perpetrated in that region. International offences such as the crimes against humanity and war crimes that have been committed in Darfur may be no less serious and heinous than genocide. [. . .] As stated above genocide is not necessarily the most serious international crime. Depending upon the circumstances, such international offences as crimes against humanity or large scale war crimes may be no less serious and heinous than genocide.[205]

The sad irony in all of this is that 'crimes against humanity' was the first term applied to prosecute perpetrators of the Holocaust. Yet its collective memory

Crimes Against Humanity, August 2010, Article 1 <https://sites.law.wustl.edu/docs/harris/cah/EnglishTreatyFinal.pdf>.

201 See Whitney R. Harris World Law Institute, Washington University School of Law, Crimes Against Humanity Initiative, Proposed International Convention on the Prevention and Punishment of Crimes Against Humanity, August 2010, Article 3 <https://sites.law.wustl.edu/docs/harris/cah/EnglishTreatyFinal.pdf>. See also the Rome Statute of the International Criminal Court, 17 July 1998, 2187 United Nations Treaty Series 3, Article 7.

202 See International Law Commission, Report on the Work of its Sixty-fifth Session (6 May to 7 June and 8 July to 9 August 2013), 68 UNGAOR, Supplement No. 10 (A/68/10), 116 and 140, Annex B.

203 See Steven R. Ratner, 'Labeling Mass Atrocity: Does and Should International Criminal Law Rank Evil?' (2008) 54 *Wayne Law Review* 569, 569.

204 See ibid 570.

205 Report of the International Commission of Inquiry on Darfur to the United Nations Secretary-General, Pursuant to Security Council Resolution 1564 of 18 September 2004, Geneva, 25 January 2005, S/2005/60, 4 and 132, para 522.

has arguably manifested itself in the word 'genocide' alone. It elevates the impact of the term on the public conscience to an almost unrivalled level.

One of the most prominent international lawyers in the field of international criminal law, William Schabas, has upheld the view that genocide is still superior, if not in terms of law,[206] at least in terms of moral gravity of the crime:

> International lawyers seem sometimes to insist in vain that the distinction between genocide and crimes against humanity is of little or no importance. The argument is not about the state of the law: it is one of symbolism and semantics. If the result of the terminological quarrel is to insist upon the supreme heinousness of 'racial hatred', for want of a better term, and to reiterate society's condemnation of the mass killings of Jews, Tutsis and Armenians, to cite the primary historical examples of the past century, the distinction retains and deserves all of its significance. From this perspective, genocide stands to crimes against humanity as premeditated murder stands to intentional homicide. Genocide deserves its title as the 'crime of crimes'.[207]

At another instance, however, he reflects and, perhaps, rescinds his original view:

> If labelling genocide the 'crime of crimes' has contributed to the difficulty in explaining the terrible seriousness of crimes against humanity which, after all, formed the basis of the 1915 allegations against the Ottomans as well as the judgments at Nuremberg, then there are solid grounds to abandon the expression.[208]

Consequently, 'the legal bifurcation does not make sense and many acts that are legally considered crimes against humanity fall sociologically within the scope of genocide'.[209]

[206] See William A. Schabas, 'Semantics or Substance? David Scheffer's Welcome Proposal to Strengthen Criminal Accountability for Atrocities' (2007) 2 *Genocide Studies and Prevention: An International Journal* 31, 35.

[207] Schabas, *Genocide in International Law* (ch 2, n 28) 15. See also Schabas, 'Semantics or Substance? David Scheffer's Welcome Proposal to Strengthen Criminal Accountability for Atrocities' (ch 2, n 206) 36.

[208] Schabas, *Genocide in International Law* (ch 2, n 28) 653.

[209] Shaw, *What Is Genocide?* (ch 1, n 36) 44.

2.7 War crimes, ethnic cleansing

This short depiction of the prohibition of genocide as it arose in international law, contrasting it with the prosecution of crimes against humanity, is but a small spotlight on the legal conceptualization of atrocities. War crimes and ethnic cleansing equally feature in the work of International Criminal Tribunals and in international relations,[210] perhaps most visible today in the broad public discussion of Vladimir Putin as a war criminal for Russia's actions against Ukraine.

But as the following chapters illustrate, an enquiry into atrocity labelling does not necessarily require a comprehensive encyclopaedic discussion of international crimes or prohibitions under international humanitarian law: the debate within Genocide Studies circles around the 'crime of crimes' alone.

[210] For example, prominently, the responsibility to protect as defined in United Nations General Assembly Resolution 60/1, '2005 World Summit Outcome', 24 October 2005, A/RES/60/1.

3

Labelling atrocities

At first glance, 'labelling' simply implies the process of attaching a certain term to a certain event in space and time. But 'atrocity labelling' is different from many other forms of branding or framing in that it applies what is essentially technical legal terminology: genocide, crimes against humanity, war crimes and so on. As illustrated in the previous chapter, each specific definition is context-driven, and its individual elements might depend on the applicability of a particular legal framework. Inadvertently, as in any term borrowed from another discipline, scholars must walk an interdisciplinary tightrope as the underlying concepts bend against their respective methodological constraints.[1]

Comparative legal methodology provides a useful framework in trying to grapple with the migration of words and concepts. In his book *Legal Transplants – An Approach to Comparative Law*, Alan Watson[2] discussed the phenomenon of legal concepts developed in one legal system and 'transplanted' into another, often alien to the original.

In his search for a proper substance of the discipline of comparative law, Watson decided that it must be 'a study of the relationship, above all the historical relationship, between legal systems or between rules of more than one system'.[3] Thereby, the process by which these rules move from one to another could take on all possible forms: they 'come in all shapes and sizes' such as 'imposed reception, solicited imposition, penetration, infiltration, crypto-reception, inoculation and so on'.[4]

1 See Tanner, 'Der Historiker und der Richter. Der Genozid an den Armeniern und die Genozidforschung aus rechtlicher und geschichtswissenschaftlicher Sicht' (ch 1, n 51) 186.
2 See Alan Watson, *Legal Transplants. An Approach to Comparative Law* (2nd edn, University of Georgia Press 1993).
3 Ibid 9.
4 Ibid 30.

Watson pointed out that terminology is sometimes simply adopted, leaving the host legal system 'largely unchanged though it has become more sophisticated'[5] and that 'usually legal rules are not devised for the particular society in which they now operate and also that this is not a matter for great concern'.[6] However, what Watson has in mind is the transplant from one legal system to another, not from an entirely different discipline to another.

But the ideas discussed by Watson can be chosen to describe, more broadly, any concept that has developed within the framework of one discipline and is then 'transplanted' into another. In this process, '[m]eaning or linguistic resources constitute the repertoires which are borrowed in the process of communications'.[7] The words saturate the discussion with the entirety of their 'conceptual baggage'.

As opposed to a simple transplant that implies a discrete event, moving a term or concept from one discipline to another, the interdisciplinary nature of Genocide Studies provides a communicative framework that encourages crossover effects. Where scholars of multiple disciplines engage in the writings of one another, creating a subject-specific epistemic community, the effects of a transplant upon the discourse can hardly be imagined as a one-way street. Each time a concept 'boomerangs' from a historian to a political scientist, to a lawyer or to a sociologist, it will take on a slightly different trajectory depending on the methodological needs of the respective discipline. It is likely that the next discipline will again throw it at a different angle it finds more suitable for its purpose. Each time though, through continuous observation, techniques will be blended for better results. As different disciplines look at new events, the common experience changes with every new move.

At the outset of Genocide Studies, be they led by historians or political and social scientists, stands the terminology of international (criminal) law,[8] as applied in different historical contexts. This already makes for different vantage points, ranging from the saturation of further enquiries with past precedent to the abstraction of concepts. The result might even be the recognition that the original application of the law appears unsatisfactory, putting into question the use of a concept in its original discipline. Thereby, scholars participate in

5 Ibid 81.
6 Ibid 96.
7 Jabri, *Discourses on Violence. Conflict Analysis Reconsidered* (ch 1, n 31) 94.
8 See Chapter 2.

a quasi-legal process, juxtaposing the prerogative of law over international crimes.[9] Whichever perspective, the process begs three questions: Why is a label chosen? How is it applied? What are the consequences?[10] The following sections of this chapter attempt to address these in turn.

3.1 Motivations

The first choice put before states, peoples, indigenous populations, minorities, groups, politicians, NGOs, activists or scholars must be, of course, whether to apply such a label in the first place: Do I catch the boomerang I have been thrown? And which one: genocide, crimes against humanity, war crimes or something other?

The use of the label 'genocide' is most illustrative of the fact that legal definitions alone are not necessarily what guides the choice towards the one or other term: 'Plainly, the genocide concept is *not only* a politically-neutral, heuristic device of social science, at least in public discourse.'[11] The labelling process 'will thrive [. . .] on a plurality of different energies that generate implicit disagreement about its basic scope, meaning, and significance'.[12]

The motivation for sticking the label 'genocide' to an event may range from a sense of immediacy and urgency to pragmatism and cynicism, from commercial interests to the support for a specific (research) agenda.[13] In 2004, the animal rights organization People for the Ethical Treatment of Animals (PETA) caused a stir with its 'Holocaust on Your Plate' campaign that contrasted images of Nazi death camps with pictures of industrial animal farming. Various groups accused PETA of relativizing the destruction of the

[9] See Chapter 1, n 85.

[10] Cf ch 1, n 74.

[11] Moses, 'Genocide and Settler Society in Australian History' (ch 1, n 14) 16, emphasis added.

[12] Meiches, *The Politics of Annihilation. A Genealogy of Genocide* (ch 1, n 23) 266.

[13] Cf Weiss-Wendt, 'Problems in Comparative Genocide Scholarship' (ch 1, n 67) 45–6. A prominent example might be Norman M. Naimark, *Stalin's Genocides* (Princeton University Press 2010). The title appears quite peculiar, considering that Naimark concludes that none of the instances in question actually amount to genocide. However, no one would doubt that it is a catchy book title (and a well-written book, for that matter), which brings up a number of (controversial and provocative) connotations to the audience, in particular the 'Historikerstreit' of the 1980s. In a later publication, Naimark alternatively suggests the term 'communist genocide'. See Naimark, *Genocide. A World History* (ch 1, n 40) 86.

European Jews,[14] and German courts banned the use of the imagery.[15] More recently, the widely popular Netflix show *Squid Game*[16] referenced the furnaces of Auschwitz[17] to add a shock factor to entertainment – with surprisingly little debate on this fact to date. Such provocative references are themselves an expression of the power of 'genocide', of its 'symbolic capital', as a gateway to the collective memory, providing reference and comparison to the Holocaust.

Scholars have discussed this phenomenon under different headings. Benjamin Meiches calls it the 'politics of genocide',[18] William Schabas has referred to it as the 'genocide mystique',[19] and Aleksandar Jokic has created a typology of what he deems 'genocidalism':

> (i) The purposeful neglect to attribute responsibility for genocide in cases when overwhelming evidence exists, and (ii) the energetic attributions of 'genocide' in less than clear cases without considering available and convincing, opposing evidence and argumentation.[20]

This typology presents a sliding scale from unjustified application to denial. Jokic further distinguishes between (i) 'genocidalism of omission' and (ii) 'genocidalism of commission', or what he calls 'the genocidal use of the word "genocide"'.[21] Such an attribution is 'camouflaged as genuine concern for the evil contained in genocide', while 'the real interest is of another sort, e.g., the outcomes may have clear propagandistic connotation'.[22]

While this book is less about the public discourse, for scholarship as well, the possible motivations should be clear, if only as a preliminary caveat in any earnest enquiry. One must therefore look to (1) the value of symbolic capital and its appropriation and (2) the potential use as a means of activism and accusation.

14 See 'Campaign Angers Holocaust Survivors' *BBC News* (1 March 2003) <http://news.bbc.co.uk/2/hi/europe/2810031.stm>.

15 For the constitutional verdict citing the original decisions, see German Constitutional Court, Decision of 20 February 2009, 1 BvR 2266/04, 1 BvR 2620/05.

16 See IMDb, Squid Game (2021) <https://www.imdb.com/title/tt10919420/>.

17 See https://www.youtube.com/watch?v=QjuB2eC7Mmc&t=606s.

18 Meiches, *The Politics of Annihilation. A Genealogy of Genocide* (ch 1, n 23) 9.

19 See Schabas, *Unimaginable Atrocities. Justice, Politics, and Rights at the War Crimes Tribunals* (ch 1, n 45) 99–124.

20 Aleksandar Jokic, 'Genocidalism' (2004) 8 *The Journal of Ethics* 251, 251.

21 Ibid.

22 Ibid 254.

3.1.1 Symbolic capital and appropriation

Depending on the agenda, the symbolic capital connected with a term can constitute the main source of attraction for atrocity labelling.[23] 'Genocide' carries all the epistemic elements necessary to invoke and appropriate it.[24]

In the 1970s, the ground was laid when 'Holocaust memory' had its 'breakthrough' and even 'gradually supplanted genocide as the main signifier of evil'.[25] Later on, '[i]n the late 1990s, the word "genocide" began to be used as a type of moral category, taking on a symbolic quality as the crime of crimes, the darkest of humanity's inhumanity',[26] 'synonymous with extreme evil'.[27] Through its uniqueness and iconicity, this word seems ideally set to capture and cement the penumbra of diffuse notions associated with atrocities.[28] Today, genocide and the Holocaust are used as if synonymous.[29]

Hence, the 'hegemony of Holocaust *as* genocide [. . .] repeatedly acts as a magnet to advocates of other human catastrophes, clamouring to the point that the "g-word" applies to theirs, too':[30]

> Important political prerogatives and much symbolism remain associated with the label genocide. Many victims are deeply disappointed when their own suffering is acknowledged as 'mere' crimes against humanity. They do not fully appreciate the validity of the legal distinctions, which are the result of a complex historical debate. [. . .] The distinction between genocide and crimes against humanity is still of great symbolic significance.[31]

23 Cf Zimmerer, 'Kolonialer Genozid? Vom Nutzen und Nachteil einer historischen Kategorie für eine Globalgeschichte des Völkermordes' (ch 1, n 14) 110.

24 Cf Dietrich Busse, 'Juristisches Wissen als institutionelle Begriffsstrukturen. Analyseansätze aus Kognitionswissenschaften und wissensanalytischer Semantik (am Beispiel von Gesetzes-Begriffen)' (2015) 101 *Archiv für Rechts- und Sozialphilosophie* 354, 356.

25 Moses, 'Introduction: The Field of Genocide Studies' (ch 1, n 30) 3. Cf Bloxham and Moses, 'Editor's Introduction: Changing Themes in the Study of Genocide' (ch 1, n 21) 3; Curthoys and Docker, 'Defining Genocide' (ch 1, n 43) 23.

26 Irvin-Erickson, *Raphaël Lemkin and the Concept of Genocide* (ch 2, n 19) 2.

27 Bazyler, *Holocaust, Genocide, and the Law. A Quest for Justice in a Post-Holocaust World* (ch 2, n 19) 37.

28 See Clavero, *Genocide or Ethnocide 1933–2007. How to Make, Unmake, and Remake Law With Words* (ch 1, n 49) 91. Cf with regard to the term 'Holocaust' in the German language Angelika Linke, 'Kulturelles Gedächtnis. Linguistische Perspektiven auf ein kulturwissenschaftliches Forschungsfeld' in Dietrich Busse, Thomas Niehr and Martin Wengeler (eds), *Brisante Semantik. Neuere Konzepte und Forschungsergebnisse einer kulturwissenschaftlichen Linguistik* (Max Niemeyer 2005) 82.

29 See Chapter 1, n 14.

30 Levene, *Genocide in the Age of the Nation-State. Volume I: The Meaning of Genocide* (ch 1, n 15) 2–3. See also Moses, 'Introduction: The Field of Genocide Studies' (ch 1, n 30) 14; Snyder, *Bloodlands. Europe Between Hitler and Stalin* (ch 2, n 107) 413.

31 Schabas, *Unimaginable Atrocities. Justice, Politics, and Rights at the War Crimes Tribunals* (ch 1, n 45) 121 and 124. Cf, however, Schabas, 'Genocide in International Law and International Relations Prior to 1948' (ch 2, n 78) 34.

The status of the crime of genocide as seen in relation to any alternatives for the conceptualization of mass atrocities is motivation enough. And it is backed up by the case law of International Criminal Tribunals, as when the ICTY elaborated on the relationship of international crimes to each other as reflected in the case law of the ICTR:

> A hierarchy of crimes seems to emerge from the case-law of the ICTR [International Criminal Tribunal for Rwanda]. The Trial Chamber seised [*sic*] of the *Kambanda* case established a complete scale of seriousness of the crimes which was taken up in the subsequent Judgements of the ICTR. The following hierarchy of crimes falling under the jurisdiction of the Tribunal may therefore be compiled:
>
> 1) 'The crime of crimes': genocide
> 2) Crimes of an extreme seriousness: crimes against humanity
> 3) Crimes of a lesser seriousness: war crimes
>
> The ICTR has thus supposedly established a genuine hierarchy of crimes and this has been used in determining sentences as witnessed by the fact that the crime of genocide was punished by life imprisonment.[32]

Genocide stands as the pinnacle at the very top of the pyramid of international crimes. This hierarchy, as elaborated by the ICTY, also suggests a scale of moral gravity in which war crimes – which according to the Rome Statute of the ICC include, among other acts, 'wilful killing', 'torture or inhuman treatment, including biological experiments', 'wilfully causing great suffering' and 'unlawful deportation'[33] – constitute 'crimes of lesser seriousness'. Perhaps it is only the wording that is unfortunate but one is left baffled by such a statement.

Scholars also adhere to the view that genocide is still superior in terms of wrongdoing.[34] It remains the threshold against which all other atrocities are measured. This goes so far that 'mass killing', 'ethnic cleansing', 'mass murder' or even 'genocidal acts' are considered a 'euphemism' for genocide.[35] The 2005 report of the International Commission of Inquiry on Darfur to

[32] *Prosecutor v. Tihomir Blaškić*, Judgement, Case No. IT-95-14-T, Judgement of 3 March 2000, para 800.
[33] See Rome Statute of the International Criminal Court, 17 July 1998, 2187 United Nations Treaty Series 3, Article 8(2).
[34] For example, Schabas, *Genocide in International Law* (ch 2, n 28) 15.
[35] See Michelle E. Ringrose, 'The Politicization of the Genocide Label: Genocide Rhetoric in the UN Security Council' (2020) 14 *Genocide Studies and Prevention: An International Journal* 124, 132 and 135.

the United Nations Secretary-General discussed in the previous chapter is symptomatic by having to emphasize that it should 'not be taken in any way as detracting from the gravity of the crimes perpetrated in that region' that only constituted 'crimes against humanity' or 'war crimes'.[36]

Against this background, 'Genocide Studies' becomes the supreme discipline dealing with mass atrocities. For scholars, this may give a morbid sense of vocation for those 'concerned about peace, human rights, and justice', since, in this 'grim but essential profession'[37] that comes with a 'moral impulse' to 'universalise the lessons of the Holocaust in light of postwar history',[38] 'here is a sense that with genocide you are confronting the "Big One", what Joseph Conrad called the "heart of darkness"'.[39] An additional attraction then lies in having found a topic or an event that nobody has yet discussed through the lens of a particular label, as perhaps the efforts at writing a 'world history of genocide' show.[40]

3.1.2 Activism and accusation

Symbolic capital and its appropriation have made atrocity labelling a much-contested process:

> The stakes are high in this area, as various individuals, groups, governments, and institutions vie to map out a narrative of the past that legitimates their agendas or desire for justice, to assert or reject the right to legal redress for and moral outrage about 'the crime of all crimes', and to acknowledge or disavow memoires, experiences, suffering, and losses linked to mass murder.[41]

As a consequence, if not already by the nature of the atrocity itself, '[t]he charge of genocide places great opprobrium on the perpetrators or alleged perpetrators and [. . .] endows the greatest moral and political capital on the

[36] Report of the International Commission of Inquiry on Darfur to the United Nations Secretary General, Pursuant to Security Council Resolution 1564 of 18 September 2004, 25 January 2005, S/2005/60, 4 and 132, para 522.

[37] David Scheffer, 'The Merits of Unifying Terms: "Atrocity Crimes" and "Atrocity Law"' (2007) 2 *Genocide Studies and Prevention: An International Journal* 91, 91.

[38] Moses, 'Introduction: The Field of Genocide Studies' (ch 1, n 30) 2.

[39] Jones, *Genocide. A Comprehensive Introduction* (ch 1, n 34) xxviii.

[40] Cf ch 1, n 40.

[41] O'Neill, 'Anthropology and Genocide' (ch 1, n 26) 182.

victims',[42] whereas '[t]he accusation of genocide can be a large rhetorical and moral club to be used against one's political opponents'.[43] As Judge Bennouna wrote in his declaration annexed to the Order of the International Court of Justice indicating provisional measures in the context of the Russian aggression against Ukraine: 'I am aware that this concept of genocide has been overused and indiscriminately employed by propagandists of all persuasions.'[44] As Russia had to learn through this case, frivolous claims of genocide can provoke surprising outcomes, such as a claim before the International Court of Justice.[45]

Already for Lemkin, the idea was not just to work out a legal concept but to create a word that would serve as a suitable vehicle for the conveyance of moral vilification.[46] This was, in the first instance, also its primary use throughout the second half of the twentieth century during the Cold War.[47] Today the term 'genocide' 'has come to be used when all other terms of opprobrium fail, when the speaker or writer means to indict a set of actions as extraordinary in their malevolence and heinousness'.[48] Being brought into connection with it may create an almost impervious stigma upon a person, an organization or a state.[49] Its use 'effectively is to make an accusation against whatever it is that one thinks is the very worst thing imaginable':[50]

> It seems that genocide has become a label to be stuck on your worst enemy, a perverse version of the Nobel Prize, part of a rhetorical arsenal that helps you vilify your adversaries while ensuring impunity for your allies.[51]

[42] Donald Beachler, *The Genocide Debate. Politicians, Academics, and Victims* (Palgrave Macmillan 2011) 5.

[43] Ibid 10. See also Barth, *Genozid. Völkermord Im 20. Jahrhundert. Geschichte, Theorien, Kontroversen* (ch 2, n 174) 44–5, with further examples; Sémelin, *Säubern und Vernichten. Die politische Dimension von Massakern und Völkermorden* (ch 1, n 25) 340.

[44] International Court of Justice, *Allegations of Genocide under the Convention on the Prevention and Punishment of the Crime of Genocide* (Ukraine *v.* Russian Federation), Declaration of Judge Bennouna to the Order of 16 March 2022, para 4.

[45] See Chapter 1, n 84.

[46] See Chapter 1, n 13.

[47] See Chapter 2, n 122.

[48] Lang, 'The Concept of Genocide' (ch 1, n 1) 115.

[49] See Kirsch, 'The Two Notions of Genocide: Distinguishing Macro Phenomena and Individual Misconduct' (ch 2, n 175) 142; Schabas, *Genocide in International Law* (ch 2, n 28) 10.

[50] Levene, *Genocide in the Age of the Nation-State. Volume I: The Meaning of Genocide* (ch 1, n 15) 37.

[51] Mamdani, 'The Politics of Naming. Genocide, Civil War, Insurgency' (ch 1, n 74) 360.

This process has become so evident that 'some cynics deprecate labelling events as genocide, viewing it just a rhetorical weapon because the concept of genocide has been so diminished, vulgarized and banalized in public rhetoric'.[52]

Equally, the label 'genocide' can be used to give impact to reports of atrocities, which would otherwise draw little attention[53] and it 'is often applied rhetorically to gain attention for different causes'.[54] An early such instance was the attempt of the Korean ambassador in 1950 to convince US president Harry S. Truman to ratify the Genocide Convention by invoking the collective memory of the Holocaust.[55] In this context, one might also recall Judge Bennouna's critical statement.[56]

The concept is seen valuable 'a normative, action-oriented concept that has historically and essentially been created for the political struggle, not for scholarly analysis', as a '*politischer Kampfbegriff*' aiming at 'unanimous condemnation' and 'made for instrumentalization, and in fact for intervention'.[57] It remains 'the "gold standard" of humanitarian emergencies'.[58] One of the most prominent proponents of the responsibility to protect, Gareth Evans finds it 'the best linguistic vehicle for energizing mass support and high-level governmental support for effective action in response to newly emerging atrocity situations'.[59]

3.2 Labels

Once a label has been chosen, there follows the question of how it is applied: In the strict legal sense? By one's own (better) definition? Or might one assume the term itself saturates the discussion or leaves some welcome ambiguity?

52 Helen Fein, 'Definition and Discontent: Labelling, Detecting, and Explaining Genocide in the Twentieth Century' in Stig Förster and Gerhard Hirschfeld (eds), *Genozid in der modernen Geschichte* (Lit Verlag 1999) 12.

53 With regard to the examples of Argentina, Côte d'Ivoire, the Democratic Republic of the Congo, Israel and Sudan, see Schabas, *Unimaginable Atrocities. Justice, Politics, and Rights at the War Crimes Tribunals* (ch 1, n 45) 99–103 and 122.

54 Helen Fein, 'Introduction' in Helen Fein (ed), *Genocide Watch* (Yale University Press 1992) 2.

55 See Irvin-Erickson, *Raphaël Lemkin and the Concept of Genocide* (ch 2, n 19) 204.

56 See Chapter 3, n 44.

57 Gerlach, 'Extremely Violent Societies. An Alternative to the Concept of Genocide' (ch 1, n 66) 452.

58 See Chapter 1, n 6.

59 Gareth Evans, 'Crimes Against Humanity and the Responsibility to Protect' in Leila Nadya Sadat (ed), *Forging a Convention for Crimes Against Humanity* (Cambridge University Press 2011) 3.

Many legal terms have seeped into everyday language where their use is largely unproblematic and the colloquial understanding only negligibly deviates from the original meaning. A 'murder' in law is usually a 'murder' in anyone's understanding. The art of legal interpretation itself first and foremost takes recourse to the 'ordinary meaning' of a term.[60]

But once you introduce the element of 'malice aforethought' to distinguish 'murder' from other forms of homicide it will become more complicated. It depends on the complexity of a concept and the extent to which colloquial use of the word or another discipline will have appropriated its elements. Transplants 'come in all shapes and sizes'[61] and do not necessarily occur lock, stock and barrel. A label might either occur or be applied in another discipline based on (1) a full transplant, (2) an adaptation or (3) a vulgarization of its original.

3.2.1 Full transplant

A full transplant of the concept of 'genocide' would require a complete understanding of the definition of Article II of the Genocide Convention (as far as this may be possible in light of different interpretations and varying national implementation, although it may be 'fair to state that genocide is by far the most standardised criminal offence worldwide'.[62]) Only events that match both the objective (primarily killing of members of a group) and subjective (intent) requirements could be labelled accordingly. The same, of course, applies to the definition of crimes against humanity or war crimes under the Rome Statute. A full transplant would require consideration of their contextual elements.

In any case, such labelling would be merely descriptive.[63] Both for historiography and the social sciences, this raises the question of analytical utility of applying the legal concept. Much speaks against a full transplant if it

[60] For example, Vienna Convention on the Law of Treaties, 23 May 1969, 1155 United Nations Treaty Series 331, Article 31(1).
[61] See Chapter 3, n 4.
[62] Kirsch, 'The Two Notions of Genocide: Distinguishing Macro Phenomena and Individual Misconduct' (ch 2, n 175) 143.
[63] Cf Gerlach, 'Extremely Violent Societies. An Alternative to the Concept of Genocide' (ch 1, n 66) 443.

cannot offer any analytical value for the host discipline,[64] even though scholars still pledge allegiance to the definition:

> Through its focus on intentionality, the fate of defined population groups, and physical annihilation, the Genocide Convention, despite its weaknesses, provides us with a fruitful working definition that can guide the study of past regimes and events.[65]

Legal definitions are not necessarily designed to produce any explanatory outcome or predictive result. They are 'designed for the ex post facto judgements of the courtroom rather than the historian's attempt to understand events as they develop', as 'a retrospective projection'.[66] Lawyers pursue different goals than historians or social scientists,[67] and neither do they 'speak the same languages, nor do they share an epistemological framework':[68]

> History is concerned with the study of past events, even if lessons are to be drawn from them. Law is concerned with past events ('rules', 'accumulated past decision'), but is concerned with their application in a formalised and normative manner today.[69]

This may be an issue, particularly, where the historical evaluation is anticipated by the specific framework of a legal provision functioning more as a rigid blueprint than result-open methodology.[70] The focus of historical analysis will revolve around the urge to fit the descriptive elements of a concept.

It is little surprising then to read of the Genocide Convention: 'Nearly everyone who considers the definition finds it insufficient for one reason or another.'[71] Accordingly, it has been found limited '[a]s a guide to historical and

[64] Cf Tanner, 'Der Historiker und der Richter. Der Genozid an den Armeniern und die Genozidforschung aus rechtlicher und geschichtswissenschaftlicher Sicht' (ch 1, n 51) 184.

[65] Weitz, *A Century of Genocide. Utopias of Race and Nation* (ch 1, n 34) 10. Cf also Kuper, *Genocide. Its Political Use in the Twentieth Century* (ch 1, n 34) 39.

[66] Donald Bloxham, 'The Armenian Genocide of 1915–1916: Cumulative Radicalization and the Development of a Destruction Policy' (2003) 181 *Past & Present* 141, 189.

[67] See Sémelin, *Säubern und Vernichten. Die politische Dimension von Massakern und Völkermorden* (ch 1, n 25) 351–2.

[68] Johannes Houwink ten Cate and Harmen van der Wilt, 'Foreword' in Harmen G. van der Wilt and others (eds), *The Genocide Convention: The Legacy of 60 Years* (Martinus Nijhoff 2012) ix.

[69] Rosalyn Higgins, 'The Identity of International Law' in Bin Cheng (ed), *International Law: Teaching and Practice* (Stevens & Sons 1982) 43.

[70] See Sémelin, *Säubern und Vernichten. Die politische Dimension von Massakern und Völkermorden* (ch 1, n 25) 338.

[71] Weitz, *A Century of Genocide. Utopias of Race and Nation* (ch 1, n 34) 9.

moral interpretation',[72] with little value 'as a tool for understanding the nature of genocide',[73] 'flawed and unsatisfactory',[74] 'too open-ended and vague',[75] 'both too broad and too narrow for scholarly comparative purposes',[76] 'at one and the same time, extremely broad and extremely narrow',[77] whereas 'others have deferred to it simply because in international law it *is* canonical'.[78]

Even for legal purposes, it has been considered 'a badly drafted definition that included a specific intent that would be hard to prove'.[79] From this springs a search for the 'discrete decision for total murder, as endlessly debated in the historiography of the Nazi "final solution"' as 'a product of the *ex post facto* ruminations of genocide scholars'.[80] Discussions often revolve around the existence of a 'master plan' for atrocities, not the objective and subjective elements of the definition.

As opposed to the expected clarity a full transplant would provide, some find that '[t]he lack of rigor in the UN definition of genocide is responsible for much of the confusion that plagues scholarly work in the field'.[81] Particularly, the social sciences have put the value of a full transplant to question: 'Social scientists and historians are well advised to address legal discussions [. . .] but [. . .] should not be unduly deferential to them.'[82] The issue is seen in the 'Convention's ambiguous status as a legal document defining a sociological concept, adopted in a political context'.[83] Hence, some have gone so far as to call the legal definition 'a purely political ploy' that 'cannot determine for use how to relate to acts of mass murder or genocide'.[84]

72 Snyder, *Bloodlands. Europe Between Hitler and Stalin* (ch 2, n 107) 413.
73 Levene, *Genocide in the Age of the Nation-State. Volume I: The Meaning of Genocide* (ch 1, n 15) 35.
74 Ibid.
75 Omer Bartov, 'Seeking the Roots of Modern Genocide. On the Macro- and Microhistory of Mass Murder' in Robert Gellately and Ben Kiernan (eds), *The Specter of Genocide. Mass Murder in Historical Perspective* (Cambridge University Press 2003) 77.
76 Melson, 'Problems in the Comparison of the Armenian Genocide and the Holocaust: Definitions, Typologies, Theories, and Fallacies' (ch 1, n 29) 27. *Verbatim* Weitz, *A Century of Genocide. Utopias of Race and Nation* (ch 1, n 34) 9.
77 William S. Parsons and Samuel Totten, 'Introduction' in William S. Parsons and Samuel Totten (eds), *Century of Genocide. Critical Essays and Eyewitness Accounts* (3rd edn, Routledge 2009) 4.
78 Levene, *Genocide in the Age of the Nation-State. Volume I: The Meaning of Genocide* (ch 1, n 15) 35.
79 Clark, 'History of Efforts to Codify Crimes Against Humanity. From the Charter of Nuremberg to the Statute of Rome' (ch 2, n 157) 14.
80 Bloxham, 'The Armenian Genocide of 1915–1916: Cumulative Radicalization and the Development of a Destruction Policy' (ch 3, n 66) 181–2.
81 Chalk and Jonassohn, *The History and Sociology of Genocide. Analyses and Case Studies* (ch 1, n 40) 10–11.
82 Shaw, *What Is Genocide?* (ch 1, n 36) 5.
83 Ibid 42.
84 Bauer, 'Comparison of Genocides' (ch 1, n 30) 33.

3.2.2 Adaptation

This controversy over the value of applying the legal definition by way of a full transplant has led to 'a merry-go-round of definitional debates'[85] and such varied adaptations that '[n]o generally accepted definition of genocide is available in the literature'[86] where 'it is hard to find two genocide scholars who adhere to the same definition':[87]

> Genocide scholars have constructed their individual definitions of genocide like the Procrustean bed of Greek mythology. They analyzed social events according to the definition they chose, stretching some points, shortening others, and in general 'cutting and pasting' the narrative to match their 'bed'.[88]

Consequently, 'one of the few things that everyone agrees on is that genocides are large-scale, violent episodes'.[89] The process towards the adaptation of different definitions in Genocide Studies can be pictured as follows:

> Genocide was regarded as a single event, and the event in question (which was generally physical annihilation) was examined from the perspective of whether or not it conformed to the 1948 Genocide Convention;
>
> Those social scientists who did not agree with the United Nations definition (whether justified or not) began proposing their own. Nearly every genocide scholar had her or his own definition and therefore most debates were focused on classification and labeling; The Holocaust occupied the central place in these debates as a sine qua non.[90]

[85] Stone, 'Introduction' (ch 1, n 35) 2.

[86] Chalk and Jonassohn, *The History and Sociology of Genocide. Analyses and Case Studies* (ch 1, n 40) xvii.

[87] Gerlach, 'Extremely Violent Societies. An Alternative to the Concept of Genocide' (ch 1, n 66) 454.

[88] Taner Akçam, *The Young Turks' Crime Against Humanity. The Armenian Genocide and Ethnic Cleansing in the Ottoman Empire* (Princeton University Press 2012) xxix. See also Israel W. Charny, 'Introduction' in Israel W. Charny (ed), *Genocide. A Critical Bibliographical Review* (Facts on File Publications 1988) xii; Parsons and Totten, 'Introduction' (ch 3, n 77) 4; Rubinstein, *Genocide: A History* (ch 1, n 40) 1–6.

[89] Shaw, *What Is Genocide?* (ch 1, n 36) 4.

[90] Akçam, *The Young Turks' Crime Against Humanity. The Armenian Genocide and Ethnic Cleansing in the Ottoman Empire* (ch 3, n 88) xxix. See also Schaller, 'Genozidforschung: Begriffe und Debatten. Einleitung' (ch 1, n 34) 14–5.

In his seminal article 'A Typology of Genocide', now seen as one of the earliest efforts in what would later come to be known as Genocide Studies, Vahakn Dadrian offered the following proposal for a new definition of genocide:

> Genocide is the successful attempt by a dominant group, vested with formal authority and/or with preponderant access to the overall resources of power, to reduce by coercion or lethal violence the number of a minority group whose ultimate extermination is held desirable and useful and whose respective vulnerability is a major factor contributing to the decision of genocide. Genocide therefore requires at least two polar elements, namely a perpetrator and a victim whose conflicting but disparate power relations yield the vulnerability of the victim group in relation to the dominant group, and consequently may also affect the pattern of genocidal victimization as a way of resolving the conflict.[91]

Within the adaptations that followed, two main trajectories have been identified where 'scholars developed their own definitions of genocide and explanatory frameworks':[92]

> In general, they have done so in two ways. One paradigm, which I call 'intentionalist', regards the Holocaust as the archetypal genocide and therefore emphasizes the official, exterminatory goal of the state to kill groups of people. The other, a reaction to the first, is 'structuralist' because it averts the issue of perpetrator agency and intention by highlighting anonymous 'genocidal processes' of cultural and physical destruction.[93]

Some thirty years after Dadrian, Martin Shaw, in his monograph *What Is Genocide?*, provides an entire list of 'new definitions' for 'genocide', 'genocidal action', 'a genocide' and 'genocidal violence'.[94] The latter should be used in cases of 'too small a scale or with too few victims to be regarded as genocide'.[95]

In its use as a 'somewhat more attenuated adjectival form',[96] the term 'genocide' becomes host to a whole range of events:[97] where there is no 'intent

[91] Dadrian, 'A Typology of Genocide' (ch 1, n 34) 201.
[92] Moses, 'Genocide and Settler Society in Australian History' (ch 1, n 14) 23.
[93] Ibid.
[94] Shaw, *What Is Genocide?* (ch 1, n 36) 193.
[95] Ibid.
[96] Chorbajian, 'Introduction' (ch 2, n 184) xvii.
[97] Cf Barth, *Genozid. Völkermord Im 20. Jahrhundert. Geschichte, Theorien, Kontroversen* (ch 2, n 174) 40–1.

to destroy a group',[98] where there are just 'some of the elements of genocide'[99] or where there is '[l]imited or localized genocidal conflict, on too small a scale or with too few victims to be regarded as genocide'.[100] As an alternative, Helen Fein suggests the term 'ideological slaughters' for cases in which only some elements of the legal definition are present.[101] Essentially, this moves the definition towards that of crimes against humanity, 'without the nexus to armed conflict'[102] – but through a focus on ideology enriching the prohibition of genocide with the contextual elements of crimes against humanity as found in the Rome Statute. In turn, Fein also distinguishes 'pogroms, lynching, collective punishments and massacre' as 'instances of collective behavior rather than organized state actions'.[103] Rarely, if ever, does anyone suggest crimes against humanity or war crimes as an alternative.

Recently, the word 'atrocity' has been popularized as a generic term in international criminal law and human rights law – prominently by one of the most eminent legal scholars on the crime of genocide, William Schabas[104] – to cover the three core crimes of the Rome Statute, 'genocide', 'crimes against humanity' and 'war crimes', including within the framework of the United Nations.[105] As one of the preeminent professional law societies, the American Society of International Law lists 'atrocity prevention' as a signature topic.[106] The UN High Commissioner for Human Rights delivered a statement on the 'Global Action Against Mass Atrocity Crimes Platform for Prevention High

[98] See Chalk and Jonassohn, *The History and Sociology of Genocide. Analyses and Case Studies* (ch 1, n 40) 26–7. See also Chalk and Jonassohn, 'The History and Sociology of Genocidal Killings' (ch 1, n 40) 40. Cf Kurt Jonassohn, 'What Is Genocide?' in Helen Fein (ed), *Genocide Watch* (Yale University Press 1992) 19–20, arguing that the term also applies when the following two elements are missing: '(2) there must be a group whose victimization threatens its survival as a group; and (3) the victimization must be one-sided'.

[99] Kuper, *Genocide. Its Political Use in the Twentieth Century* (ch 1, n 34) 10.

[100] Shaw, *What Is Genocide?* (ch 1, n 36) 193.

[101] See Helen Fein, 'Scenarios of Genocide: Models of Genocide and Critical Responses' in Israel W. Charny (ed), *Toward the Understanding and Prevention of Genocide. Proceedings of the International Conference on the Holocaust and Genocide* (Westview Press 1984) 4.

[102] Schabas, *Unimaginable Atrocities. Justice, Politics, and Rights at the War Crimes Tribunals* (ch 1, n 45) 122.

[103] Fein, 'Scenarios of Genocide: Models of Genocide and Critical Responses' (ch 3, n 101) 4.

[104] See already the title of the publication by Schabas, *Unimaginable Atrocities. Justice, Politics, and Rights at the War Crimes Tribunals* (ch 1, n 45).

[105] For example, United Nations, Framework of Analysis for Atrocity Crimes. A Tool for Prevention, October 2014, 1–2 <https://www.un.org/en/genocideprevention/documents/about-us/Doc.3_Framework%20of%20Analysis%20for%20Atrocity%20Crimes_EN.pdf>. For earlier proposals in this direction, see Schabas, 'Semantics or Substance? David Scheffer's Welcome Proposal to Strengthen Criminal Accountability for Atrocities' (ch 2, n 206) 31, fn 1.

[106] See American Society of International Law, 'Signature Topics – Atrocity Prevention' <https://www.asil.org/related-terms-vocabulary/signature-topics-atrocity-prevention>.

Level Dialogue on Atrocity Prevention' on 16 November 2020.[107] Instead of focussing on particular crimes in an exclusionary manner, the idea is to deal with violence on a broader and open scale.[108]

Irrespective of such propositions, there has been observed 'a continuum, running from narrow and restrictive, all the way to broad and inclusive' in the use of definitions 'in the specialist literature',[109] with the spectrum ranging from Israel Charny's over-inclusive 'humanistic definition of genocide'[110] to Stephan Katz's over-exclusive definition of genocide, ultimately reducing its application to the Holocaust.[111] What has been referred to as 'the inclusivist camp'[112] would end any further terminological discussions by simply using the term as a *pars pro toto* for all atrocity crimes.[113] In effect though, a 'more relaxed definition makes genocide a common historical event'.[114]

Others adapt not just the definition but the word itself: 'classicide', 'democide', 'ethnocide', 'gendercide', 'humanicide',[115] 'linguicide'[116] and so on have all been suggested[117] – and again rejected[118] – in the literature. Additional neologisms

[107] See United Nations Human Rights Office of the High Commissioner, Global Action Against Mass Atrocity Crimes Platform for Prevention, High Level Dialogue on Atrocity Prevention, Statement by Michelle Bachelet, UN High Commissioner for Human Rights, 16 November 2020 <https://www.ohchr.org/EN/NewsEvents/Pages/DisplayNews.aspx?NewsID=26507&LangID=E>.

[108] See David Scheffer, 'The Future of Atrocity Law' 25 *Suffolk Transnational Law Review* 389; David Scheffer, 'Genocide and Atrocity Crimes' (2006) 1 *Genocide Studies and Prevention: An International Journal* 229. Although international criminal lawyers have criticized the term for supposedly excluding the crime of aggression.

[109] Gellately and Kiernan, 'Investigating Genocide' (ch 1, n 36) 377.

[110] Charny, 'Introduction' (ch 3, n 88) xii and xxiv.

[111] See Sémelin, *Säubern und Vernichten. Die politische Dimension von Massakern und Völkermorden* (ch 1, n 25) 341–3; Shaw, *What Is Genocide?* (ch 1, n 36) 54–5; Henry C. Theriault, 'Genocidal Mutation and the Challenge of Definition' (2010) 41 *Metaphilosophy* 481, 482.

[112] Levene, *Genocide in the Age of the Nation-State. Volume I: The Meaning of Genocide* (ch 1, n 15) 38.

[113] For example, Genocide Prevention Task Force, *Preventing Genocide. A Blueprint for U.S. Policymakers* (United States Holocaust Memorial Museum, The American Academy of Diplomacy, and the Endowment of the United States Institute of Peace 2008) xxii: 'The colloquial description of large-scale and deliberate attacks on civilians is buttressed by a framework in international law that has been accepted by the United States and other governments and that defines serious crimes meriting special international concern. We use the term genocide in this report as a shorthand expression for this wider category of crimes.' Cf Stone, 'Introduction' (ch 1, n 35) 2.

[114] Ellman, 'Stalin and the Soviet Famine of 1932–33 Revisited' (ch 1, n 75) 691.

[115] See Pieter N. Drost, *The Crime of State. Penal Protection for Fundamental Freedoms of Persons and Peoples. Book I. Humanicide. International Governmental Crime Against Individual Human Rights.*

[116] See Jaroslav B. Rudnyckyj, 'Linguicide: Concept and Definition' in Israel W. Charny (ed), *Toward the Understanding and Prevention of Genocide. Proceedings of the International Conference on the Holocaust and Genocide* (Westview Press 1984).

[117] For overviews, see Clavero, *Genocide or Ethnocide 1933–2007. How to Make, Unmake, and Remake Law With Words* (ch 1, n 49) 8 and 111–22; Jones, *Genocide. A Comprehensive Introduction* (ch 1, n 34) 34–7; Shaw, *What Is Genocide?* (ch 1, n 36) 84–100.

[118] Cf Clavero, *Genocide or Ethnocide 1933–2007. How to Make, Unmake, and Remake Law With Words* (ch 1, n 49) 203–4; Gellately and Kiernan, 'Investigating Genocide' (ch 1, n 36) 277; Irving L. Horowitz, 'Science, Modernity and Authorized Terror: Reconsidering the Genocidal State' in Levon

may rather carry further potential for confusion[119] than aiding in comparative analysis.[120]

Confusion increases where adaptations are aimed at producing a normative result (e.g. the inclusion of political groups)[121] or where they are used in contradiction to or partially blended with the original legal definition.[122]

When Chalk and Jonassohn, in their guided reading on genocide, rely on their 'own definition',[123] they deliberately stick with 'genocide', 'partly because we have not been able to think of an adequate alternate term and partly because the term *genocide* is by now so widely accepted'.[124] Thereby, they follow the suggestion that 'scholars who disagree with the breadth of the UN definition of genocide, in describing a particular case as a tragedy falling short of genocide' should at least 'make clear that they are not exercising a legal judgment that might diminish the rights of redress on the part of the victims'.[125]

Once scholars have come up with their own definition, this is often the end of it and rarely do other scholars build on their work.[126] Too great, perhaps, is the temptation to leave a mark by creating one's own definition and be the first to get it right. As Helen Fein remarks on her own 'formula': 'It appears to work so far.'[127] Scholars of Genocide Studies are aware of these uncoupled efforts to create a new working definition and have discussed how these relate to the original definition of the Genocide Convention.[128] Judging from these

Chorbajian and George Shirinian (eds), *Studies in Comparative Genocide* (Palgrave Macmillan/St Martin's Press 1999) 15.

119 See Förster and Hirschfeld, 'Einleitung' (ch 1, n 14) 7; Gellately and Kiernan, 'Investigating Genocide' (ch 1, n 36) 377.

120 See Förster and Hirschfeld, 'Einleitung' (ch 1, n 14) 8. Cf, however, Chalk and Jonassohn, *The History and Sociology of Genocide. Analyses and Case Studies* (ch 1, n 40) 23 with regard to 'ethnocide'.

121 For example, Beth Van Schaack, 'The Crime of Political Genocide: Repairing the Genocide Convention's Blind Spot' (1996) 106 *Yale Law Journal* 2259.

122 See Horowitz, *Taking Lives. Genocide and State Power* (ch 1, n 26) 14.

123 Chalk and Jonassohn, *The History and Sociology of Genocide. Analyses and Case Studies* (ch 1, n 40) xvii and 23. See also already Chalk and Jonassohn, 'The History and Sociology of Genocidal Killings' (ch 1, n 40) 40.

124 Chalk and Jonassohn, *The History and Sociology of Genocide. Analyses and Case Studies* (ch 1, n 40) 23, emphasis in original.

125 Gellately and Kiernan, 'Investigating Genocide' (ch 1, n 36) 380.

126 For example, Horowitz, *Taking Lives. Genocide and State Power* (ch 1, n 26) 14–5, relying on the definition given by Chalk and Jonassohn. Or Ternon, *L'État Criminel. Les Génocides au XXe Siècle* (ch 1, n 36), relying on various definitions throughout his book.

127 Fein, 'Definition and Discontent: Labelling, Detecting, and Explaining Genocide in the Twentieth Century' (ch 3, n 52) 15.

128 For example, Barth, *Genozid. Völkermord Im 20. Jahrhundert. Geschichte, Theorien, Kontroversen* (ch 2, n 174) 21–5; Chalk and Jonassohn, *The History and Sociology of Genocide. Analyses and Case Studies* (ch 1, n 40) 12–23; Fein, 'Introduction' (ch 3, n 54) 2–5; Fein, 'Definition and Discontent: Labelling, Detecting, and Explaining Genocide in the Twentieth Century' (ch 3, n 52) 15–7; Jones, *Genocide. A*

assessments, it appears quite unlikely that amalgamations or synergies can be expected in the near future. Rather it is symptomatic of a circularity within Genocide Studies, a recurring struggle with the definition and what it is one wishes to accomplish.

3.2.3 Vulgarization

Finally, simplification extracts the term from its original discipline without regard to its originally accepted – one could say state of the art – definition, while at the same time failing to supply an alternative. This naturally goes hand in hand with the popularization of a label. Hence, the third possibility of transplant is an '"ordinary" understanding of genocide'[129] or, more bluntly put, its vulgarization.

Once scientific terminology seeps into the public discourse, the attached connotations can take over and determine the use of the word:

> A significant, albeit often ignored, difference exists between everyday discourse and scientific discourse. The language we use in everyday usage does not require and does not benefit from precise definitions; this is so because we want to communicate not only information, but also feelings, attitudes and opinions. Scientists too have feelings, attitudes, and opinions, of course, but they also have an overriding need to separate them from their data, concepts, and research findings. Therefore, the scientist requires a language that includes precise definitions of the terms he uses and that separates the cognitive content of his communication from the emotional and evaluative content. This distinction between everyday discourse and scientific discourse is becoming increasingly difficult to establish and maintain for several reasons: the spread of education, of the mass media, and of the popularization of science allow scientific terminology to filter into daily discourse. In this process it acquires new meanings that detract from its utility in scientific language. The problem is compounded in the case of concepts that acquire a political loading; when this happens, the polemical use of a term may overshadow its original meaning and increase

Comprehensive Introduction (ch 1, n 34) 23–7; Ben Kiernan, 'Genocide and "Ethnic Cleansing"' in Stig Förster and Gerhard Hirschfeld (eds), *Genozid in der modernen Geschichte* (Lit Verlag 1999) 37; Rubinstein, *Genocide: A History* (ch 1, n 40) 2–6; Sémelin, *Säubern und Vernichten. Die politische Dimension von Massakern und Völkermorden* (ch 1, n 25) 346–51; Shaw, *What Is Genocide?* (ch 1, n 36) 46–50.

[129] Kirsch, 'The Two Notions of Genocide: Distinguishing Macro Phenomena and Individual Misconduct' (ch 2, n 175) 141.

the difficulty of precise communication. The term *genocide* has become an almost classic illustration of this process.[130]

Already the Whitaker Report of the United Nations pointed out in 1985 that '"genocide" in popular modern usage covers many more cases of mass killings than those covered in the Convention'.[131]

In some instances, the simplification is veiled by a reference to the definition of Article II of the Genocide Convention, only to be followed by a misrepresentation through false or irrelevant arguments in the conversation over whether the label fits. Similarly, the analysis may continue without any further mention of or regard to the actual scope of the definition.

3.3 Consequences

The fact that terminology is adopted by different actors in different ways could be expected. The appropriation of symbolic capital, be it as an instrument for accusation or activism, may not surprise. But what is the added value of these statements – 'why does it matter'?[132] As Alex Alvarez rightly points out, 'the reality is that the term used to describe a people's suffering and/or victimization is ultimately irrelevant to their lived experience as human beings'.[133] But there are other consequences which make atrocity labelling relevant and call for a better understanding of the process.

Expected or not, with or without surprise, the use of transplants has both (1) diluted their meaning and (2) great caution is applied today when publicly labelling atrocities. Parts of the literature suggest (3) a different use for words such as 'genocide' altogether, reimagining them in the 'borrowing', 'host' discipline and leaving the donor 'conceptless'.

130 Chalk and Jonassohn, *The History and Sociology of Genocide. Analyses and Case Studies* (ch 1, n 40) 3. See also Lang, 'The Concept of Genocide' (ch 1, n 1) 115.

131 United Nations Economic and Social Council, Commission on Human Rights, Sub-Commission on Prevention of Discrimination and Protection of Minorities, 'Revised and Updated Report on the Question of the Prevention and Punishment of the Crime of Genocide', 2 July 1985, E/CN.4/Sub.2/1985/6, 20, para 42.

132 See Kelly, 'Genocide – The Power of a Label' (ch 1, n 74) 148.

133 Alex Alvarez, *Native America and the Question of Genocide* (Rowman & Littlefield 2014) 167.

3.3.1 Dilution

The ambiguity of different use of labels reflects on the use of the term 'genocide'. The multiplicity of definitions has led to a watering down of the concept.[134] Since 'the media as well as historians tend to use the term simply to describe the occurrence of mass killings or ethnic cleansing based on discriminatory motives',[135] in a way, 'genocide has become for many writers little more than mass murder'.[136] Adaptation and vulgarization have made it 'a much contested and overused term' that is '[s]ometimes [. . .] uttered with thoughtless abandon'.[137] That the term is 'overused and indiscriminately employed' is found by Judge Bennouna in his declaration annexed to the Order of the International Court of Justice indicating provisional measures in the context of the Russian aggression against Ukraine as 'neither in the interest of the human groups under serious threat of destruction, nor in the interest of the credibility and efficiency of the 1948 Convention'.[138] The use of the term becomes 'trivialized'[139] and 'fraught with ambiguities, possibly because it became a catchphrase for the dispossessed'.[140] If undefined or left to blur, 'the term becomes devoid of all cognitive content and communicates nothing but the author's disapproval'.[141]

Mark Levene goes so far to say that 'the term now is so broadly used and abused that it has become much less a tool for understanding and more a millstone around our necks':[142] 'One can only conclude that "genocide" has become, on the one hand, so ubiquitous a term, yet on the other, so unmalleable

[134] Cf Schaller, 'Genozidforschung: Begriffe und Debatten. Einleitung' (ch 1, n 34) 15.

[135] Kirsch, 'The Two Notions of Genocide: Distinguishing Macro Phenomena and Individual Misconduct' (ch 2, n 175) 141.

[136] Shaw, *What Is Genocide?* (ch 1, n 36) 8.

[137] Weitz, *A Century of Genocide. Utopias of Race and Nation* (ch 1, n 34) 8.

[138] International Court of Justice, *Allegations of Genocide under the Convention on the Prevention and Punishment of the Crime of Genocide* (Ukraine *v.* Russian Federation), Declaration of Judge Bennouna to the Order of 16 March 2022, para 4.

[139] Chalk and Jonassohn, 'Conceptualizations of Genocide and Ethnocide' (ch 1, n 34) 182.

[140] Barbara Harff, 'Recognizing Genocides and Politicides' in Helen Fein (ed), *Genocide Watch* (Yale University Press 1992) 28. See also Bazyler, Bazyler, *Holocaust, Genocide, and the Law. A Quest for Justice in a Post-Holocaust World* (ch 2, n 19) 59; Jürgen Zimmerer, 'Holocaust und Kolonialismus. Beitrag zu einer Archäologie des genozidalen Gedankens' in Jürgen Zimmerer (ed), *Von Windhuk nach Auschwitz? Beiträge zum Verhältnis von Kolonialismus und Holocaust* (Lit Verlag 2011) 144.

[141] Chalk and Jonassohn, *The History and Sociology of Genocide. Analyses and Case Studies* (ch 1, n 40) 3. See also Eckart Conze and Christoph Safferling, 'The Genocide Convention Sixty Years After Its Adoption' in Eckart Conze and Christoph Safferling (eds), *The Genocide Convention Sixty Years After its Adoption* (TMC Asser Press 2010) 7.

[142] Levene, *Genocide in the Age of the Nation-State. Volume I: The Meaning of Genocide* (ch 1, n 15) 37.

to interrogation, that is [*sic*] has completely lost any descriptive value.'[143] It becomes either too fuzzy or too contentious for any proper analytical scope.[144] Benjamin Meiches begins his book *The Politics of Annihilation: A Genealogy of Genocide* with a quote from Friedrich Nietzsche's *On the Genealogy of Morals*: 'All concepts in which an entire process is semiotically concentrated elude definition; only that which has no history is definable.'[145]

Of course, '[h]istorians' and politicians' wording is not law's wording. The media's language is not courts' language.'[146] But at the level of international law it could be the language of international relations, of states, of the United Nations or of NGOs. And, thereby, the 'boomerang' of international legal concepts returns to its original discipline. Trying to make it fit, Genocide Studies have chipped away at their main research object.

3.3.2 Humanitarian inertia

This dilution carries broader consequences when it comes to the necessity for humanitarian action by the international community:

> It has become apparent that there are undesirable consequences to enlarging or diluting the definition of genocide. This weakens the terrible stigma associated with the crime and demeans the suffering of its victims. It is also likely to enfeeble whatever commitment States may believe they have to prevent the crime. The broader and more uncertain the definition, the less responsibility States will be prepared to assume.[147]

But even without such dilution, states have, in the past, become uncomfortable using the term to assert a humanitarian crisis. In the international political theatre, the implications of applying the term – either legally or politically – have, at times, led to skirting around the term 'genocide' by government administrations.[148]

[143] Ibid 37–8.

[144] See Zimmerer, 'Kolonialer Genozid? Vom Nutzen und Nachteil einer historischen Kategorie für eine Globalgeschichte des Völkermordes' (ch 1, n 14) 109.

[145] Meiches, *The Politics of Annihilation. A Genealogy of Genocide* (ch 1, n 23) 1.

[146] Clavero, *Genocide or Ethnocide 1933–2007. How to Make, Unmake, and Remake Law With Words* (ch 1, n 49) 93.

[147] Schabas, *Genocide in International Law* (ch 2, n 28) 10.

[148] See Akçam, *The Young Turks' Crime Against Humanity. The Armenian Genocide and Ethnic Cleansing in the Ottoman Empire* (ch 3, n 88) xxviii; Bazyler, *Holocaust, Genocide, and the Law. A Quest for Justice in a Post-Holocaust World* (ch 2, n 19) 60; Gerlach, 'Extremely Violent Societies. An Alternative to

This becomes a humanitarian Groundhog Day: 'Whenever new challenges arise the same confused debate occurs over whether attacks on civilians constitute "genocide", "ethnic cleansing" or just the excess of a dirty "civil war".'[149] Here, atrocity labelling demarcates the path towards different decisions whenever humanitarian action is required.[150] The process of atrocity labelling is cause for additional hesitation or perhaps even a welcome proxy discussion and 'the effects of applying the label can truncate options for dealing with the situation'.[151]

Therefore, atrocity labelling is relevant because its effects can be critical:[152] 'Too often the debate over whether genocide is occurring has become more important than taking action to reverse the situation and prevent further violations.'[153] Scholarly attempts have been made to 'liberate' governments from 'the Genocide Factor',[154] suggesting the use of the term 'atrocity crime' as an alternative:[155]

> Just as the term 'genocide' originally captured what Raphael Lemkin recognized as the essence of a particular crime against humanity requiring special identification in public, legal, and historical terms, so too does the term 'atrocity crimes' describe a basket of particularly heinous crimes that are suitable for criminal prosecution before international tribunals and national courts and for which states and certain non-state organizations and groups should be held responsible. Atrocity crimes also are collectively executed crimes of such magnitude and destructive character as to be particularly prominent and logically inconsistent with the protection of human rights and the maintenance of international peace and security in an increasingly interdependent and sophisticated global society.[156]

the Concept of Genocide' (ch 1, n 66) 452–3; Power, *A Problem from Hell. America and the Age of Genocide* (ch 1, n 13) XVIII; Ringrose, 'The Politicization of the Genocide Label: Genocide Rhetoric in the UN Security Council' (ch 3, n 35) 124; Sémelin, *Säubern und Vernichten. Die politische Dimension von Massakern und Völkermorden* (ch 1, n 25) 338–40.

[149] Shaw, *What Is Genocide?* (ch 1, n 36) 1.

[150] See Harff, 'Recognizing Genocides and Politicides' (ch 3, n 140) 146–7.

[151] Kelly, 'Genocide – The Power of a Label' (ch 1, n 74) 148.

[152] Jäger suggests this should be a criterion for the selection of the object of any critical discourse analysis. See Jäger, *Kritische Diskursanalyse. Eine Einführung* (ch 1, n 96) 91.

[153] Juan E. Méndez, 'The United Nations and the Prevention of Genocide' in Ralph Henham and Paul Behrens (eds), *The Criminal Law of Genocide. International, Comparative and Contextual Aspects* (Ashgate 2007) 228.

[154] See Scheffer, 'Genocide and Atrocity Crimes' (ch 3, n 108) 229–39. Cf also already Scheffer, 'The Future of Atrocity Law' (ch 3, n 108) 419.

[155] Scheffer, 'The Future of Atrocity Law' (ch 3, n 108) 398–400; Scheffer, 'Genocide and Atrocity Crimes' (ch 3, n 108) 237. Cf also Kelly, 'Genocide – The Power of a Label' (ch 1, n 74) 157.

[156] Scheffer, 'Genocide and Atrocity Crimes' (ch 3, n 108) 238.

However, it has also been said that 'alternative categorizations have only marginal impact on meaningful action where there is a failure of political will'.[157] But this still leads directly into the third and final consequences of atrocity labelling.

3.3.3 Reimagination

International legal concepts may be reimagined within their 'host' discipline. It has been suggested that the term 'genocide' 'in the coming years and decades, will prove more significant as *an intellectual and scholarly framework* [. . .] and as *a tool of advocacy and mobilization*'[158] so that its 'most significant deployment [. . .] may *not* be as a legal-prosecutorial device, but as an intellectual concept and [. . .] an advocacy tool to arouse public concern, shame perpetrators, and press for intervention'.[159] In turn, '[t]his may also free the term from its unnecessarily restrictive framing in the UN Genocide Convention, with its limited target groups and high evidentiary requirement of genocidal intent'.[160] It will have left the legal domain to transform into a political slogan,[161] no longer relevant for lawyers, judges and international legal scholars (except those of legal history).

However, the intensification of scholarly preoccupation with international criminal law makes this full shift towards a political category an unlikely one, and it risks giving up the only international crime backed by an international treaty conferring jurisdiction of the International Court of Justice. But it has also indeed been observed that scholarship has moved in the direction of considering the three core crimes, genocide, crimes against humanity and war crimes to be 'of equal gravity',[162] evident also in the inclusion of genocide alongside crimes against humanity and war crimes – as well as 'ethnic cleansing' – triggering the 'responsibility to protect'.[163]

[157] Payam Akhavan, 'Proliferation of Terminology and the Illusion of Progress' (2007) 2 *Genocide Studies and Prevention: An International Journal* 73, 73.
[158] Jones, *Genocide. A Comprehensive Introduction* (ch 1, n 34) 34. See also Shaw, *What Is Genocide?* (ch 1, n 36) 1.
[159] Jones, *Genocide. A Comprehensive Introduction* (ch 1, n 34) 712, emphasis in original.
[160] Ibid 712.
[161] Zimmerer, 'Kolonialer Genozid? Vom Nutzen und Nachteil einer historischen Kategorie für eine Globalgeschichte des Völkermordes' (ch 1, n 14) 109.
[162] Schabas, *Genocide in International Law* (ch 2, n 28) 652–3. Cf Chapter 3, n 32.
[163] See United Nations General Assembly Resolution 60/1, '2005 World Summit Outcome', 24 October 2005, UN Doc A/RES/60/1, paras 138–9. See also David Scheffer, 'Atrocity Crimes Framing the Responsibility to Protect' (2007) 40 *Case Western Reserve Journal of International Law* 111, 115.

Others see 'a subtle but noticeable shift in international tribunals away from genocide and toward crimes against humanity as the preferred legal framework'.[164] Alternatively, a new category of atrocity crime could be envisioned to reconceptualize the legal framework under a different heading.[165]

[164] Jones, *Genocide. A Comprehensive Introduction* (ch 1, n 34) 711.
[165] See Chapter 3, n 104–8.

4

Colonialism, transformation and the process of labelling

Having discussed the use of different terms, the motivations for their selection, and the possible consequences in the abstract, how might one now imagine atrocity labelling 'in practice'? This chapter peeks over the shoulders of historians, political and social scientists – the scholars of Genocide Studies – to better learn what guides the process.

Four case studies have been selected in the search for common denominators of atrocity labelling: the Belgian rubber exploitation in the Congo under King Leopold II; the campaign against the Herero and Nama peoples in German South-West Africa at the outset of the twentieth century; the expulsion of the Armenians in Asia Minor during the First World War; and the famine in Ukraine of the early 1930s, known commonly as the Holodomor.[1]

These cases also stand representative of two circumstances considered in the literature as inducive to genocide: colonialism and transformation. Mass atrocities have been found closely connected to events of societal upheaval, both in a transformative and colonial context. The classic phenomenology of genocide preconditions the existence of modern ethnic nation states. Multiple works have focused on the systems of nationalism and totalitarianism as fertile

[1] The corpus for each case study was selected based on presence in the discussions, taking into account citations, bibliographies and (online) research guides. While journalistic and popular non-fictions were considered, news articles and opinion pieces were, as a rule, not taken into account. Neither were other forms of reception such as fiction or poetry. Primary sources and so-called ego-documents such as eyewitness accounts and memoire literature were also excluded. Languages were restricted to English, French and German. Although it should go without saying, none of the works were intentionally selected to target or discredit specific authors. The aim is not to 'name and shame' – although nationalist or revisionist motifs should be highlighted where they shine through the text – but to draw conclusions that might help address the main research question of this book.

ground for atrocities.[2] Struggles for political and economic transformation have proven catalysts for the escalation of slumbering tensions.[3] The decline and fall of both the Ottoman and Russian Empires not only brought these to surface but the ensuing chaos was met by totalitarian response.[4]

Hence, 'it was not accidental that the Armenian genocide occurred in the crisis setting of World War I; that the Soviet purge of nationalities began during the decade of the "great transformation," when the immense upheavals of crash industrialization and forced collectivization created social havoc':[5] 'The connection between genocides and extreme societal crisis is so critical because both war and revolution break standard codes of human interaction.'[6] Adding to this, societies and regimes undergoing rapid changes and processes of modernization have also seen achievements and progress in dual-use for the commission of atrocities.[7] The railway remains a sad symbol of twentieth-century ethnic cleansing and genocide.

Going hand in hand with a turn towards 'Colonial Studies', genocide has also been increasingly discussed as a colonial phenomenon.[8] There is probably no instance of colonialism[9] that is not in some way connected to discrimination and repression

2 For example, Horowitz, *Taking Lives. Genocide and State Power* (ch 1, n 26); Kuper, *Genocide. Its Political Use in the Twentieth Century* (ch 1, n 34); Rudolph J. Rummel, *Statistics of Democide. Genocide and Mass Murder since 1900* (Lit Verlag 1998). Cf Hannah Arendt, *The Origins of Totalitarianism* (Harcourt, Brace and Company 1951); Zygmunt Bauman, *Modernity and the Holocaust* (Polity Press 1989).

3 See Harff, 'No Lessons Learned from the Holocaust? Assessing Risks of Genocide and Political Mass Murder since 1955' (ch 1, n 35) 61–9.

4 See Tessa Hofmann, 'Christenverfolgung in Armenien (1894–1941). Die Synergie von nationalistischem Völkermord und stalinistischer Religionsunterdrückung' in Georg Plasger and Heinz-Günther Stobbe (eds), *Gewalt Gegen Christen. Formen, Gründe, Hintergründe* (Evangelische Verlagsanstalt 2014) 159; Horowitz, 'Science, Modernity and Authorized Terror: Reconsidering the Genocidal State' (ch 3, n 118) 22; Norman M. Naimark, *Fires of Hatred. Ethnic Cleansing in Twentieth-Century Europe* (Harvard University Press 2001) 9, 17, and 24; Rubinstein, *Genocide: A History* (ch 1, n 40) 127–33. Cf with regard to the Armenian case Donald Bloxham, 'Internal Colonization, Inter-Imperial Conflict and the Armenian Genocide' in A. Dirk Moses (ed), *Empire, Colony Genocide. Conquest, Occupation, and Subaltern Resistance in World History* (Berghahn Books 2008).

5 Weitz, *A Century of Genocide. Utopias of Race and Nation* (ch 1, n 34) 250.

6 Ibid. 251. See also Alexander J. Motyl, 'Looking at the Holodomor Through the Lens of the Holocaust' in Lubomyr Y. Luciuk (ed), *Holodomor: Reflections on the Great Famine of 1932–1933 in Soviet Ukraine* (Kashtan Press 2008) 175.

7 See Naimark, *Fires of Hatred. Ethnic Cleansing in Twentieth-Century Europe* (ch 4, n 4) 9.

8 Cf Elazar Barkan, 'Genocides of Indigenous Peoples. Rhetoric of Human Rights' in Robert Gellately and Ben Kiernan (eds), *The Specter of Genocide. Mass Murder in Historical Perspective* (Cambridge University Press 2003) 133–9; Barth, *Genozid. Völkermord Im 20. Jahrhundert. Geschichte, Theorien, Kontroversen* (ch 2, n 174) 134; Cooper, *Raphael Lemkin and the Struggle for the Genocide Convention* (ch 1, n 43) ix; Kuper, *Genocide. Its Political Use in the Twentieth Century* (ch 1, n 34) 14–5; Leo Kuper, 'Other Selected Cases of Genocide and Genocidal Massacres: Types of Genocide' in Israel W. Charny (ed), *Genocide. A Critical Bibliographical Review* (Facts on File Publications 1988) 156–7.

9 For a definition of 'colonialism', see Jan C. Jansen and Jürgen Osterhammel, *Kolonialismus. Geschichte, Formen, Folgen* (7th edn, CH Beck 2012).

against the existing (indigenous) population, irrespective of the underlying rationale.[10] In extreme cases, this culminated in mass atrocities or annihilation.[11] The concept of genocide as a dominant group driving another towards submission or destruction offers itself as a lens through which to view these events.

Jean-Paul Sartre had already highlighted the close relationship between genocide and colonialism in his 1968 essay 'On Genocide'.[12] Since then, this has been continuously reemphasized[13] on the basis that 'the two phenomena are profoundly connected, as many examples from around the world illustrate'.[14] Beyond the two examples in this book, one might think of the fate of the indigenous populations of the Americas or Australia.[15]

Drawing the line back to the classic phenomenology of genocide as preconditioning the existence of modern ethnic nation states, 'the prototype for developmental genocides may have occurred in the interaction between European settlers and the natives of the Americas, Australia, New Zealand, and South Africa'.[16] Returning to Lemkin's original conception of genocide in *Axis Rule in Occupied Europe*, the idea of cultural genocide comes to mind and has been invoked in the literature.[17]

[10] See Roger W. Smith, 'State Power and Genocidal Intent: On the Uses of Genocide in the Twentieth Century' in Levon Chorbajian and George Shirinian (eds), *Studies in Comparative Genocide* (Palgrave Macmillan/St Martin's Press 1999) 10–1.

[11] See Robert K. Hitchcock and Samuel Totten, 'Introduction. The Genocide of Indigenous Peoples' in Robert K. Hitchcock and Samuel Totten (eds), *Genocide of Indigenous Peoples. A Critical Bibliographic Review* (Transaction Publishers 2011) 1.

[12] See Jean-Paul Sartre, 'On Genocide' (1968) VI *Ramparts* 37–9. See also already on colonialism as a basis for totalitarian ideology Arendt, *The Origins of Totalitarianism* (ch 4, n 2). Cf Kuper, *Genocide. Its Political Use in the Twentieth Century* (ch 1, n 34) 44; Kuper, 'Other Selected Cases of Genocide and Genocidal Massacres: Types of Genocide' (ch 4, n 8) 156; Ternon, *L'État Criminel. Les Génocides au XXe Siècle* (ch 1, n 36) 72–4.

[13] For example, Levene, *Genocide in the Age of the Nation-State. Volume II: The Rise of the West and the Coming of Genocide*; United Nations Economic and Social Council, Commission on Human Rights, Sub-Commission on Prevention of Discrimination and Protection of Minorities, 'Revised and Updated Report on the Question of the Prevention and Punishment of the Crime of Genocide', 2 July 1985, E/CN.4/Sub.2/1985/6, 7, para 21.

[14] A. Dirk Moses and Dan Stone, 'Introduction', *Colonialism and Genocide* (Routledge 2007) xiv.

[15] Cf Alvarez, *Native America and the Question of Genocide* (ch 3, n 133); Jeff Benvenuto, Alexander Laban Hinton and Andrew Woolford (eds), *Colonial Genocide in Indigenous North America* (Duke University Press 2014); A. Dirk Moses (ed), *Genocide and Settler Society. Frontier Violence and Stolen Indigenous Children in Australian History* (Berghahn Books 2004); A. Dirk Moses (ed), *Empire, Colony Genocide. Conquest, Occupation, and Subaltern Resistance in World History* (Berghahn Books 2008); Jeffrey Ostler, *Surviving Genocide. Native Nations and the United States from the American Revolution to Bleeding Kansas* (Yale University Press 2019); David E. Stannard, *American Holocaust. The Conquest of the New World* (Oxford University Press 1992).

[16] Fein, 'Scenarios of Genocide: Models of Genocide and Critical Responses' (ch 3, n 101) 8.

[17] For example, Dominik J. Schaller, 'Genocide and Mass Violence in "The Heart of Darkness": Africa in the Colonial Period' in Donald Bloxham and A. Dirk Moses (eds), *The Oxford Handbook of Genocide* (Oxford University Press 2010) 360–1.

The colonial perspective goes beyond the obvious focus on (European) settler societies. As Dominik Schaller puts forward, 'not only are genocides always colonial, but colonial rule and colonialism as such are constantly genocidal'.[18] Already '[t]he inventor of the term "genocide," Raphael Lemkin, certainly conceived of the Nazi project in Europe as colonial',[19] he viewed the Holocaust through the lens of colonialism.[20] This line of thought has been spun into comparison, suggesting that 'the number of tribal peoples who died because they built no houses and dug no wells amounts to one of the great acts of human destruction, comparable to the Nazi Holocaust, or the Stalinist purges of the Soviet Union, or the mass slaughters of communist China'.[21]

But there has been some backlash, too. The category of 'colonial genocide' as a distinct phenomenon is criticized and rejected for its apparent suggestion that no 'genocide' proper took place:

> The murder of the Ottoman Armenians by the Young Turks during World War I and the Holocaust are widely perceived as ideal types of genocide because of the perpetrators' alleged 'irrational' motives: nationalism and racism. The perpetrators of colonial mass violence, by contrast, are believed to be driven by 'rational' motives like greed and revenge. Such artificially constructed distinction ignores the fact that génocidaires never rely on a single motive, and it leads to the distorted but widespread conclusion that the category 'colonial genocide' is analytically useless, and that no genocides occurred in colonial Africa.[22]

Others have suggested to abandon the category alltogether.[23] For the purpose of this book, the debate may rest aside. The idea of a colonial perspective is not used here to qualify the character of atrocities committed within a colonial

18 Dominik J. Schaller, 'From Conquest to Genocide. Colonial Rule in German Southwest Africa and German East Africa' in A. Dirk Moses (ed), *Empire, Colony Genocide. Conquest, Occupation, and Subaltern Resistance in World History* (Berghahn Books 2008) 317.

19 A Dirk Moses, 'Preface' in A. Dirk Moses (ed), *Genocide and Settler Society. Frontier Violence and Stolen Indigenous Children in Australian History* (Berghahn Books 2004) xiv. See also Irvin-Erickson, *Raphaël Lemkin and the Concept of Genocide* (ch 2, n 19) 82; Moses, 'Genocide and Settler Society in Australian History' (ch 1, n 14) 27–8.

20 He also spoke of a 'policy of deliberate extermination' with regard to German South-West Africa. See Cooper, *Raphael Lemkin and the Struggle for the Genocide Convention* (ch 1, n 43) 244; Dominik J. Schaller, 'Genocide in Colonial South-West Africa: The German War against the Herero and Nama, 1904–1907' in Robert K. Hitchcock and Samuel Totten (eds), *Genocide of Indigenous Peoples. A Critical Bibliographic Review* (Routledge 2011) 38–9.

21 Mark Cocker, *Rivers of Blood, Rivers of Gold* (Pimlico 1999) 364–5.

22 Schaller, 'Genocide and Mass Violence in "The Heart of Darkness": Africa in the Colonial Period' (ch 4, n 17) 346. See also Moses, 'Genocide and Settler Society in Australian History' (ch 1, n 14) 25.

23 See Zimmerer, 'Kolonialer Genozid? Vom Nutzen und Nachteil einer historischen Kategorie für eine Globalgeschichte des Völkermordes' (ch 1, n 14) 109, 123, and 219–20.

setting but to acknowledge and engage with the process of atrocity labelling as it appears against the background of such events and the historiography produced through Colonial Studies.

With this in mind, this chapter considers four cases, two of which fit clearly within the classic phenomenology of genocide – the fate of the Armenians in Asia Minor and the famine in Ukraine of the early 1930s – and two that have only been explored more closely since the 'colonial turn' – the Belgian rubber exploitation in the Congo and the conflict between the Herero and Nama peoples in German South-West Africa and their 'colonial masters'.

This categorization of events is not mutually exclusive. Neither vantage point would provide a useful analytical framework if it descriptively threw the net over obvious examples. Both the Herero and Nama genocide and the Armenian genocide have been viewed as 'a signifier of modernity'.[24] Equally, the Armenian genocide and the Holodomor have been discussed through the lens of colonialism.[25] On the Ukrainian famine, Niall Ferguson writes that it 'was possible because the Ukraine was in effect being run as a Russian colony'.[26]

In any case, it appears quite clear that the context of transformation and colonialism offer themselves for the study of atrocities. Still, why these four cases?

First and foremost, all four of the cases are mainstream references in Genocide Studies. To make this apparent, one only has to open Adam Jones's introductory textbook *Genocide Studies*[27] or the *Oxford Handbook on Genocide Studies*.[28] All the four cases also share entries in the *Encyclopedia of Genocide and Crimes against Humanity*,[29] and they are all listed in various research guides on genocide.[30]

[24] Bartov, 'Seeking the Roots of Modern Genocide. On the Macro- and Microhistory of Mass Murder' (ch 3, n 75) 76.

[25] For example, Mark von Hagen, 'Wartime Occupation and Peacetime Alien Rule: "Notes and Materials" Toward a(n) (Anti-) (Post-) Colonial History of Ukraine' (2015) 34 *Harvard Ukrainian Studies* 153; Jürgen Zimmerer, 'Der erste Genozid des 20. Jahrhunderts. Der deutsche Vernichtungskrieg in Südwestafrika (1904–1908) und die Globalgeschichte des Genozids' in Jürgen Zimmerer (ed), *Von Windhuk nach Auschwitz? Beiträge zum Verhältnis von Kolonialismus und Holocaust* (Lit Verlag 2011) 66–7.

[26] Niall Ferguson, *The War of the World. History's Age of Hatred* (Penguin Books 2007) 217.

[27] See Jones, *Genocide. A Comprehensive Introduction* (ch 1, n 34).

[28] See Bloxham and Moses, *The Oxford Handbook of Genocide Studies* (ch 1, n 30).

[29] Dinah L. Shelton (ed), *Encyclopedia of Genocide and Crimes Against Humanity* (Thomson Gale 2005).

[30] For example, Georgetown Law Library, War Crimes Research Guide <http://guides.ll.georgetown.edu/c.php?g=365751&p=2471267>; Monash University, Holocaust and Genocide Studies, <http://guides.lib.monash.edu/c.php?g=219731&p=1452958>; Rutgers, Genocide Studies <http://libguides.rutgers.edu/genocide>; Yale University, Genocide Studies Program, <http://gsp.yale.edu/>.

Second, it is also not the first time that these events have been discussed together, having already been considered by Lemkin in his unpublished book on the history of genocides.[31] In fact, they commonly serve as comparative references to one another, building a natural corpus within Genocide Studies. As Dominik Schaller writes in the *Oxford Handbook of Genocide*: 'Two of the most brutal and inhuman regimes of forced labour were practised in German South West Africa and in the Belgian Congo'[32] which 'have become symbols for the exploitative character of European colonial rule in Africa'.[33] With regard to German South-West Africa and the Armenian genocide, Norman Naimark's *Genocide – A World History* emphasizes that 'the German army and state were implicated in both'.[34]

Third, all four cases have captured broader public interest beyond academic preoccupation alone, shaping public debate. Two non-fiction bestsellers, Adam Hochschild's *King Leopold's Ghost*[35] and Robert Conquest's *Harvest of Sorrow*,[36] stand as representatives for the Belgian 'Rubber Terror' under Leopold II in the Congo and the Ukrainian famine of 1932 to 1933, respectively. The 'Rubber Terror' had already received its literary monument in Joseph Conrad's *Heart of Darkness*[37] – and, of course, through its big screen adaptation in Francis Ford Coppola's *Apocalypse Now* where the events are transposed to the Vietnam War[38] – while the Armenian genocide was immortalized in literary history by Franz Werfel's *The Forty Days of Musa Dagh*.[39] The atrocities committed

[31] On the two colonial cases, see Dominik J. Schaller, 'Raphael Lemkin's View of European Colonial Rule in Africa: Between Condemnation and Admiration' (2005) 7 *Journal of Genocide Research* 531. On the Armenian genocide, see Peter Balakian, 'Raphael Lemkin, Cultural Destruction, and the Armenian Genocide' (2013) 27 *Holocaust and Genocide Studies* 57, 60–1. On the Holodomor, see Roman Serbyn, 'Lemkin on Genocide of Nations' (2009) 7 *Journal of International Criminal Justice* 123.

[32] Schaller, 'Genocide and Mass Violence in "The Heart of Darkness": Africa in the Colonial Period' (ch 4, n 17) 362. Cf, however, on the use of the term 'Belgian Congo' with regard to the Congo Free State, Jean Stengers, 'The Congo Free State and the Belgian Congo Before 1914' in Peter Duignan and Lewis H. Gann (eds), *Colonialism in Africa 1870–1960. Volume 1. The History and Politics of Colonialism 1870–1914* (Cambridge University Press 1969) 261–2.

[33] Schaller, 'Genocide and Mass Violence in "The Heart of Darkness": Africa in the Colonial Period' (ch 4, n 17) 362.

[34] Naimark, *Genocide. A World History* (ch 1, n 40) 69.

[35] Adam Hochschild, *King Leopold's Ghost. A Story of Greed, Terror and Heroism in Colonial Africa* (Pan Books 2012). Cf Marouf Hasian, *Restorative Justice, Humanitarian Rhetorics, and Public Memories of Colonial Camp Cultures* (Palgrave Macmillan 2014) 193.

[36] Robert Conquest, *The Harvest of Sorrow. Soviet Collectivization and the Terror-Famine* (Oxford University Press 1986).

[37] Joseph Conrad, *Heart of Darkness* (Blackwood's Magazine 1899).

[38] IMDb, Apocalypse Now (1979) <https://www.imdb.com/title/tt0078788/>.

[39] Franz Werfel, *Die vierzig Tage des Musa Dagh* (Paul Zsolnay 1933).

against the Herero in German South-West Africa continue to appear repeatedly in the daily news against the background of reparation claims, while the Ukrainian famine stands firm within the narrative of a Ukrainian struggle for emancipation from Russian oppression.[40]

Fourth, all the events took place before the 'invention' of the term 'genocide'. None of them carries the suspicion of having been labelled to garner political or humanitarian support during the actual course of events. Since words load past events with all their 'conceptual baggage', governments also avoid labelling past events as genocide on the cynical, albeit legal argument that there is no crime and that there can be no punishment without a corresponding legal provision existing at the time of the act[41] (the obvious exception to this line of argumentation being the Holocaust, as it was the event that triggered the conception of the crime of genocide in the first place).

Fifth, the cases allow for comparing and contrasting contested with uncontested labels (although the purpose is less a comparative study of genocides than an attempt at extrapolating common patterns and tendencies in atrocity labelling). While the cases of German South-West Africa[42] and the fate of the Armenians in Asia Minor are commonly discussed as genocide today, the label continues to be hotly debated in the case of the Ukrainian famine[43] and is not in common use at all for the atrocities that took place within the Congo Free State. The so-called Whitaker Report of the United Nations specifically mentions 'the German massacre of Hereros in 1904' and 'the Ottoman massacre of Armenians in 1915-1916' as examples of genocide.[44]

[40] See Kerstin Jobst, *Geschichte Der Ukraine* (2nd edn, Reclam 2015) 234.

[41] Even if claims for reparations are put forward today, this cannot be based on a violation of the prohibition of genocide or crimes against humanity in their legal sense. Claims for reparations must seek other routes in intertemporal law. As the United Kingdom Foreign & Commonwealth Office argues, 'whilst the term can be applied to tragedies that occurred subsequent to the holocaust, such as Rwanda, it cannot be applied retrospectively'. Cited from Geoffrey Robertson, 'Was There an Armenian Genocide? Geoffrey Robertson QC's Opinion with Reference to Foreign & Commonwealth Office Documents Which Show How British Ministers, Parliament and People Have Been Misled', para 65 <http://groong.usc.edu/Geoffrey-Robertson-QC-Genocide.pdf>. See also Schabas, *Unimaginable Atrocities. Justice, Politics, and Rights at the War Crimes Tribunals* (ch 1, n 45) 63.

[42] Cf, however, Manus I. Midlarsky, *The Killing Trap. Genocide in the Twentieth Century* (Cambridge University Press 2005) 30–4.

[43] Cf, however, Asbjørn Eide, 'Famine' in Dinah L. Shelton (ed), *Encyclopedia of Genocide and Crimes Against Humanity. Vol. 1 [A-H]* (Thomson Gale 2005) 349.

[44] See United Nations Economic and Social Council, Commission on Human Rights, Sub-Commission on Prevention of Discrimination and Protection of Minorities, 'Revised and Updated Report on the Question of the Prevention and Punishment of the Crime of Genocide', 2 July 1985, E/CN.4/Sub.2/1985/6, 9, para 24. Cf James E. Mace, 'Is the Ukrainian Genocide a Myth?' in

But, assessments vary. German historian Boris Barth, in his book on genocide in the twentieth century, lists the Armenian genocide alongside the Holocaust and the genocide in Rwanda as an unequivocal case of genocide. In contrast, he sees the Holodomor and the killing of Herero and Nama peoples in German South-West Africa as cases only with a mere 'suspicion of genocide' ('Fälle mit Genozidverdacht').[45]

Finally, less recent cases allow for a more consolidated record of factual events, as often only the passage of time may lay bare the truth in politically contested circumstances. With, perhaps, the exception of the Holodomor,[46] there is a chance that archival evidence and oral history have reached a certain stage of consolidation.

Each of the following sections begins with (1) a short recollection of the course of events – the horrors of which are recounted in great and greater details throughout the many works referred to in this book – before (2) reviewing the death toll estimates given throughout the literature. This is followed by (3) a discussion of the process of atrocity labelling, (4) highlighting direct references or comparisons to the Holocaust. It ends with (5) a brief assessment, feeding into the overall conclusion.

4.1 Belgian rubber exploitation in the Congo

4.1.1 Course of events

The 'Rubber Terror' already found its literary monument in Joseph Conrad's *Heart of Darkness*. Today, the sad reality behind this fictional account is no longer an obscure footnote of colonial history for the preoccupation of expert academics,[47] but has been brought to greater public attention thanks to a well-received monograph, Adam Hochschild's *King Leopold's Ghost*, together with its follow-up documentary.[48]

Lubomyr Y. Luciuk (ed), *Holodomor: Reflections on the Great Famine of 1932–1933 in Soviet Ukraine* (Kashtan Press 2008) 50.

45 See Barth, *Genozid. Völkermord Im 20. Jahrhundert. Geschichte, Theorien, Kontroversen* (ch 2, n 174) 62.

46 See pp 155 ff.

47 Cf Hochschild, *King Leopold's Ghost. A Story of Greed, Terror and Heroism in Colonial Africa* (ch 4, n 35) 3.

48 IMDb, 'King Leopold's Ghost' <https://www.imdb.com/title/tt0455581/>.

Throughout the last two decades, this increasing interest has also led to a debate within Belgian civil society, finally resulting in an official apology.[49] This is not to say that the events had not previously been subject to historical analysis,[50] just not in the public space or within the mainstream of Genocide Studies.[51]

The atrocities, described as 'the worst instance of colonial exploitation in tropical Africa under the aegis of the new imperialism',[52] took place largely between 1885 and 1908, after which Leopold's Congo became an 'official' Belgian colony, no longer privately held by the king alone. The territory of the Congo had remained unclaimed up until the personal efforts of King Leopold II. Having founded the Association International Africaine in 1876 to underpin his 'humanitarian' interest in the continent, just two years later, British journalist and explorer Henry Morton Stanley offered the claim to the territory of central Africa he had explored. In 1879, Leopold began exercising control through the Comité d'Études du Haut-Congo, later replaced by the Association Internationale du Congo, with Stanley concluding agreements and establishing outposts on his behalf.

At the Berlin Conference – sometimes also referred to as the 'Congo Conference' – held from 15 November 1884 until 26 February 1885 under the aegis of Otto von Bismarck – and after much lobbying throughout Germany, France and the United States[53] – Leopold, who never had and never would visit the Congo, managed to fulfil his desire to secure for himself a privately

[49] See on the state of affairs prior to the publication of *King Leopold's Ghost* and the ensuing debate Hochschild, *King Leopold's Ghost. A Story of Greed, Terror and Heroism in Colonial Africa* (ch 4, n 35) 309–13. See also Jacques Depelchin, *From the Congo Free State to Zaire: How Belgium Privatized the Economy. A History of Belgian Stock Companies in Congo-Zaïre from 1885 to 1974* (Codesria Book Series 1992) 63, fn 23; Guy Vanthemsche, *Belgium and the Congo, 1885–1980* (Cambridge University Press 2012) 9–10. Cf, however, critically Matthew G. Stanard, *Selling the Congo. A History of European Pro-Empire Propaganda and the Making of Belgian Imperialism* (University of Nebraska Press 2011) 8–10.

[50] For example, Neal Ascherson, *The King Incorporated. Leopold the Second and the Congo* (Granta Books 1999) originally published in 1963; William Roger Louis and Jean Stengers (eds), *E.D. Morel's History of the Congo Reform Movement* (Clarendon Press 1968); Ruth Slade, *King Leopold's Congo. Aspects of the Development of Race Relations in the Congo Independent State* (Greenwood Press 1962) 178–81.

[51] See Beachler, *The Genocide Debate. Politicians, Academics, and Victims* (ch 3, n 42) 13.

[52] Peter Duignan and Lewis H. Gann, 'Introduction' in Peter Duignan and Lewis H. Gann (eds), *Colonialism in Africa 1870–1960. Volume 1. The History and Politics of Colonialism 1870–1914* (Cambridge University Press 1969) 20.

[53] See Hochschild, *King Leopold's Ghost. A Story of Greed, Terror and Heroism in Colonial Africa* (ch 4, n 35) 75–87.

held 'Congo Free State'.[54] The conference 'marked the end of an old phase in the history of the exploitation of the human and material resources of the African continent, as well as the beginning of a new phase'.[55] A new phase of exploitation, however.

While Leopold veiled his efforts under a philanthropic guise and under the banner of abolishing the Arab slave trade, the other parties to the Berlin Conference were mainly interested in the designation of the Congo Basin as a free trade zone,[56] the economically relevant natural resource alongside ivory being rubber.[57] Alluding to the blood spilt in its harvest, the British journalist Edmund Dene Morel, who had visited the Congo Free State, gave his account of the atrocities in his book titled *Red Rubber*,[58] – a term still applied to the atrocities committed in the course of its exploitation.

One of the 'signature atrocities' signifying the horrors of King Leopold's reign was mutilation by cutting off hands, also as proof that gun cartridges had not been wasted but actually put to use against a human being.[59] Already by 1899, newspapers had used the term 'atrocity' to refer to what was happening in the Congo[60] and, from 1904 onwards, it started to gain broader public attention, in particular through the efforts of the Congo Reform Association founded by Morel.

As early as 1907, British parliamentary debates referred to atrocities committed in the Congo as 'crimes against humanity'.[61] All of this resulted in a commission of enquiry into the practices in the Congo Free State that

[54] As pointed out by Barbara Emerson, *Leopold II of the Belgians. King of Colonialism* (Weidenfeld and Nicolson 1979) xii.

[55] Depelchin, *From the Congo Free State to Zaire: How Belgium Privatized the Economy. A History of Belgian Stock Companies in Congo-Zaïre from 1885 to 1974* (ch 4, n 49) 35.

[56] Hochschild, *King Leopold's Ghost. A Story of Greed, Terror and Heroism in Colonial Africa* (ch 4, n 35) 86. The King's interests were, obviously, more economic in nature. See Depelchin, *From the Congo Free State to Zaire: How Belgium Privatized the Economy. A History of Belgian Stock Companies in Congo-Zaïre from 1885 to 1974* (ch 4, n 49) 37; Emerson, *Leopold II of the Belgians. King of Colonialism* (ch 4, n 54) 98, 108–9, and 115.

[57] See Depelchin, *From the Congo Free State to Zaire: How Belgium Privatized the Economy. A History of Belgian Stock Companies in Congo-Zaïre from 1885 to 1974* (ch 4, n 49) 120.

[58] Edmund D. Morel, *Red Rubber. The Story of the Rubber Slave Trade Flourishing on the Congo in the Year of Grace 1906* (The Nassau Print 1906).

[59] See Martin Ewans, *European Atrocity, African Catastrophe. Leopold II, the Congo Free State and Its Aftermath* (Routledge Curzon 2002) 164 and 177–8; Hochschild, *King Leopold's Ghost. A Story of Greed, Terror and Heroism in Colonial Africa* (ch 4, n 35) 225–6 and 254; Jean Stengers, 'Morel and Belgium' in William Roger Louis and Jean Stengers (eds), *E.D. Morel's History of the Congo Reform Movement* (Clarendon Press 1968) 247–9.

[60] See Emerson, *Leopold II of the Belgians. King of Colonialism* (ch 4, n 54) 239.

[61] See Schabas, *Unimaginable Atrocities. Justice, Politics, and Rights at the War Crimes Tribunals* (ch 1, n 45) 53.

ultimately forced Leopold to 'secede' the territory to Belgium as a colony in 1908. However, this did little to alleviate the conditions of the local population; the consequences of which can be felt until this day.[62]

The case of the Congo is worth exploring in the present context: it stands out due to its vast scope yet, *arguendo*, lack of genocidal intent. For the deaths of Congolese were simply accepted as collateral damage in the course of economic exploitation.

4.1.2 Numbers

Most estimates of the victims of the atrocities are so high that they seem difficult to grasp or fathom. According to Dominik Schaller, the colonial regime in the Congo Free State led to 'a population decline of fifty per cent or, in absolute numbers, in the deaths of several million Congolese'.[63] David Lewis holds that 'the Congolese population dropped by eight million in fifty years'[64] and Joe Jackson that '[d]uring the fifteen years of Leopold's stewardship, the population in the Congo Free State dropped from 25 million to 10 million – 15 million dead for approximately 75,000 tons of rubber'.[65] Adam Hochschild concludes 'that during the Leopold period and its immediate aftermath the population of the territory dropped by approximately ten million people'.[66] This is also echoed by Georges Nzongola-Ntalaja.[67]

These gargantuan figures have since been criticized by William Rubinstein:[68] 'On balance, it is possible that, say, 1.0-1.5 million persons died in the Congo under Leopold's rule, reducing the net population by 1 million or so.'[69] Mark Cocker speaks of 'evidence for the hundreds of thousands, and probably

[62] Cf Depelchin, *From the Congo Free State to Zaire: How Belgium Privatized the Economy. A History of Belgian Stock Companies in Congo-Zaïre from 1885 to 1974* (ch 4, n 49).

[63] Schaller, 'Genocide and Mass Violence in "The Heart of Darkness": Africa in the Colonial Period' (ch 4, n 17) 362.

[64] David Levering Lewis, *The Race to Fashoda. European Colonialism and African Resistance in the Scramble for Africa* (Bloomsbury 1988) 92, supposedly counting from the inauguration of the Congo Free State.

[65] Joe Jackson, *The Thief at the End of the World. Rubber, Power, and the Seeds of Empire* (Viking 2008) 257.

[66] Hochschild, *King Leopold's Ghost. A Story of Greed, Terror and Heroism in Colonial Africa* (ch 4, n 35) 233.

[67] See Georges Nzongola-Ntalaja, *The Congo. From Leopold to Kabila. A People's History* (Zed Books 2002) 22.

[68] See Rubinstein, *Genocide: A History* (ch 1, n 40) 98–9.

[69] Ibid 99.

Table 4.1 Death Toll Estimates – Leopold's Reign (from High to Low)

Author	Number
Joe Jackson	15 million
Adam Hochschild	10 million
Georges Nzongola-Ntalaja	10 million
David Lewis	8 million
Dominik Schaller	several million
William Rubinstein	1–1.5 million
Mark Cocker	Hundreds of thousands, probably millions

millions of Africans who died in the Belgian Congo as a consequence of the Belgian King Leopold's frenzied quest for rubber and ivory'.[70]

4.1.3 Genocide

The first person to bring the events into the purview of Genocide Studies was Adam Hochschild. In *King Leopold's Ghost*, he refers to the contemporaneous assessment of the events as 'crimes against humanity'.[71] The index also has one entry for 'genocide', referring to the events in German South-West Africa, but which also points the reader to 'murders'. This entry includes the category 'extent of' and, again, a cross-reference to 'genocide'.

But far from suggesting that Hochschild added some sophisticated, subliminal scheme to convey to the reader a 'sense of genocide' – and the author may not have necessarily compiled the index himself – these connotations find themselves inserted throughout the book. In assessing the death toll of the Rubber Terror, Hochschild writes of 'genocidal proportions', even if 'it was not, strictly speaking, a genocide':

> The Congo state was not deliberately trying to eliminate one particular ethnic group from the face of the Earth. Instead, like the slave dealers who raided Africa for centuries before them, Leopold's men were looking for labor. If, in the course of their finding and using that labor, millions of people died, that to them was incidental.[72]

[70] Cocker, *Rivers of Blood, Rivers of Gold* (ch 4, n 21) 6.
[71] See Hochschild, *King Leopold's Ghost. A Story of Greed, Terror and Heroism in Colonial Africa* (ch 4, n 35) 112.
[72] Ibid 225–6.

Highlighting the distinction of intent, he appears to have worked from the legal definition of genocide. But the 'not, strictly speaking' leaves his assessment ambiguous: in light of the sheer extent of the death toll, the 'Rubber Terror' should perhaps at least be viewed on a par with a genocide in the sense of the word. This is underlined by the reference not just to the 'genocidal proportions' but also, at the very beginning of his book, to 'Holocaust dimensions'.[73] Hochschild holsters the 'conceptual baggage', while adding a disclaimer that the legal definition does not apply in the present case. The reader is left to judge.

Similarly, Neal Ascherson, in a foreword to a new edition of his 1963 book *The King Incorporated*, writes that 'while not a case of genocide, in the strict sense, this was one of the most appalling slaughters known to have been brought about by human agency'.[74] Along those lines, John Wellington put forward in 1967 that the Congo Free State 'was the scene of some of the most deplorable atrocities in the world's history'.[75] Roughly thirty years later, in a contribution on twentieth-century genocides, Martin Gilbert writes: 'What [Morel] described had all the hallmarks of genocide: Belgian punitive expeditions which, on their return to base, brought baskets of human hands as proof of their ruthlessness.'[76] All these assessments bring out the connotations of genocide without its 'strict' application.

Others apply the term, if only by implication. John Cooper, in his biography of Raphaël Lemkin, raises the question 'whether the Belgian regime perpetrated genocide in the Congo when it first colonized this region'.[77] After invoking the victim estimates of Hochschild and Rubinstein, he draws a parallel between the atrocities in the Congo Free State and the fate of the Herero and Nama in German South-West Africa: 'The system of forced labour in the German colonies in East and South West Africa was equally pernicious and bore many similarities to conditions in the Congo.'[78] By then categorizing the events in German South-West Africa as 'the first genocide of the twentieth century',[79] Cooper justifies discussing the Congo Free State in the purview of Genocide

[73] Ibid 4.
[74] Ascherson, *The King Incorporated. Leopold the Second and the Congo* (ch 4, n 50) 8–9.
[75] John H. Wellington, *South West Africa and Its Human Issues* (The Clarendon Press 1967) 228.
[76] Martin Gilbert, 'Twentieth Century Genocides' in Jay Winter (ed), *America and the Armenian Genocide of 1915* (Cambridge University Press 2003) 12.
[77] Cooper, *Raphael Lemkin and the Struggle for the Genocide Convention* (ch 1, n 43) 248.
[78] Ibid 249.
[79] Ibid.

Studies. William Rubinstein, in his book *Genocide: A History*, even finds that 'in recent years [it] has become one of the best-known and most widely discussed instances of nineteenth-century colonial genocide'.[80]

While the sheer numbers and the incredibly gruesome details of atrocities evoke the image of genocide and other mass atrocities, a number of scholars have emphasized the collateral nature of the Congolese victims. Mark Levene, in his *Genocide in the Age of the Nation-State*, has held that 'the colonial agenda here was still predicated on the continuing existence of a Congolese population, if only to provide extractive labour'.[81] In comparing the events with the campaign against the Herero and Nama in German South-West Africa, Boris Barth, in his history of twentieth-century genocides, finds that the atrocities were the consequence of economic exploitation of the land and its population.[82] But this should not detract from the scope of atrocities, as Donald Beachler writes in *The Genocide Debate*:

> It is obvious that some killings of genocidal proportions generate considerably more attention and interest than others. A striking example of a neglected human catastrophe is the mass murder inflicted on the Congo by Belgian king Leopold II as he exploited the resources of the central African land during the decades surrounding the turn of the twentieth century. While Leopold's primary objective was not to eliminate the Congolese people, outright killings and the harsh conditions imposed on the indigenous people by the Belgians resulted in several million deaths.[83]

Other attempts at properly categorizing the events seem less helpful through their revisionist approach. Michel Dumoulin, in his book *Léopold II un roi génocidaire?*, published in 2004, in reaction to the television documentary *White King, Red Rubber, Black Death*,[84] seeks to counter the negative perception of Belgian colonial history by critically appraising the sources used in the documentary.[85] While he fails to answer the question posed by his title explicitly, the implicit answer seems to be 'no'. But Dumoulin's central claim appears to

[80] Rubinstein, *Genocide: A History* (ch 1, n 40) 95.

[81] Levene, *Genocide in the Age of the Nation-State. Volume I: The Meaning of Genocide* (ch 1, n 15) 230.

[82] See Barth, *Genozid. Völkermord Im 20. Jahrhundert. Geschichte, Theorien, Kontroversen* (ch 2, n 174) 134.

[83] Beachler, *The Genocide Debate. Politicians, Academics, and Victims* (ch 3, n 42) 13.

[84] IMDb, 'White King, Red Rubber, Black Death' <https://www.imdb.com/title/tt0404551/>. Cf Stanard, *Selling the Congo. A History of European Pro-Empire Propaganda and the Making of Belgian Imperialism* (ch 4, n 49) 267.

[85] See Michel Dumoulin, *Léopold II un Roi Génocidaire?* (Académie Royale de Belgique 2005) 17–28.

be that the discussions regarding the character of Belgian colonialism in the Congo boil down to a misperception of Joseph Conrad's book as non-fiction.[86] Much earlier still, Barbara Emerson, in her 1979 biography of Leopold II, criticized notions of an intentional cruel Belgian, holding that 'to claim that Leopold deliberately instituted a system he knew to be cruel is a distortion'.[87]

But even before Hochschild, scholars such as David Lewis in his 1988 book *The Race to Fashoda* had countered any such monarchist or revisionist narratives with accounts of the dire situation within which the Congolese found themselves:

> Compelled to tend rubber trees and carry ivory for faceless syndicates to whom Léopold profitably leased much of the Congo, Africans were systematically maimed and murdered both as warning and punishment for 'trespassing' on the crown's domain; for failing to work off taxes with exemplary industry; and, above all, for the felony of diverting to their own use the least bit of rubber and ivory chugging down the Congo for shipment to Europe.[88]

4.1.4 Holocaust

In the foreword to *King Leopold's Ghost*, Hochschild writes that the Congo during the 'Rubber Terror' had witnessed 'a death toll of Holocaust dimensions'.[89] The French title of his book builds on this with its subtitle *Un Holocauste Oublié*.[90] When speaking of the discrepancy between men and women in village headcounts made in 1907, Hochschild further compares reviewing the figures 'to sifting through an Auschwitz crematorium': 'They do not tell you precise death tolls, but they reek of mass murder.'[91]

Under the heading 'King Leopold II and the Congo holocaust',[92] Georges Nzongola-Ntalaja, in his history of the Congo, writes that '[i]t was the

86 See ibid 74–82.
87 Emerson, *Leopold II of the Belgians. King of Colonialism* (ch 4, n 54) 241.
88 Lewis, *The Race to Fashoda. European Colonialism and African Resistance in the Scramble for Africa* (ch 4, n 64) 92.
89 Hochschild, *King Leopold's Ghost. A Story of Greed, Terror and Heroism in Colonial Africa* (ch 4, n 35) 4.
90 Adam Hochschild, *Les Fantômes du Roi Léopold. Un Holocauste Oublié* (Belfond 1998).
91 Hochschild, *King Leopold's Ghost. A Story of Greed, Terror and Heroism in Colonial Africa* (ch 4, n 35) 232.
92 Nzongola-Ntalaja, *The Congo. From Leopold to Kabila. A People's History* (ch 4, n 67) 20.

collection of wild rubber that resulted in the depopulation of entire villages and the perpetration of heinous crimes against humanity in the Congo':[93]

> Villages unwilling or unable to meet the assigned daily quotas of production were subject to rape, arson, bodily mutilation and murder. Although this violence did not meet the definition of *genocide* in international law as 'acts committed with intent to destroy, in whole or in part, a national, ethnic, racial or religious group', it resulted in a death toll of holocaust proportions that is estimated to be as high as 10 million people.[94]

He also speaks of a 'cruel and inhumane enterprise'[95] (perhaps a reference to the prohibition of torture under international law[96] while drawing on the contextual elements of crimes against humanity). Later on in his book, Nzongola-Ntalaja refers to 'King Leopold's holocaust of the Congolese people'[97] and points out the contemporary description of the atrocities as 'crimes against humanity' as already cited by Hochschild.[98]

Similarly, with regard to the estimates given by Hochschild, David Renton and others, in their book *The Congo – Plunder & Resistance*, relate the number of victims of Leopold's reign to both the Holocaust and the genocide in Rwanda:

> As a proportion of the total population (the numbers that could have been killed) such a number is comparable to the well-known genocides of the twentieth century, the Nazi holocaust, the murders in Rwanda. As an absolute number of deaths, the figure in the Congo may be higher than each.[99]

Robert Weisbord, in an article in the *Journal of Genocide Research* on the role of the Vatican in relation to the Congo Free State, calls the atrocities 'a holocaust before Hitler's Holocaust'.[100]

93 Ibid 22.
94 Ibid.
95 Ibid.
96 See the Convention against and Other Cruel, Inhuman or Degrading Treatment or Punishment, New York, 10 December 1984, 1465 United Nations Treaty Series 85, Article 16.
97 Nzongola-Ntalaja, *The Congo. From Leopold to Kabila. A People's History* (ch 4, n 67) 23.
98 See ibid. See Hochschild, *King Leopold's Ghost. A Story of Greed, Terror and Heroism in Colonial Africa* (ch 4, n 35) 112.
99 David Renton, David Seddon and Leo Zeilig, *The Congo. Plunder & Resistance* (Zed Books 2007) 31.
100 Robert G. Weisbord, 'The King, the Cardinal and the Pope: Leopold II's Genocide in the Congo and the Vatican' (2003) 5 *Journal of Genocide Research* 35, 35.

Belgian historian Guy Vanthemsche, in his book *Belgium and the Congo, 1885-1980*, has criticized this form of comparison, however, also emphasizing the collateral nature of the Congolese victims:

> Hochschild's book tells of a 'holocaust' perpetrated in the Congo, setting the number of victims at ten million. The term *holocaust*, associated in the public mind with genocide, seems inappropriate in this case. No one sought to systematically exterminate the native population; who, then, would have provided the labour on which the exploitation was based? Hochschild's estimate remains conjectural. No one knows the exact figure of the population of central Africa at the end of the nineteenth century. [. . .] We should tread cautiously.[101]

4.1.5 Assessment

None of the works on the Belgian 'Rubber Terror' deal with the definition of genocide or crimes against humanity in detail in their analysis. They all seem to apply an ordinary meaning, only suggesting through a focus on Belgian intent a full transplant of the legal definition. Particularly, the works critical of genocide or Holocaust comparisons emphasize the exploitative goals of Belgian colonial policy over the destruction of the indigenous Congolese population. Since there is not even a cursory discussion of the application of the term, it does not allow for a proper assessment of terminology.

What seems apparent is the purpose of instilling a sense of the scope of the atrocities committed during the 'Rubber Terror' through comparisons with other 'colonial genocides' or the Holocaust, be it in passing or relating to the dimensions and proportions. The mention of additional symbols such as Auschwitz or the consideration of the Belgian Congo as a precursor to twentieth-century genocide consolidates this impression with the reader.

The vast disparity between estimates provided in the literature has probably to do with the lack of documentation paired with difficulty in distinguishing between mortality due to violent deaths or poor health and living circumstances, as well as a drop in fertility. In the literature, these different

[101] Vanthemsche, *Belgium and the Congo, 1885–1980* (ch 4, n 49) 9–10. See also already Louis and Stengers, *E.D. Morel's History of the Congo Reform Movement* (ch 4, n 50) 252–6.

aspects contributing to the population decline from the creation to the end of the Congo Free State are not always made entirely clear to the reader.

4.2 The Herero and the Nama in German South-West Africa

4.2.1 Course of events

The atrocities committed against the Herero and Nama peoples by their 'colonial masters' are widely undisputed as instances of genocide today. Indeed, Germany itself has recognized it.[102] Here is also a rare instance where genocidal intent can be directly inferred from an actual written order, the 'Vernichtungsbefehl'[103] of General Lothar von Trotha[104] and his other writings.[105]

The events, originally neglected in historiography[106] – arguably for having been dwarfed by the later German crimes of the twentieth century[107] – have entered the public debate against the background of claims for reparations by the descendants of the Herero and Nama peoples against Germany, resulting in 2021 in an agreement on the recognition of the genocide by Germany together with *ex gratia* (= voluntary) payments in the form of development aid.[108]

Starting as a protectorate over Lüderitz Bay in the South-West of modern-day Namibia in 1884, Germany immediately began concluding treaties with the indigenous population. Just as in the case of the Congo Free State, Germany had secured colonial claims at the Berlin Conference, the previously

[102] See Marina Adami, 'Germany Recognizes Herero and Nama Genocide' *Politico* (28 May 2021) <https://www.politico.eu/article/germany-recognizes-colonial-herero-nama-genocide/>. Cf Auswärtiges Amt, 'Außenminister Maas zum Abschluss der Verhandlungen mit Namibia' (28 May 2021) <https://www.auswaertiges-amt.de/de/newsroom/-/2463396>.

[103] 'Destruction order'.

[104] See Das Bundesarchiv, 'Der Krieg Gegen Die Herero 1904' <https://www.bundesarchiv.de/DE/Content/Virtuelle-Ausstellungen/Der-Krieg-Gegen-Die-Herero-1904/der-krieg-gegen-die-herero-1904.html>.

[105] See Dominik J. Schaller, 'Kolonialkrieg, Völkermord und Zwangsarbeit in "Deutsch-Südwestafrika"' in Vivianne Berg and others (eds), *Enteignet – Vertrieben – Ermordet. Beiträge zur Genozidforschung* (Chronos 2004) 167–8; Zimmerer, 'Der erste Genozid des 20. Jahrhunderts. Der deutsche Vernichtungskrieg in Südwestafrika (1904–1908) und die Globalgeschichte des Genozids' (ch 4, n 25) 51–4.

[106] See Schaller, 'Kolonialkrieg, Völkermord und Zwangsarbeit in "Deutsch-Südwestafrika"' (ch 4, n 105) 147–8. For a bibliography of works published prior to 1990, see Chalk and Jonassohn, *The History and Sociology of Genocide. Analyses and Case Studies* (ch 1, n 40) 438.

[107] See Zimmerer, 'Der erste Genozid des 20. Jahrhunderts. Der deutsche Vernichtungskrieg in Südwestafrika (1904–1908) und die Globalgeschichte des Genozids' (ch 4, n 25) 41.

[108] See Chapter 4 n 102.

mentioned 'Congo Conference'. Soon after, the territory was transferred to the private German Colonial Society for South-West Africa ('Deutsche Kolonialgesellschaft für Südwestafrika').

A first major confrontation between Germany and the indigenous population took place between 1893 and 1894, when Germany initiated an operation against Nama resistance, resulting in a new treaty between them and the colonial government. Following multiple smaller revolts by the Herero as a consequence of the loss of much of their subsistence through a cattle plague in 1897 and their ensuing lack of economic perspective under German rule, the beginning of the year 1904 saw a major uprising.[109]

Germany sent troops led by von Trotha as commander-in-chief and soon installed him as the new governor of German South-West Africa to ensure he properly quash the rebellion in 'arguably one of the most brutal colonial wars ever fought in history'.[110] Following the defeat of the Herero at the Battle of Waterberg on 11 August 1904, the remaining survivors were driven into the Omaheke desert, and water holes were occupied by German troops. Initiating 'the most shameful atrocity of the war in South West Africa', on 2 October of that same year,[111] von Trotha issued the infamous 'proclamation of extermination (*Vernichtungsbefehl*)'[112] addressed to the Herero and from which historians today derive the genocidal intent of his campaign.[113] When

[109] For an overview of the discussion on the succession of events and the underlying reasons, see Jan-Bart Gewald, *Herero Heroes. A Socio-Political History of the Herero of Namibia, 1890–1923* (Boydell & Brewer 1999) 10–170, with a more critical view of the common narrative; Nils Ole Oermann, *Mission, Church and State Relations in South West Africa Under German Rule (1884–1915)* (Franz Steiner Verlag 1999) 93–7; Karla Poewe, *The Namibian Herero. A History of Their Psychosocial Disintegration and Survival* (Edwin Mellen Press 1985) 56–7, offering a psychological explanation. For earlier appraisals, see Helmut Bley, *Kolonialherrschaft und Sozialstruktur in Deutsch-Südwestafrika 1894–1914* (Leibniz-Verlag 1968) 164–85; Wellington, *South West Africa and Its Human Issues* (ch 4, n 75) 174–200. Cf also the somewhat revisionist J. H. Esterhuyse, *South West Africa 1880–1894. The Establishment of German Authority in South West Africa* (C Struik 1968).

[110] Jürgen Zimmerer, 'Colonial Genocide: The Herero and Nama War (1904–8) in German South West Africa and Its Significance' in Dan Stone (ed), *The Historiography of Genocide* (Palgrave Macmillan 2008) 325.

[111] Cf Gert Sudholt, *Die deutsche Eingeborenenpolitik in Südwestafrika. Von den Anfängen bis 1904* (Georg Olms Verlag 1975) 187. Indeed, eight weeks after the Battle of Waterberg. However, this does not necessarily rebut the argument of intent.

[112] Robert Cornevin, 'The Germans in Africa Before 1918' in Peter Duignan and Lewis H. Gann (eds), *Colonialism in Africa 1870–1960. Volume 1. The History and Politics of Colonialism 1870–1914* (Cambridge University Press 1969) 388.

[113] Reproduced at Das Bundesarchiv, 'Der Krieg Gegen Die Herero 1904' (ch 4, n 104): 'Ich der große General der Deutschen Soldaten sende diesen Brief an das Volk der Herero. Die Herero sind nicht mehr Deutsche Untertanen. Sie haben gemordet und gestohlen, haben verwundeten Soldaten Ohren und Nasen und andere Körperteile abgeschnitten und wollen jetzt aus Feigheit nicht mehr kämpfen. Ich sage dem Volk: Jeder der einen der Kapitäne an eine meiner Stationen als Gefangenen

the Nama also saw themselves driven to an uprising in early October 1904, the consequence was full retaliation.[114]

Eventually, upon pressure from Berlin, von Trotha had to renege on his 'Vernichtungsbefehl' in December of that same year. It has been pointed out, though, that colonialism requires a historicized definition of the state, and redress to the policy of the German Kaiser should not distract from the premodern structure of the colonial state in which intermediaries often determined the picture.[115] In any case, it was also the Kaiser's Germany that had brought von Trotha to South-West Africa in the first place.

Although the state of war ended in 1907, sporadic guerrilla warfare against the colonial government continued. During that time and beyond, many captives succumbed to the concentration and labour camps, the most infamous being that in operation on Shark Island in Lüderitz Bay from 1904 to 1908.[116]

What had started as an uprising against German rule had brought the full force of colonial power upon the Herero and Nama peoples: 'The sense of mission and paternalism of Europeans at home and in the colonies could turn hard and vengeful when peoples like the Hereros rose in armed rebellion.'[117]

abliefert erhält tausend Mark, wer Samuel Maherero bringt erhält fünftausend Mark. Das Volk der Herero muß jedoch das Land verlassen. Wenn das Volk dies nicht tut, so werde ich es mit dem Groot Rohr [cannon] dazu zwingen. Innerhalb der Deutschen Grenze wird jeder Herero mit oder ohne Gewehr, mit oder ohne Vieh erschossen, ich nehme keine Weiber und keine Kinder mehr auf, treibe sie zu ihrem Volke zurück oder lasse auch auf sie schießen. Dies sind meine Worte an das Volk der Herero. Der große General des mächtigen Deutschen Kaisers. / Dieser Erlaß ist bei den Appels den Truppen mitzuteilen mit dem Hinzufügen, daß auch der Truppe, die einen der Kapitäne fängt, die entsprechende Belohnung zu teil wird, und daß das Schießen auf Weiber und Kinder so zu verstehen ist, daß über sie hinweggeschossen wird, um sie zum Laufen zu zwingen. Ich nehme mit Bestimmtheit an daß dieser Erlass dazu führen wird, keine männliche Gefangene mehr zu machen, aber nicht zu Grausamkeiten gegen Weiber und Kinder ausartet. Diese werden schon fortlaufen, wenn zweimal über sie hinweggeschossen wird. Die Truppe wird sich des guten Rufes der Deutschen Soldaten bewußt bleiben. Der Kommandeur. gez. v. Trotha Generalleutnant.'

[114] See Isabel V. Hull, 'Military Culture and the Production of "Final Solutions" in the Colonies', *The Specter of Genocide. Mass Murder in Historical Perspective* (Cambridge University Press 2003) 144.

[115] See Zimmerer, 'Kolonialer Genozid? Vom Nutzen und Nachteil einer historischen Kategorie für eine Globalgeschichte des Völkermordes' (ch 1, n 14) 120; Jürgen Zimmerer, 'Colonialism and the Holocaust. Towards an Archeology of Genocide' in A. Dirk Moses (ed), *Genocide and Settler Society. Frontier Violence and Stolen Indigenous Children in Australian History* (Berghahn Books 2004) 63–4. Cf, however, Schaller, 'Genocide in Colonial South-West Africa: The German War against the Herero and Nama, 1904–1907' (ch 4, n 20) 45, who argues that support was only dropped due to economic considerations.

[116] See Joachim Zeller and Jürgen Zimmerer, 'Vorwort' in Joachim Zeller and Jürgen Zimmerer (eds), *Völkermord in Deutsch-Südwestafrika. Der Kolonialkrieg (1904–1908) in Namibia und seine Folgen* (Ch Links 2003) 10.

[117] Chalk and Jonassohn, *The History and Sociology of Genocide. Analyses and Case Studies* (ch 1, n 40) 230.

What followed was the creation of a racist system that supposedly served as a template for the later South African apartheid regime.[118]

4.2.2 Numbers

There is, overall, large consistency in the literature when it comes to the number of victims of von Trotha's campaign. German historian Horst Drechsler already established that quite precise estimates could be given based on the documents of the German Reichskolonialamt.[119] He takes the 1911 census as a starting point to find that of the formerly 80,000 Herero only 15,130 and of the 20,000 Nama only 9,781 were alive in 1911, meaning that 80 per cent of the Herero and 50 per cent of the Nama population had fallen victim to German colonial rule.[120] This is echoed by Gilbert Schrank.[121] Thomas Pakenham equally cites the 1911 census to conclude that 'only half the Nama estimated a decade before (9,800 out of 20,000) and less than a quarter of the original number of Herero (15,000 out of 80,000) were found to have survived the war'.[122] Similarly, Marc Cocker concludes 'that approximately three-quarters of the Herero and more than half the Nama died in the three-year period'.[123] Overall, he comes up with 'about 75,000 African inhabitants perished in the war'.[124]

Sven Lindqvist writes: 'Almost the entire people – about eighty thousand human beings – died in the deserts.'[125] Robert Cornevin states: 'Out of an estimated 80,000 Herero in 1903, no more than 20,000 remained within German territory by 1906.'[126] Chalk and Jonassohn assume as many as 65,000 deaths.[127] For Timothy Stapleton, 'likely around 60,000 Herero and 10,000 Nama

[118] See Fatima El-Tayeb, *Schwarze Deutsche. Der Diskurs um 'Rasse' und nationale Identität 1890–1933* (Campus 2001) 82–3.

[119] See Horst Drechsler, *Südwestafrika unter Deutscher Kolonialherrschaft. Der Kampf der Herero und Nama gegen den deutschen Imperialismus* (2nd edn, Akademie Verlag 1984) 213.

[120] See ibid 214.

[121] See Gilbert I. Schrank, 'German South West Africa: Social and Economic Aspects of Its History, 1884–1915' (PhD, New York University 1974) 188.

[122] Thomas Pakenham, *The Scramble for Africa. White Man's Conquest of the Dark Continent From 1876 to 1912* (Avon Books 1992) 615.

[123] Cocker, *Rivers of Blood, Rivers of Gold* (ch 4, n 21) 346. See also ibid 342.

[124] Cocker, *Rivers of Blood, Rivers of Gold* (ch 4, n 21) 346.

[125] Sven Lindqvist, *Exterminate All the Brutes* (Granta Books 1996) 149.

[126] Cornevin, 'The Germans in Africa before 1918' (ch 4, n 112) 388.

[127] See Chalk and Jonassohn, *The History and Sociology of Genocide. Analyses and Case Studies* (ch 1, n 40) 231.

Table 4.2 Death Toll Estimates – 1904–8 (from High to Low)

Author(s)	Number
Sven Lindqvist	80,000
Horst Drechsler	75,000 / 50–80% (Herero and Nama)
Thomas Pakenham	75,000 / 50–80% (Herero and Nama)
Marc Cocker	75,000 / 50–75% (Herero and Nama)
Timothy Stapleton	70,000 (Herero and Nama)
German Federal Archive	65,000 (Herero)
Frank Chalk / Kurt Jonassohn	65,000 (Herero)
Ruth First	65,000 (Herero)
Norman Naimark	65,000 (Herero)
Walter Nuhn	63,000–64,000 (Herero)
Jeremy Sarkin	60,000–70,000
Dominik Schaller	60,000–70,000
Robert Cornevin	60,000 (Herero)

died during the conflict, which represented a large part of each population'.[128] Dominik Schaller echoes that number[129] and, in another instance, speaks of approximately 60,000 to 70,000 deaths between 1904 and 1907.[130]

Schaller finds that mortality of African prisoners in German South-West Africa 'during and immediately after the 1904-1908 war was almost fifty per cent according to official German documentation'.[131] Jeremy Sarkin speaks of 'the genocide of between 60 000 and 100 000 indigenous Herero people'[132] and Nuhn of devastating numbers, leaving only around 16,000 to 17,000 survivors among the Herero.[133] In comparison to the previous population strengths given by him,[134] this leaves a population loss of between 63,000 and 64,000.

However, Israel Goldblatt, in his *History of South West Africa*, writes that '[i]t is impossible to arrive at any reliable figure of the number of Hereros who

[128] Timothy J. Stapleton, *A Military History of Africa. Volume 2. The Colonial Period: From the Scramble for Africa to the Algerian Independence War (ca. 1870–1963)* (Praeger 2013) 112. See also Timothy J. Stapleton, 'Herero and Nama Genocide (1904–1907)' in Timothy J. Stapleton (ed), *Encyclopedia of African Colonial Conflicts. Volume I: A-H* (ABC-CLIO 2017) 346.

[129] See Schaller, 'Genocide in Colonial South-West Africa: The German War against the Herero and Nama, 1904–1907' (ch 4, n 20) 37; Schaller, 'From Conquest to Genocide. Colonial Rule in German Southwest Africa and German East Africa' (ch 4, n 18) 296.

[130] See Schaller, 'Kolonialkrieg, Völkermord und Zwangsarbeit in "Deutsch-Südwestafrika"' (ch 4, n 105) 147.

[131] Schaller, 'Genocide and Mass Violence in "The Heart of Darkness": Africa in the Colonial Period' (ch 4, n 17) 359.

[132] Jeremy Sarkin, *Germany's Genocide of the Herero: Kaiser Wilhelm II, His General, His Settlers, His Soldiers* (UCT Press/James Currey 2011) 1.

[133] See Walter Nuhn, *Sturm Über Südwest. Der Hereroaufstand von 1904 – Ein Düsteres Kapitel Der Deutschen Kolonialen Vergangenheit Namibias* (Bernard & Graefe Verlag 1989) 315.

[134] See ibid 26.

were killed or who died during the campaign and it is therefore impossible to be able to state, as has been claimed in some quarters, that only one-tenth of the Herero population survived'.[135] But he does concede that 'whatever the actual figures may be, the Hereros suffered a vast reduction in their numbers, and those who did survive were in a sickly condition'.[136] Gert Sudholt, in his book *Die deutsche Eingeborenenpolitik in Südwestafrika* has also sown doubt on the numbers.[137]

Relating to today's debates on the true nature of events and the process of atrocity labelling, Marc Cocker holds: 'Clearly, the greater the number of casualties, the more firmly could Germany's accusers press the charge of genocide.'[138] Jan-Bart Gewald already in 1999 commented quite critically, though, that the debate on the genocide of the Herero and Nama peoples 'has been reduced to the rather unfortunate business of debating numbers killed, and has continued to rage in ever more meaningless ways'.[139]

Today, the German Federal Archive states on its website that of the originally 80,000 Herero, only 15,000 survived the 'genocide' ('Völkermord') of the confrontation and concentration camps[140] (an estimate also given in the literature by Ruth First[141] and Norman Naimark[142]).

4.2.3 Genocide

The 'genocide thesis' was reputedly first put forward by Horst Drechsler in his book *Südwestafrika Unter Deutscher Kolonialherrschaft*.[143] That Drechsler's account was characterized by Karla Poewe as a 'competent account by the left'[144] illustrates that the earliest discussions were also divided along ideological fault

135 Israel Goldblatt, *History of South West Africa. From the Beginning of the Nineteenth Century* (Juta & Company Limited 1971) 133.
136 Ibid.
137 See Sudholt, *Die deutsche Eingeborenenpolitik in Südwestafrika. Von den Anfängen bis 1904* (ch 4, n 111) 186. Nuhn speaks of the 'very low estimates of Sudholt'. See Nuhn, *Sturm Über Südwest. Der Hereroaufstand von 1904 – Ein Düsteres Kapitel Der Deutschen Kolonialen Vergangenheit Namibias* (ch 4, n 133) 314.
138 Cocker, *Rivers of Blood, Rivers of Gold* (ch 4, n 21) 345.
139 Gewald, *Herero Heroes. A Socio-Political History of the Herero of Namibia, 1890–1923* (ch 4, n 109) 2.
140 See Das Bundesarchiv, 'Der Krieg Gegen Die Herero 1904' (ch 4, n 104).
141 See Ruth First, *South West Africa* (Penguin Books 1963) 82.
142 See Naimark, *Genocide. A World History* (ch 1, n 40) 69.
143 See Barth, *Genozid. Völkermord Im 20. Jahrhundert. Geschichte, Theorien, Kontroversen* (ch 2, n 174) 128.
144 See, *The Namibian Herero. A History of Their Psychosocial Disintegration and Survival* (ch 4, n 109) 55.

lines between the Federal Republic of Germany and the German Democratic Republic.[145]

Depicting the 'pogrom atmosphere against the Herero' ('Pogromstimmung gegen die Herero') following the uprising[146] and a 'German policy of extermination' ('deutsche Ausrottungspolitik'),[147] Drechsler recounted German violations of the laws of war:[148] Von Trotha driven by nothing other than the annihilation of the Herero,[149] his policy one of destruction ('Throthasche Vernichtungspolitik').[150] What remained of humanitarian restraints or international law was thrown overboard[151] (a comment also made by Gilbert Schrank in his PhD thesis on *German South West Africa*).[152]

In Drechsler's view, von Trotha thought he could most easily rid himself of the Herero by driving them into the Omaheke desert.[153] When the 'Vernichtungsbefehl' ordered to shoot over the heads of women and children, this was not to spare them but to ensure a gradual death from hunger and thirst.[154] In fact, Drechsler even suggests that the order was not followed by the German forces, but that Herero were killed, no matter man, woman or child.[155]

But not enough: once the rebellion of the Herero had been quashed, German soldiers undertook outright eradication campaigns ('regelrechte Ausrottungszüge') from time to time.[156] Viewed together with the actions taken against the Nama, there was organized genocide in South-West Africa ('organisierter Völkermord in Südwestafrika'), according to Drechsler.[157] There was genocide against the Herero in the desert ('Völkermord an den Herero

145 Cf Zimmerer, 'Colonial Genocide: The Herero and Nama War (1904–8) in German South West Africa and Its Significance' (ch 4, n 110) 330–1.

146 Jürgen Zimmerer, *Von Windhuk nach Auschwitz? Beiträge zum Verhältnis von Kolonialismus und Holocaust* (Lit Verlag 2011) 147.

147 Ibid 161.

148 See, in this regard, also Cocker, *Rivers of Blood, Rivers of Gold* (ch 4, n 21) 331–2.

149 See Drechsler, *Südwestafrika unter Deutscher Kolonialherrschaft. Der Kampf der Herero und Nama gegen den deutschen Imperialismus* (ch 4, n 119) 154 and 157.

150 Ibid 165 and 167–8.

151 See ibid 154.

152 See Schrank, 'German South West Africa: Social and Economic Aspects of Its History, 1884–1915' (ch 4, n 121) 157.

153 See Drechsler, *Südwestafrika unter Deutscher Kolonialherrschaft. Der Kampf der Herero und Nama gegen den deutschen Imperialismus* (ch 4, n 119) 157.

154 See ibid 159.

155 Ibid. See also Schrank, 'German South West Africa: Social and Economic Aspects of Its History, 1884–1915' (ch 4, n 121) 161.

156 Drechsler, *Südwestafrika unter Deutscher Kolonialherrschaft. Der Kampf der Herero und Nama gegen den deutschen Imperialismus* (ch 4, n 119) 170.

157 Ibid 206.

in der Omaheke') and a policy of extermination against the Nama ('deutsche Ausrottungspolitik gegenüber Nama und Bergdamara').[158] No label other than genocide could be given to such a crime.[159]

This proposition was also taken up by Western German scholarship. Shortly after Drechsler's publication, in his detailed study of the German colonial system in the period between 1894 and 1914, *Kolonialherrschaft und Sozialstruktur in Deutsch-Südwestafrika 1894-1914*, Helmut Bley wrote about the 'Trothasche Vernichtungspolitik', illustrated by the number of casualties during the fight and continued by slow death in the camps. He emphasizes patterns of domination and modern efficiency at play that would only later reach the 'motherland', drawing a red line to the crimes of Nazi Germany.[160]

Bley specifically invokes Hannah Arendt's idea of the colonial origins of totalitarianism, finding the case of German South-West Africa already a transgression and aggravation of Arendt's theory.[161] On the other hand, while remaining critical from the outset of colonial disregard to local territorial arrangements,[162] Bley does paint the picture of German relations with their colonial subjects as – at least originally – more differentiated than in other colonial systems.[163]

The 'genocide thesis' has gained acceptance since these early contributions. In fact, Gert Sudholt critically remarked as early as 1975 that it had entered common parlance.[164] Today, this is surely true. But even before Drechsler, Jon Bridgman had written in *The Revolt of the Hereros* that the events 'disappeared from history'[165] and argued that '[i]t was their Marathon, their Cannae, their Sedan, their Hiroshima'.[166] John Wellington, in *South West Africa and Its Human Issues*, spoke of 'inhuman butchery'[167] and 'annihilation'.[168] And Leo Kuper, in his book on Genocide as a political instrument in the twentieth

[158] Ibid 209.
[159] See ibid 157.
[160] Bley, *Kolonialherrschaft und Sozialstruktur in Deutsch-Südwestafrika 1894–1914* (ch 4, n 109) 191–2 and 314–6.
[161] Ibid 314.
[162] Ibid 21.
[163] Ibid 163.
[164] See Sudholt, *Die deutsche Eingeborenenpolitik in Südwestafrika. Von den Anfängen bis 1904* (ch 4, n 111) 186.
[165] Jon M. Bridgman, *The Revolt of the Hereros* (University of California Press 1981) 1.
[166] Ibid.
[167] Wellington, *South West Africa and Its Human Issues* (ch 4, n 75) 208.
[168] Ibid 212.

century, found '[t]he slaughter of the Herero by the German rulers of South West Africa in 1904 [. . .] among the most exterminatory and horrifying of the reprisals for rebellion'.[169]

More recently, Ben Kiernan called the suppression of the indigenous population of German South-West Africa '[t]he first genocide of the twentieth century'[170] and Norman Naimark, in his *Genocide. A World History*, sees it as 'the first genocide of the modern period'.[171] Joachim Zeller and Jürgen Zimmerer, in their edited volume on the genocide in South-West Africa, consider it the 'first genocide committed by Germans', where 'the European "violent man" learnt the art of "extinction" in the colonies'.[172]

Timothy Stapleton, writing in the *Encyclopedia of African Colonial Conflicts*, finds: 'Although the German campaign against the Herero and Nama in South West Africa [. . .] took place before the term *genocide* was coined, it corresponds to this definition and happened within the context of European conquest in Africa.'[173] In his book *Herero Heroes*, Jan-Bart Gewald speaks of 'a genocidal colonial war',[174] a 'deliberate policy of genocide'[175] and that '[w]hen the war finally ended in 1908, Herero society, as it had existed prior to 1904, had been completely destroyed'.[176] Chalk and Jonassohn, in their *History and Sociology of Genocide*, see 'the German killing of Herero noncombatants after their warriors had been defeated' as 'the core of the genocide'.[177]

Some authors also emphasize the consensus in labelling the atrocities committed against the Herero and Nama peoples as genocide. Mark Levene, in his *Genocide in the Age of the Nation-State*, holds that '[t]he term genocide, where it appears in history books at all, with reference to the Scramble for

[169] Kuper, *Genocide. Its Political Use in the Twentieth Century* (ch 1, n 34) 16.

[170] Ben Kiernan, 'Twentieth-Century Genocides. Underlying Ideological Themes from Armenia to East Timor' in Robert Gellately and Ben Kiernan (eds), *The Specter of Genocide. Mass Murder in Historical Perspective* (Cambridge University Press 2003) 29. See also *verbatim* Cooper, *Raphael Lemkin and the Struggle for the Genocide Convention* (ch 1, n 43) 249.

[171] Naimark, *Genocide. A World History* (ch 1, n 40) 66.

[172] See Zeller and Zimmerer, 'Vorwort' (ch 4, n 116) 9. See also Jürgen Zimmerer, 'Krieg, KZ und Völkermord in Südwestafrika. Der erste deutsche Genozid' in Joachim Zeller and Jürgen Zimmerer (eds), *Völkermord in Deutsch-Südwestafrika. Der Kolonialkrieg (1904–1908) in Namibia und seine Folgen* (Ch Links 2003) 45; Zimmerer, 'Colonialism and the Holocaust. Towards an Archeology of Genocide' (ch 4, n 115) 61.

[173] Stapleton, *A Military History of Africa. Volume 2. The Colonial Period: From the Scramble for Africa to the Algerian Independence War (ca. 1870–1963)* (ch 4, n 128) 343.

[174] Gewald, *Herero Heroes. A Socio-Political History of the Herero of Namibia, 1890–1923* (ch 4, n 109) 1.

[175] Ibid 2. See also ibid 288.

[176] Gewald, *Herero Heroes. A Socio-Political History of the Herero of Namibia, 1890–1923* (ch 4, n 109) 141.

[177] Chalk and Jonassohn, *The History and Sociology of Genocide. Analyses and Case Studies* (ch 1, n 40) 230.

Africa, is usually only reserved for one single case'.[178] In *King Leopold's Ghost*, Adam Hochschild also mentions the atrocities committed against the Herero and Nama, referring to them as 'mass murder by the percentage of the population killed' and that 'the toll was even worse among the Hereros in German South West Africa, today's Namibia'.[179] His verdict is clear: 'It was genocide, pure and simple, starkly announced in advance.'[180] Jeremy Sarkin, in his book *Germany's Genocide of the Herero*, puts the events into an overall context of violence, finding that '[a]lthough the Herero war appears to be the only "genocide" Germany conducted within its colonies, it exercised brutality in many', that it was 'actually no aberration'.[181]

However, Drechsler's and others' conclusions have also been subject to criticism. Karla Poewe counters the idea with *ad hominem* arguments, attributing Drechsler a 'Marxist-Leninist bias' and as lacking 'a better "feeling" for the situation'.[182] She argues that von Trotha's 'Vernichtungsbefehl' with its verb 'vernichten' does not properly translate as 'exterminate' and was rather aimed at psychological warfare than anything else.[183] Boris Barth suggests in his book on genocide in the twentieth century that von Trotha's order should not be read as proof of genocide but as the intent to ethnically cleanse German South-West Africa from the Herero, seeing genocide and ethnic cleansing as related, yet separate concepts.[184] This approach is equally inferred by Norman Naimark.[185]

Where these arguments take on a revisionist spin, the process of atrocity labelling shifts from analysis to result-oriented denial. A prominent example is Claus Nordbruch's *Völkermord an den Herero in Deusch-Südwestafrika? Widerlegung einer Lüge*. It starts off with a dedication to the memory of Heinrich Schnee, the last governor of German East Africa, praising him for having rebuked the lie of colonial guilt of Germany ('koloniale

[178] Levene, *Genocide in the Age of the Nation-State. Volume I: The Meaning of Genocide* (ch 1, n 15) 228.
[179] Hochschild, *King Leopold's Ghost. A Story of Greed, Terror and Heroism in Colonial Africa* (ch 4, n 35) 281.
[180] Ibid.
[181] Sarkin, *Germany's Genocide of the Herero: Kaiser Wilhelm II, His General, His Settlers, His Soldiers* (ch 4, n 132) 4.
[182] See Poewe, *The Namibian Herero. A History of Their Psychosocial Disintegration and Survival* (ch 4, n 109) 58.
[183] See ibid 60–6.
[184] See Barth, *Genozid. Völkermord Im 20. Jahrhundert. Geschichte, Theorien, Kontroversen* (ch 2, n 174) 130. For an attempt at conceptual differentiation, see Naimark, *Fires of Hatred. Ethnic Cleansing in Twentieth-Century Europe* (ch 4, n 4) 3–4. Cf, however, critically, Shaw, *What Is Genocide?* (ch 1, n 36) 66–83.
[185] See Naimark, *Fires of Hatred. Ethnic Cleansing in Twentieth-Century Europe* (ch 4, n 4) 6.

Schuldlüge Deutschlands') as early as the 1920s.[186] Of course, the idea of the 'Kriegsschuldlüge' that Germany was wrongly framed as responsible for the aggression of the First World War reverberates in this statement.

In stark opposition to the 'genocide thesis', Nordbruch starts off by questioning the high estimates of Herero population prior to 1904[187] and at the Waterberg.[188] Interestingly, Nordbruch does acknowledge von Trotha's intent, 'merely' disputing that a genocide was actually carried out.[189] Further examples of varying levels of academic quality can be found in the 'journal' *Befunde und Berichte zur deutschen Kolonialgeschichte* (and for that reason no further consideration has been given these).

There are also mere implicit recognitions of genocide within the literature. Nils Oermann, in *Mission, Church and State Relations in South West Africa Under German Rule (1884-1915)*, recounts the discussion on 'whether von Trotha intended a genocide policy', holding that he will not 'add another viewpoint to a military issue which has already been extensively discussed' and that he 'will not analyse the justification of the label "extermination order"'.[190] However, through his criticism of what he calls '"apologetic revisionist" writers' and his dismissal of von Trotha's order actually sparing women and children,[191] he implicitly pushes the events into the proximity of the 'genocide thesis', even if he does not apply the word beyond speaking of a 'genocide policy'. In a contribution on genocide in the twentieth century, Martin Gilbert calls the action taken against the Herero 'a more sustained attempt to destroy a whole people' compared to atrocities committed against the Boers by the British.[192]

Others again try to avoid applying the full label, instead resorting to the adjective 'genocidal'. Yves Ternon, in his work on the criminal state and the genocides of the twentieth century, finds that the measures taken against the Herero mark the outermost limit in allowing for a distinction between genocidal massacre and genocide ('marque la limite extrême entre massacre

[186] See Claus Nordbruch, *Völkermord an den Herero in Deutsch-Südwestafrika? Widerlegung einer Lüge* (Grabert 2004) 6.
[187] See ibid 14–7.
[188] See ibid 17–20 and 84–6.
[189] See ibid 124.
[190] Oermann, *Mission, Church and State Relations in South West Africa Under German Rule (1884–1915)* (ch 4, n 109) 97–8.
[191] See ibid 99.
[192] Gilbert, 'Twentieth Century Genocides' (ch 4, n 76) 11.

génocidaire et génocide'),[193] although he also writes that von Trotha had no other goal than to destroy the Herero nation ('détruire la nation herero').[194] Ultimately, he leaves the final categorization open (although the case does suggestively figure in the chapter 'Massacres génocidaires'). Along the same lines, Joachim Zeller, in a contribution in the already mentioned volume edited together with Jürgen Zimmerer, finds that the Battle of Waterberg is rightly categorized as a 'genocide campaign' ('Völkermord-Aktion').[195] In the same volume, Andreas Eckert speaks of a 'war led with a genocidal urge for destruction' ('mit genozidalem Vernichtungswillen geführte Krieg').[196]

William Rubinstein, in the chapter on 'Genocide in the Colonial Age' of his book *Genocide: A History*, writes that 'the activities of the German military authorities towards the Herero of German South-West Africa would certainly be termed genocidal by most observers'.[197] In the corresponding footnote, he adds: 'The murder and enslavement of African tribes by African slaving middlemen and local kings, under European direction, might well also be described as genocidal in the commonly accepted sense.'[198] Marouf Hasian, in his book *Restorative Justice, Humanitarian Rhetorics, and Public Memories of Colonial Camp Cultures*, specifically calls the camps in which the survivors were left to succumb to 'genocidal'.[199]

4.2.4 Holocaust

Building on the 'genocide thesis', scholars have also put the events in relation to the Holocaust by either drawing a red thread from the underlying policy, the military apparatus and its officers or even a general German mentality. In this narrative, the atrocities are portrayed either as a blueprint for later events or as the German 'original sin' that inevitably led to the Holocaust.

[193] Ternon, *L'État Criminel. Les Génocides au XXe Siècle* (ch 1, n 36) 311.

[194] Ibid 312.

[195] Joachim Zeller, '"Ombepera i koza – Die Kälte tötet mich". Zur Geschichte des Konzentrationslagers in Swakopmund (1904–1908)' in Joachim Zeller and Jürgen Zimmerer (eds), *Völkermord in Deutsch-Südwestafrika. Der Kolonialkrieg (1904–1908) in Namibia und seine Folgen* (Ch Links 2003) 65.

[196] Andreas Eckert, 'Namibia – ein deutscher Sonderweg in Afrika? Anmerkungen zur internationalen Diskussion' in Joachim Zeller and Jürgen Zimmerer (eds), *Völkermord in Deutsch-Südwestafrika. Der Kolonialkrieg (1904–1908) in Namibia und seine Folgen* (Ch Links 2003) 231.

[197] Rubinstein, *Genocide: A History* (ch 1, n 40) 103.

[198] Ibid 124, fn 124.

[199] Hasian, *Restorative Justice, Humanitarian Rhetorics, and Public Memories of Colonial Camp Cultures* (ch 4, n 35) 112–3.

In the introduction to his book on the period of South-West Africa under German colonial rule, Drechsler writes that the war against the Herero and Nama was the first instance of German imperialism practicing 'methods of genocide through which it would later reach sad acclaim'.[200] He connects the colonial period with Nazi Germany through a thread of German imperialist policy. This idea was also explored by Dominik Schaller,[201] who finds that 'German settlers had for a long time been waiting for the elimination of the Africans as autonomous actors and their complete subjugation'[202] and that it 'is widely recognized as *the* imperial genocide'[203] (however, in another instance he seems to deny intent, at least with regard to the concentration and labour camps where casualties were accepted as collateral damage).[204]

Jürgen Zimmerer, building on Drechsler's ideas,[205] sees commonalities not just in German imperialism but in a pre-existing genocidal tendency, perhaps even a genocidal mentality ('Ausdruck einer bereits vorhandenen genozidalen Tendenz, vielleicht sogar einer genozidalen Mentalität').[206] The campaign in German South-West Africa appears to bear all elements of a 'race war'[207] with the destruction of the Herero and Nama as the only possible result for Germany.[208]

[200] Drechsler, *Südwestafrika unter Deutscher Kolonialherrschaft. Der Kampf der Herero und Nama gegen den deutschen Imperialismus* (ch 4, n 119) 20. See also Horst Kühne, 'Die Ausrottungsfeldzüge der Kaiserlichen Schutztruppen in Afrika' in Commission Internationale d'Histoire Militaire (ed), *Actes du 4. Colloque International d'Historie Militaire (Ottawa, 23–25 VIII 1978)* (1979) 215–6.

[201] See Schaller, 'Kolonialkrieg, Völkermord und Zwangsarbeit in "Deutsch-Südwestafrika"' (ch 4, n 105) 184–95 with further references.

[202] Schaller, 'Genocide in Colonial South-West Africa: The German War against the Herero and Nama, 1904–1907' (ch 4, n 20) 42–3.

[203] Ibid 47.

[204] Schaller, 'Genozidforschung: Begriffe und Debatten. Einleitung' (ch 1, n 34) 14.

[205] For example, Zimmerer, *Von Windhuk nach Auschwitz? Beiträge zum Verhältnis von Kolonialismus und Holocaust* (ch 4, n 146). See, on this discussion with regard to the idea of concentration camps, also Hasian, *Restorative Justice, Humanitarian Rhetorics, and Public Memories of Colonial Camp Cultures* (ch 4, n 35) 90–127. Cf Eckert, 'Namibia - ein deutscher Sonderweg in Afrika? Anmerkungen zur internationalen Diskussion' (ch 4, n 196) 232.

[206] See Jürgen Zimmerer, 'Nationalsozialismus postkolonial. Plädoyer zur Globalisierung der deutschen Gewaltgeschichte' in Jürgen Zimmerer (ed), *Von Windhuk nach Auschwitz? Beiträge zum Verhältnis von Kolonialismus und Holocaust* (Lit Verlag 2011) 23.

[207] See Zimmerer, 'Kolonialer Genozid? Vom Nutzen und Nachteil einer historischen Kategorie für eine Globalgeschichte des Völkermordes' (ch 1, n 14) 121–2; Jürgen Zimmerer, *Deutsche Herrschaft über Afrikaner. Staatlicher Machtanspruch und Wirklichkeit im kolonialen Namibia* (Lit Verlag 2001) 31 and 37.

[208] See Zimmerer, 'Kolonialer Genozid? Vom Nutzen und Nachteil einer historischen Kategorie für eine Globalgeschichte des Völkermordes' (ch 1, n 14) 118.

Similarly, Mark Cocker, in *Rivers of Blood, Rivers of Gold*, emphasizes the racial hatred embodied in the extermination order[209] and writes of an effort to have women and children transferred from the camps of Shark Island: 'With all the frozen inhumanity of an SS officer or, indeed, of a British official in charge of concentration camps in the Boer War [. . .] the request was turned down, on the grounds that it endangered security in the colony.'[210] The 'frozen inhumanity' of German policy in South-West Africa springs from the same mentality that later allowed for the existence of Nazi Germany, the genesis of racist policies and cold killing supposedly something 'uniquely German' and 'Teutonic':

> Yet there was one dimension to the policies in South West Africa that seemed both distinct and uniquely German. Once relations between the Teutonic colonists and their African subjects had descended into a state of open conflict, the crisis opened the way for German officers whose views on race and on Africans in particular gave rise to policies of outright genocide. Rather than suggesting some process of imperial atavism, the deliberate, almost clinical methods and detached attitudes towards the issue of racial extermination contained a deeply modern element. Rather than a return to the anarchic brutalities of the Spanish *conquistadores*, German atrocities in Africa seem to anticipate the radical, systematic inhumanity of a later holocaust – that against the Jews during Hitler's Third Reich.[211]

Isabel Hull argues a general tendency towards 'final solutions' within the German military apparatus, even though she does not specifically put forward the claim that the German actions in German South-West Africa constituted genocide[212] (she ultimately labels the killing at Waterberg as a 'massacre'[213]). But, by speaking of 'final solutions', she already attaches the connotation of the Holocaust.[214]

[209] Cocker, *Rivers of Blood, Rivers of Gold* (ch 4, n 21) 333.
[210] Ibid 345.
[211] See ibid 292–3.
[212] See Hull, 'Military Culture and the Production of "Final Solutions" in the Colonies' (ch 4, n 114) 141–62. Cf, however, ibid 143–4.
[213] Hull, 'Military Culture and the Production of "Final Solutions" in the Colonies' (ch 4, n 114) 154.
[214] However, she distinguishes the idea of a 'final solution' from 'genocide': 'Applied to human society, final solutions dictate the disappearance of the problem population, which may occur via cultural assimilation, deportation, or physical annihilation (genocide). Genocide is therefore the most radical but not the only form of a final solution.' See ibid 143.

Stapleton writes of the Herero and Nama who perished in labour camps that 'their decapitated heads were studied by German scientists fascinated by racial theories',[215] and Hasian, in his book *Restorative Justice*, suggests evidence of eugenics,[216] effectively drawing the line to Nazi medical experiments.

Aside from continuity in method and mentality, the atrocities committed against the Herero and Nama are framed as Germany's 'original sin', inevitably paving the way towards the Holocaust. In his biography of Raphaël Lemkin, Cooper writes that 'Wilhelmine rule in their colony in South West Africa conditioned the population of Imperial Germany to accept the new norms of mass murder and the war of annihilation'.[217] Zimmerer further sees the killing of the Herero and Nama as a link between the genocides of indigenous peoples and the crimes of National Socialism, calling the events in German South-West Africa a 'precursor to the Holocaust'.[218] Stapleton holds: 'The German response to the Herero and Nama rebellions was the first genocide of the 20th century and foreshadowed the Holocaust four decades later.'[219] William Rubinstein, in his book *Genocide*, finds that the events 'unite the colonial period with the Age of Totalitarianism, a bridge to the genocide of the Armenians (carried out by the Turks with some German assistance) a decade later, and then to the horrors of the Nazi regime'.[220] Zeller and Zimmerer write that 'concentration camps and genocide within the German colonies already point to the crimes of the Third Reich'.[221] In another publication, Zeller adds

[215] Stapleton, *A Military History of Africa. Volume 2. The Colonial Period: From the Scramble for Africa to the Algerian Independence War (ca. 1870–1963)* (ch 4, n 128) 346.

[216] See also Hasian, *Restorative Justice, Humanitarian Rhetorics, and Public Memories of Colonial Camp Cultures* (ch 4, n 35) 19. Ibid at 19.

[217] Cooper, *Raphael Lemkin and the Struggle for the Genocide Convention* (ch 1, n 43) 258.

[218] Zimmerer, 'Krieg, KZ und Völkermord in Südwestafrika. Der erste deutsche Genozid' (ch 4, n 172) 60: 'Bedeutsam ist der Völkermord in Deutsch-Südwestafrika auch als Vorgeschichte des Holocaust. Schon allein durch Begriffe wie Konzentrationslager und Völkermord deutet sich eine Verbindung zu den Massenverbrechen während des Dritten Reiches an'. See, generally, ibid 60–3. Zimmerer, 'Colonialism and the Holocaust. Towards an Archeology of Genocide' (ch 4, n 115) 64–5 and 67; Zimmerer, 'Kolonialer Genozid? Vom Nutzen und Nachteil einer historischen Kategorie für eine Globalgeschichte des Völkermordes' (ch 1, n 14) 121–2.

[219] Stapleton, *A Military History of Africa. Volume 2. The Colonial Period: From the Scramble for Africa to the Algerian Independence War (ca. 1870–1963)* (ch 4, n 128) 346.

[220] Rubinstein, *Genocide: A History* (ch 1, n 40) 102.

[221] See Zeller and Zimmerer, 'Vorwort' (ch 4, n 116) 9. See also Zimmerer, 'Krieg, KZ und Völkermord in Südwestafrika. Der erste deutsche Genozid' (ch 4, n 172) 45; Zimmerer, 'Colonialism and the Holocaust. Towards an Archeology of Genocide' (ch 4, n 115) 61.

some nuance, finding comparisons to Buchenwald and Dachau, but not to the death camp of Auschwitz.[222]

Although Jon Bridgman does not use the word 'genocide' in his book *The Revolt of the Hereros*, he speaks, at one point, of 'the holocaust of rebellion and its ruthless suppression'.[223] In 2010, with *The Kaiser's Holocaust: Germany's Forgotten Genocide*, the word entered a book title on the German atrocities,[224] encouraging other scholars to engage with what is 'now called the forgotten Herero "holocaust"'.[225]

4.2.5 Assessment

None of the publications provide any form of in-depth discussion of the Genocide Convention or their applied definition of genocide (or any other crime for that matter), even though Drechsler circles his discussion around the question of intent – perhaps naturally so, considering the 'Vernichtungsbefehl' – and a number of authors specifically invoke this element of the definition of the Genocide Convention.[226] Hull, at least, seems to draw her definition from an amalgamation of the adaptations by Chalk and Jonassohn, Charny, and Dadrian, to whom she all refers.[227]

Alongside intent, organization and scope are offered to support the 'genocide thesis' or at least a 'genocidal policy'. While colonialism and totalitarianism are intertwined, comparisons and causation are offered, ranging from the formation of a genocidal tendency in the German state or military apparatus, to an existing mentality or to individual crimes that have become symbolic of the Holocaust already preconceived and committed against the Herero

[222] See Zeller, '"Ombepera i koza – Die Kälte tötet mich". Zur Geschichte des Konzentrationslagers in Swakopmund (1904–1908)' (ch 4, n 195) 76–8.

[223] Bridgman, *The Revolt of the Hereros* (ch 4, n 165) 6.

[224] Casper W. Erichsen and David Olusoga, *The Kaiser's Holocaust. Germany's Forgotten Genocide and the Colonial Roots of Nazism* (Faber and Faber 2010).

[225] Hasian, *Restorative Justice, Humanitarian Rhetorics, and Public Memories of Colonial Camp Cultures* (ch 4, n 35) 2. See also, more differentiated, ibid 90–1. Overall, Hasian concurs both with the genocide thesis and the link between these events and the Holocaust. See ibid 125.

[226] For example, Stapleton, *A Military History of Africa. Volume 2. The Colonial Period: From the Scramble for Africa to the Algerian Independence War (ca. 1870–1963)* (ch 4, n 128) 343; Zimmerer, 'Krieg, KZ und Völkermord in Südwestafrika. Der erste deutsche Genozid' (ch 4, n 172) 52–3; Zimmerer, 'Kolonialer Genozid? Vom Nutzen und Nachteil einer historischen Kategorie für eine Globalgeschichte des Völkermordes' (ch 1, n 14) 113–4.

[227] See Hull, 'Military Culture and the Production of "Final Solutions" in the Colonies' (ch 4, n 114) 143, fn 11.

and Nama as the 'original sin'. The atrocities become part of a line of events stretching from the Armenian genocide to the destruction of the European Jews.[228]

An awareness of this particular aspect of the labelling process is indeed present within the literature. Eric Weitz calls the claim of continuity between the atrocities of German South-West Africa and the Holocaust 'a links-in-the-chain kind of argument, one genocide setting the stage for another'.[229] Dominik Schaller sees this as an instrument for the strategic litigation of reparation claims: 'In order to increase moral pressure and fuel public emotions, the Herero emphasized that the murder of their ancestors had to be seen as an important precursor of the Holocaust.' He criticizes the suggestion of 'a simplified monocausal connection from the murder of the Herero to the Nazis' persecution of European Jewry', in particular as it is 'Eurocentric and neglects African agency'.[230] In the future, official recognition by the German government might move the question of labelling and framing from questions of responsibility for reparations to an analytical endeavour to better comprehend the actual links that do exist in individual biographies of the German military.

4.3 The Armenians in Asia Minor

4.3.1 Course of events

With the historical territories of Armenia falling under Ottoman rule, the Armenians came to exist as a minority within the Ottoman Empire from its very beginnings. Issues arose increasingly with the aggravation of the 'Eastern Question' in the second half of the nineteenth century. Following the Russo-Turkish War of 1877–8, the treatment of Armenian minorities became a

[228] Meiches takes a contrary position, giving the events as an example for 'colonial and postcolonial events that challenge the progressive trajectory of the narrative'. See Meiches, *The Politics of Annihilation. A Genealogy of Genocide* (ch 1, n 23) 7.

[229] Weitz, *A Century of Genocide. Utopias of Race and Nation* (ch 1, n 34) xi.

[230] Schaller, 'Genocide in Colonial South-West Africa: The German War against the Herero and Nama, 1904–1907' (ch 4, n 20) 47–8.

bargaining chip on the table of international diplomacy.[231] Article 16 of the Treaty of San Stefano of 1878 read:

> As the evacuation by the Russian troops of the territory which they occupy in Armenia, and which is to be restored to Turkey, might give rise to conflicts and complications detrimental to the maintenance of good relations between the two countries, the Sublime Porte engages to carry into effect, without further delay, the improvements and reforms demanded by local requirements in the provinces inhabited by Armenians, and to guarantee their security from Kurds and Circassians.[232]

However, the following Congress of Berlin of 1878 (not to be mistaken with the later 'Congo Conference', which featured in the previous two case studies) brought a revision of terms, and Article 61 of the Treaty of Berlin of that same year effectively tuned down what was originally a condition to a mere reporting requirement:

> The Sublime Porte undertakes to carry out, without further delay, improvements and reforms demanded by local requirements in the provinces inhabited by the Armenians, and to guarantee their security against the Circassians and Kurds. It will periodically make known the steps taken to this effect to the Powers, who will superintend their application.[233]

It seems that these attempts at minority protection only exacerbated the problems with atrocities against Armenians occurring – as a result of 'European

[231] See Donald Bloxham, *The Great Game of Genocide. Imperialism, Nationalism, and the Destruction of the Ottoman Armenians* (Oxford University Press 2005) 16; Richard G. Hovannisian, *Armenia on the Road to Independence 1918* (University of California Press 1967) 26; Richard G. Hovannisian, 'The Historical Dimensions of the Armenian Question, 1878–1923' in Richard G. Hovannisian (ed), *The Armenian Genocide in Perspective* (Transaction Books 1986) 22–4; Hilmar Kaiser, 'Genocide at the Twilight of the Ottoman Empire' in Donald Bloxham and A. Dirk Moses (eds), *The Oxford Handbook of Genocide Studies* (Oxford University Press 2010) 367–8; Naimark, *Fires of Hatred. Ethnic Cleansing in Twentieth-Century Europe* (ch 4, n 4) 21; Dominik J. Schaller, 'Der Völkermord an den Armeniern im Osmanischen Reich, 1915–1917. Ereignis Historiographie und Vergleich' in Vivianne Berg and others (eds), *Enteignet – Vertrieben – Ermordet. Beiträge zur Genozidforschung* (Chronos 2004) 235.

[232] 'Preliminary Treaty of Peace between Russia and Turkey: Signed at San Stefano, February 9/ March 3, 1878' (1908) 2 *American Journal of International Law* 387, 396.

[233] 'Treaty between Great Britain, Germany, Austria, France, Italy, Russia, and Turkey for the Settlement of Affairs in the East: Signed at Berlin, July 13, 1878' (1908) 2 *American Journal of International Law* 401, 422.

meddling'[234] or not – in various places throughout the Ottoman Empire.[235] The first of these took place in 1894, following Armenian opposition to local overtaxation.[236] When 'the rugged villagers of the Sasun district in the province of Bitlis refused to continue paying an extortionary protection tax to Kurdish chieftains', the resistance was broken and 'several thousand Armenians were put to the sword without regard to age or sex'.[237] As Britain, France and Russia pushed for the implementation of a reform by the Ottoman Empire in the fall of 1895, further atrocities ensued, lasting into the year 1896.[238]

The Sasun uprising of 1904 and the following reprisals are rarely mentioned among these early atrocities committed against the Armenians.[239] But when the conflict between the Sultan and the Young Turk movement in the encore of the Young Turk Revolution of 1908 culminated in an attempt to restore the Sultan to his original position in 1909, this gave rise to another episode of atrocities committed against Armenians throughout Cilicia,[240] reprisals for their support of the modernization of Turkey.

But all of this appears as a mere prelude against the shadow cast by later events. The period considered when talking about the 'Armenian genocide' or 'Genocide of Christians'[241] in the Ottoman Empire falls within the years 1914–16, whereas the main act can be placed in 1915.[242] Franz Werfel immortalized the paralysis of the Armenian people in the face of imminent danger and the ensuing atrocities in his *The Forty Days of Musa Dagh*.

[234] Richard G. Hovannisian, 'The Armenian Genocide' in Israel W. Charny (ed), *Genocide. A Critical Bibliographical Review* (Facts on File Publications 1988) 93. See also Kaiser, 'Genocide at the Twilight of the Ottoman Empire' (ch 4, n 231) 368; Levene, *Genocide in the Age of the Nation-State. Volume II: The Rise of the West and the Coming of Genocide* (ch 4, n 13) 225–6 and 320.

[235] For a concise overview of these and the following events, see Naimark, *Fires of Hatred. Ethnic Cleansing in Twentieth-Century Europe* (ch 4, n 4) 22–35.

[236] See Bloxham, *The Great Game of Genocide. Imperialism, Nationalism, and the Destruction of the Ottoman Armenians* (ch 4, n 231) 51; Kaiser, 'Genocide at the Twilight of the Ottoman Empire' (ch 4, n 231) 368.

[237] Hovannisian, 'The Historical Dimensions of the Armenian Question, 1878–1923' (ch 4, n 231) 24.

[238] See Bloxham, *The Great Game of Genocide. Imperialism, Nationalism, and the Destruction of the Ottoman Armenians* (ch 4, n 231) 51; Hovannisian, 'The Historical Dimensions of the Armenian Question, 1878–1923' (ch 4, n 231) 25; Kaiser, 'Genocide at the Twilight of the Ottoman Empire' (ch 4, n 231) 368.

[239] Cf Michael Hesemann, *Völkermord an den Armeniern. Mit unveröffentlichten Dokumenten aus dem Geheimarchiv des Vatikans über das größte Verbrechen des Ersten Weltkriegs* (HERBiG 2015) 111–12.

[240] See Hovannisian, 'The Historical Dimensions of the Armenian Question, 1878–1923' (ch 4, n 231) 26–7; Kaiser, 'Genocide at the Twilight of the Ottoman Empire' (ch 4, n 231) 368–9.

[241] See Uğur Ümit Üngör, *The Making of Modern Turkey. Nation and State in Eastern Anatolia, 1913–1950* (Oxford University Press 2012).

[242] For example, Bloxham, *The Great Game of Genocide. Imperialism, Nationalism, and the Destruction of the Ottoman Armenians* (ch 4, n 231) 1.

The first atrocities committed during this period followed the retreat of the Ottoman army from an attack against Russia in late 1914 and later the defeat on the battlefield of Iranian Azerbaijan. Perceived as a fifth column during the First World War, disarmament and deportations of Armenians commenced from 8 April 1915 onwards. The community in the city of Van was attacked on 20 April 1915, and while the attack on the city itself failed due to the organization of a sturdy Armenian defence, Ottoman forces roamed the surrounding villages, free to commit atrocities.

On 24 April 1915, a new phase of measures commenced, and large numbers of the Armenian elite were arrested in Istanbul and elsewhere. Many of them were led directly to their death in extra-judicial killings or murdered during their ensuing ordeals. In May 1915, orders for the deportation of the communities followed. From then onwards, Armenians were supposedly given the choice of converting to Islam in order to avoid deportation, albeit oftentimes to no avail.[243] The process of ethnic cleansing of the Armenians from their historic territories consisted of long treks, railway lines and camps, where victims were either killed or succumbed to their ordeals, falling sick or dying of thirst or starvation.

Overall, two phases of the genocide can be identified in Ottoman state policy: the first being the arrest, torture and killing of the Armenian elite, as well as the ensuing deportation and murder of the Armenian minority; the second being the treatment of survivors in 'dying camps' ('Sterbelager') and their systematic liquidation in 1916 by massacring these refugees.[244]

4.3.2 Numbers

Estimates as to the victims of the 1915 genocide vary from around half to one and a half million, with most authors providing ranges for their estimates. It is sometimes difficult to assess the exact time period in question since killings commenced before the main events and loss of life continued well beyond the year 1915 with further massacres in the desert camps.

[243] See Hofmann, 'Christenverfolgung in Armenien (1894–1941). Die Synergie von nationalistischem Völkermord und stalinistischer Religionsunterdrückung' (ch 4, n 4) 175.

[244] Hans-Lukas Kieser, 'Einleitung: Der Völkermord an den Armeniern, die Türkei und Europa' in Hans-Lukas Kieser and Elmar Plozza (eds), *Der Völkermord an den Armeniern, die Türkei und Europa / The Armenian Genocide, Turkey and Europe* (Chronos 2006) 8–9.

Leo Kuper assumes 'as many as 800,000 or more'.[245] Donald Bloxham writes: 'A total of at least one million Armenians died, more than two-thirds of those deported.'[246] In another instance, he holds that '[n]ot counting the Armenian soldiers who died in combat in Ottoman ranks, the Armenian people lost between eight hundred thousand – a figure accepted in 1919 by Kemal himself – and one and a half million of their number, with a more precise probable range lying between one million and twelve hundred thousand'.[247]

William Rubinstein writes that '[a] figure of 800,000 Armenians deported, of whom 600,000 perished, seems reasonable' and that '[i]t is also likely that several hundred thousand more Armenians died, chiefly in massacres, between 1916 and 1923, making the total number of Armenian deaths at [*sic*] about 1 million'.[248] Jay Winter assumes 'between 500,000 and 1 million'.[249] Manus Midlarsky speaks of 'approximately 1,000,000'[250] and Eric Weitz of 'around a million' deaths.[251]

Nial Ferguson writes that '[t]he number of Armenian men, women and children who were killed or died prematurely may have been even higher than a million',[252] and Roger Smith assumes 'over a million between 1915 and 1917'.[253] Hilmar Kaiser gives the number of '1.1 million'.[254] Jennifer Balint writes of an 'estimated 1.2 million'.[255]

[245] Kuper, *Genocide. Its Political Use in the Twentieth Century* (ch 1, n 34) 105. The number 800,000 is also a contemporary estimate, see James Bryce, 'The Armenian Massacres', *Arnold J. Toynbee, Armenian Atrocities. The Murder of a Nation* (Hodder & Stoughton 1915) 6. For further estimates, see Toynbee, *Armenian Atrocities. The Murder of a Nation* (ch 2, n 18) 113–4. Kuper, *Genocide. Its Political Use in the Twentieth Century* (ch 1, n 34) 113–4. At another instance, Kuper speaks of 'as many as one million or more – half the Armenian population'. See Kuper, 'Types of Genocide and Mass Murder' (ch 1, n 25) 37.

[246] Bloxham, 'The Armenian Genocide of 1915–1916: Cumulative Radicalization and the Development of a Destruction Policy' (ch 3, n 66) 141.

[247] Bloxham, *The Great Game of Genocide. Imperialism, Nationalism, and the Destruction of the Ottoman Armenians* (ch 4, n 231) 10.

[248] Rubinstein, *Genocide: A History* (ch 1, n 40) 139. For further estimates, see ibid 139–40.

[249] Jay Winter, 'Under Cover of War: The Armenian Genocide in the Context of Total War' in Robert Gellately and Ben Kiernan (eds), *The Specter of Genocide. Mass Murder in Historical Perspective* (Cambridge University Press 2003) 207.

[250] Midlarsky, *The Killing Trap. Genocide in the Twentieth Century* (ch 4, n 42) 36.

[251] Weitz, *A Century of Genocide. Utopias of Race and Nation* (ch 1, n 34) 5.

[252] Ferguson, *The War of the World. History's Age of Hatred* (ch 4, n 26) 179.

[253] Smith, 'State Power and Genocidal Intent: On the Uses of Genocide in the Twentieth Century' (ch 4, n 10) 10.

[254] Kaiser, 'Genocide at the Twilight of the Ottoman Empire' (ch 4, n 231) 382.

[255] Balint, 'The Ottoman State Special Military Tribunal for the Genocide of the Armenians: "Doing Government Business"' (ch 2, n 23) 82.

Following the argument that reliable data does not exist, Dominik Schaller suggests a broad estimate of 800,000 to 1.4 million.[256] Daniel Segesser points to the numbers of 800,000 to 1.5 million.[257] Also, Vahakn Dadrian sees 'the range of estimates vary between one and one and a half million',[258] which is also the estimate given by Yves Ternon.[259] Michael Hesemann assumes even more than 1.5 million.[260]

Other authors work with more individual estimates, such as Tessa Hofmann, who writes that only 870,000[261] of the deported population reached Mesopotamia.[262] At the same time, massacres and, even applying the landscape as a killing trap, mass burnings in caves filled with raw oil deposits left another 200,000 dead.[263] In total, her estimates assume that 630,000 of the 870,000 perished.[264]

Numbers given for the atrocities preceding the 1915 genocide equally oscillate from high to low, with wide ranges in between. Mark Levene observes that 'estimates on the number of fatalities diverge widely, between a low of 50,000 and a high of 300,000'.[265]

William Rubinstein writes that in the first attack in Sasun, '8,000 Armenians were killed' and '[s]oon afterward [. . .] widespread massacres of Armenians throughout the Ottoman Empire [occurred], with somewhere between 50,000 and 300,000 killed'.[266] Helen Fein speaks of 10,000 deaths at Sasun.[267]

256 See Schaller, 'Der Völkermord an den Armeniern im Osmanischen Reich, 1915–1917. Ereignis Historiographie und Vergleich' (ch 4, n 231) 239.

257 Segesser, *Recht statt Rache oder Rache durch Recht? Die Ahndung von Kriegsverbrechen in der internationalen wissenschaftlichen Debatte 1872–1945* (ch 2, n 5) 206.

258 Dadrian, 'A Typology of Genocide' (ch 1, n 34) 211.

259 Ternon, *L'État Criminel. Les Génocides au XXe Siècle* (ch 1, n 36) 187.

260 Hesemann, *Völkermord an den Armeniern. Mit unveröffentlichten Dokumenten aus dem Geheimarchiv des Vatikans über das größte Verbrechen des Ersten Weltkriegs* (ch 4, n 239) 219. A hand-out given to the present author on the campus of Columbia University by a group of students raising awareness for the Armenian genocide states: 'An estimated 1,500,000 Armenians, more than half of the Armenian population living on its historic homeland'. See UACLA, 'The Armenian Genocide', hand-out on file with the author.

261 See Hofmann, 'Christenverfolgung in Armenien (1894–1941). Die Synergie von nationalistischem Völkermord und stalinistischer Religionsunterdrückung' (ch 4, n 4) 174.

262 See ibid.

263 See ibid 175.

264 Ibid.

265 Levene, *Genocide in the Age of the Nation-State. Volume II: The Rise of the West and the Coming of Genocide* (ch 4, n 13) 309.

266 Rubinstein, *Genocide: A History* (ch 1, n 40) 129.

267 See Fein, *Accounting for Genocide. National Responses and Jewish Victimization During the Holocaust* (ch 1, n 8) 12.

Table 4.3 Death Toll Estimates – 1915 Genocide (from High to Low)

Author	Number
Michael Hesemann	Over 1.5 million
Vahakn Dadrian	1–1.5 million
Yves Ternon	1–1.5 million
Jennifer Balint	1.2 million
Hilmar Kaiser	1.1 million
Roger Smith	Over a million
Nial Ferguson	May have been even higher than a million
Donald Bloxham[1]	At least 1 million / more than two-thirds
Manus Midlarsky	Approximately 1 million
Eric Weitz	Around 1 million
Donald Bloxham[2]	800,000–1.5 million / 1–1.2 million
Daniel Segesser	800,000–1.5 million
Dominik Schaller	800,000–1.4 million
Leo Kuper	800,000
William Rubinstein	600,000–1 million
Jay Winter	500,000–1 million

Michael Hesemann assumes between 8,000 and 16,000 victims there[268] and finds estimates for later massacres too low with 100,000, listing 300,000 as the estimate of the Armenian Patriarchy.[269]

Martin Gilbert, William Rubinstein and Dominik Schaller assume around 100,000 victims of the Hamidian massacres of the 1890s,[270] and Donald Bloxham writes that the events 'took 80-100,000 Armenian lives directly and tens of thousands indirectly in 1894-1896'.[271] Richard Hovannisian and Leo Kuper have estimated between 100,000 and 200,000,[272] and Levon Chorbajian assumes that the '[o]rganized massacres from 1894 to 1986 claimed 150,000-200,000 Armenian victims'.[273] Manus Midlarsky speaks of 'approximately

[268] See Hesemann, *Völkermord an den Armeniern. Mit unveröffentlichten Dokumenten aus dem Geheimarchiv des Vatikans über das größte Verbrechen des Ersten Weltkriegs* (ch 4, n 239) 78.

[269] See ibid 109.

[270] See Gilbert, 'Twentieth Century Genocides' (ch 4, n 76) 9–10; Rubinstein, *Genocide: A History* (ch 1, n 40) 129; Schaller, 'Der Völkermord an den Armeniern im Osmanischen Reich, 1915–1917. Ereignis Historiographie und Vergleich' (ch 4, n 231) 236.

[271] Bloxham, *The Great Game of Genocide. Imperialism, Nationalism, and the Destruction of the Ottoman Armenians* (ch 4, n 231) 51. See also Bloxham, 'The Armenian Genocide of 1915–1916: Cumulative Radicalization and the Development of a Destruction Policy' (ch 3, n 66) 149.

[272] See Hovannisian, *Armenia on the Road to Independence 1918* (ch 4, n 231) 28. See also Hovannisian, 'The Historical Dimensions of the Armenian Question, 1878–1923' (ch 4, n 231) 25; Hovannisian, 'The Armenian Genocide' (ch 4, n 234) 93–4; Kuper, 'Types of Genocide and Mass Murder' (ch 1, n 25) 36.

[273] Chorbajian, 'Introduction' (ch 2, n 184) xxiii.

Table 4.4 Death Toll Estimates – 1894–6 Massacres (from High to Low)

Author(s)	Number
Tessa Hofmann	300,000
Roger Smith	300,000 (including 1909)
Manus Midlarsky	200,000
Norman Naimark	200,000
Yves Ternon	200,000
Michael Hesemann	8,000–16,000 (Sasun) / 100,000–300,000 overall
Levon Chorbajian	150,000–200,000
Richard Hovannisian	100,000–200,000
Leo Kuper	100,000–200,000
Martin Gilbert et al.	100,000 overall
Donald Bloxham	80,000–100,000
Mark Levene	50,000–300,000 (assessment of the literature)
Helen Fein	10,000 (Sasun) / 100,000 overall (including 1909)
William Rubinstein	8,000 (Sasun) / 50,000–300,000 overall

200,000 Armenians',[274] Norman Naimark of 'some 200,000',[275] as does Yves Ternon.[276] Tessa Hofmann writes that, due to these atrocities committed against the Armenian population as well as lost harvests and resulting famine, around 300,000 died, and another 100,000 emigrated between 1895 and 1896.[277]

For 1909, Richard Hovannisian speaks of 'between fifteen and twenty thousand'[278] and at another instance of 'some 20,000',[279] which Naimark echoes.[280] According to Donald Bloxham and Dominik Schaller, approximately 20,000 lost their lives.[281] Michael Hesemann assumes more than 20,000[282] and

[274] Midlarsky, *The Killing Trap. Genocide in the Twentieth Century* (ch 4, n 42) 5.
[275] Naimark, *Fires of Hatred. Ethnic Cleansing in Twentieth-Century Europe* (ch 4, n 4) 23. See also Naimark, *Genocide. A World History* (ch 1, n 40) 71.
[276] See Ternon, *L'État Criminel. Les Génocides au XXe Siècle* (ch 1, n 36) 182.
[277] See Hofmann, 'Christenverfolgung in Armenien (1894–1941). Die Synergie von nationalistischem Völkermord und stalinistischer Religionsunterdrückung' (ch 4, n 4) 165.
[278] Hovannisian, *Armenia on the Road to Independence 1918* (ch 4, n 231) 30.
[279] Hovannisian, 'The Historical Dimensions of the Armenian Question, 1878–1923' (ch 4, n 231) 27; Hovannisian, 'The Armenian Genocide' (ch 4, n 234) 94. Cf also Hovannisian, 'The Historical Dimensions of the Armenian Question, 1878–1923' (ch 4, n 231) 27 where he speaks of the year 1908.
[280] See Naimark, *Genocide. A World History* (ch 1, n 40) 71.
[281] See Bloxham, *The Great Game of Genocide. Imperialism, Nationalism, and the Destruction of the Ottoman Armenians* (ch 4, n 231) 60; Bloxham, 'The Armenian Genocide of 1915–1916: Cumulative Radicalization and the Development of a Destruction Policy' (ch 3, n 66) 149; Schaller, 'Der Völkermord an den Armeniern im Osmanischen Reich, 1915–1917. Ereignis Historiographie und Vergleich' (ch 4, n 231) 236.
[282] See Hesemann, *Völkermord an den Armeniern. Mit unveröffentlichten Dokumenten aus dem Geheimarchiv des Vatikans über das größte Verbrechen des Ersten Weltkriegs* (ch 4, n 239) 128.

Table 4.5 Death Toll Estimates – 1909 Massacres (from High to Low)

Author(s)	Number
Yves Ternon	30,000
Levon Chorbajian	25,000
Donald Bloxham and Dominik Schaller	20,000
Michael Hesemann	20,000
Norman Naimark	20,000
Richard Hovannisian	15,000–20,000

Levon Chorbajian writes that the 'further killings in 1909 left an additional 25,000 Armenian dead'.[283] Yves Ternon sets the number at 30,000.[284]

Lumping together the events, Helen Fein estimates that '100,000 Armenians were killed between 1895 and 1909'.[285] Roger Smith speaks of a total of '300,000 Armenians between 1895 and 1908 [*sic*!]'.[286]

4.3.3 Genocide

In 1982, Leo Kuper could still speak of 'the "forgotten genocide" of the twentieth century, remembered mainly by Armenians'.[287] Up into the twenty-first century, it has been found that 'one of the striking facts about the Armenian genocide is that it is so little known'.[288] Today, this statement surely no longer holds (although its validity, of course, depends upon the audience).[289] With the exception of the Holocaust, the Armenian genocide – 'Meds Yeghern', the 'great crime', in Armenian[290] or 'Armenocide' in the neologism of some

[283] Chorbajian, 'Introduction' (ch 2, n 184) xxiii.
[284] Ternon, *L'État Criminel. Les Génocides au XXe Siècle* (ch 1, n 36) 183.
[285] Fein, *Accounting for Genocide. National Responses and Jewish Victimization During the Holocaust* (ch 1, n 8) 6. Cf, however, ibid 12: 'While massacres of Armenians were rare in the first half of the nineteenth century, 10,000 were slain at Sassoon in 1894 and a minimum of 100,000 were estimated to have been killed between 1895 and 1908 [*sic*] when the Sultan's despotism was ended.' See, in this regard, also the following footnote and accompanying text.
[286] Smith, 'State Power and Genocidal Intent: On the Uses of Genocide in the Twentieth Century' (ch 4, n 10) 10.
[287] Kuper, *Genocide. Its Political Use in the Twentieth Century* (ch 1, n 34) 105. See also Richard G. Hovannisian, 'Foreword' in Richard G. Hovannisian (ed), *The Armenian Genocide in Perspective* (Transaction Books 1986) 1; Hovannisian, 'The Armenian Genocide' (ch 4, n 234) 89–90 and 98.
[288] Bloxham, *The Great Game of Genocide. Imperialism, Nationalism, and the Destruction of the Ottoman Armenians* (ch 4, n 231) 6. On the absence of the topic in Ottoman historiography, see also Akçam, *The Young Turks' Crime Against Humanity. The Armenian Genocide and Ethnic Cleansing in the Ottoman Empire* (ch 3, n 88) xxv–xxvi.
[289] Cf Bazyler, *Holocaust, Genocide, and the Law. A Quest for Justice in a Post-Holocaust World* (ch 2, n 19) 64.
[290] Cf Jones, *Genocide. A Comprehensive Introduction* (ch 1, n 34) 30.

historians[291] – is possibly the most well-known atrocity committed against a particular ethnic group alongside the Holocaust.

No serious historian would argue today that the events of 1915 leading to the large-scale disappearance of the Armenian population – and even entire cities – from what is modern-day Turkey did not take place, let alone that the atrocities – and the policy under which they were committed – did not seek to eradicate the minority from that territory.[292]

[291] For example, Hesemann, *Völkermord an den Armeniern. Mit unveröffentlichten Dokumenten aus dem Geheimarchiv des Vatikans über das größte Verbrechen des Ersten Weltkriegs* (ch 4, n 239) 19.

[292] See Beachler, *The Genocide Debate. Politicians, Academics, and Victims* (ch 3, n 42) 89–91; Ferguson, *The War of the World. History's Age of Hatred* (ch 4, n 26) 178. On the historiography, in general, see Schaller, 'Der Völkermord an den Armeniern im Osmanischen Reich, 1915–1917. Ereignis Historiographie und Vergleich' (ch 4, n 231) 248–53. For an overview of the debate in Turkey as well as among Ottoman historians, see Akçam, *The Young Turks' Crime Against Humanity. The Armenian Genocide and Ethnic Cleansing in the Ottoman Empire* (ch 3, n 88) xi–xii; Beachler, *The Genocide Debate. Politicians, Academics, and Victims* (ch 3, n 42) 97–104; Donald Bloxham and Fatma Müge Göçek, 'The Armenian Genocide' in Dan Stone (ed), *The Historiography of Genocide* (Palgrave Macmillan 2008); Gabriel Goltz, 'Das Jahr 2005: ein Meilenstein in der Debatte in der Türkei über das Schicksal der Armenier im Osmanischen Reich 1915/1916' in Hans-Lukas Kieser and Elmar Plozza (eds), *Der Völkermord an den Armeniern, die Türkei und Europa / The Armenian Genocide, Turkey and Europe* (Chronos 2006) 21–35. For an early appraisal of 'Rationalization, Revision, and Denial' literature, see Richard G. Hovannisian, 'The Armenian Genocide and Patterns of Denial' in Richard G. Hovannisian (ed), *The Armenian Genocide in Perspective* (Transaction Books 1986) 112–31; Hovannisian, 'The Armenian Genocide' (ch 4, n 234) 112–15. On the denialist arguments themselves, see Akçam, *The Young Turks' Crime Against Humanity. The Armenian Genocide and Ethnic Cleansing in the Ottoman Empire* (ch 3, n 88) 373–447; Vigen Guroian, 'Collective Responsibility and Official Excuse Making: The Case of the Turkish Genocide of the Armenians' in Richard G. Hovannisian (ed), *The Armenian Genocide in Perspective* (Transaction Books 1986) 135–49; Hesemann, *Völkermord an den Armeniern. Mit unveröffentlichten Dokumenten aus dem Geheimarchiv des Vatikans über das größte Verbrechen des Ersten Weltkriegs* (ch 4, n 239) 21–8; Anush Hovanissian, 'Turkey: A Cultural Genocide' in Levon Chorbajian and George Shirinian (eds), *Studies in Comparative Genocide* (Palgrave Macmillan/St Martin's Press 1999) 149–53; Richard G. Hovannisian, 'Genocide and Denial: The Armenian Case' in Israel W. Charny (ed), *Toward the Understanding and Prevention of Genocide. Proceedings of the International Conference on the Holocaust and Genocide* (Westview Press 1984) 89–96; Hovannisian, 'The Armenian Genocide' (ch 4, n 234) 98–101; Roger W. Smith, 'Denial of the Armenian Genocide' in Israel W. Charny (ed), *Genocide. A Critical Bibliographical Review. Volume Two* (Facts on File Publications 1991) 63–73; Ternon, *L'État Criminel. Les Génocides au XXe Siècle* (ch 1, n 36) 194–6. For an exploration of the reasons for the Turkish position, see Taner Akçam, 'The Genocide of the Armenians and the Silence of the Turks' in Levon Chorbajian and George Shirinian (eds), *Studies in Comparative Genocide* (Palgrave Macmillan/St Martin's Press 1999) 125–44; Henry R. Huttenbach, 'The Psychology and Politics of Genocide Denial: A Comparison of Four Case Studies' in Levon Chorbajian and George Shirinian (eds), *Studies in Comparative Genocide* (Palgrave Macmillan/St Martin's Press 1999) 217–20. Entire volumes have appeared that seek to compile documents to counter these views. For example, Artem Ohandjanian, *1915. Irrefutable Evidence. The Austrian Documents on the Armenian Genocide* (Republic of Armenia National Academy of Sciences Museum-Institute of the Armenian Genocide 2006). For a comprehensive catalogue of available material, see Vahakn N. Dadrian, 'Documentation of the Armenian Genocide in Turkish Sources' in Israel W. Charny (ed), *Genocide. A Critical Bibliographical Review. Volume Two* (Facts on File Publications 1991) 86–138. See also the further references given by Akçam, *The Young Turks' Crime Against Humanity. The Armenian Genocide and Ethnic Cleansing in the Ottoman Empire* (ch 3, n 88) 373–447; Chorbajian, 'Introduction' (ch 2, n 184) xxxi–xxxii, fn 25; Schaller, 'Der Völkermord an den Armeniern im Osmanischen Reich, 1915–1917. Ereignis Historiographie und Vergleich' (ch 4, n 231) 253–5.

The Joint Declaration of 15 May 1915 by the Entente powers, France, Great Britain and Russia, had already labelled the atrocities a 'crime against humanity',[293] and news reports spoke of massacres, deportations and extermination.[294] The term 'genocide' did not, of course, yet exist. Today, nobody discusses whether the events constitute crimes against humanity but agree that it would constitute genocide if it were to be judged by the benchmark of the Genocide Convention definition.

Donald Bloxham, in an article on 'The Armenian Genocide of 1915-1916' writes that 'every aspect of the United Nations' definition of the crime is applicable'.[295] Leo Kuper, in a contribution on 'The Turkish Genocide of Armenians, 1915-1917', lifts the events beyond categorization when he holds that 'the precise definition of genocide is not significant in the present case':[296] 'Whatever tenable definition is applied to the massacres of Armenians in World War I, they would clearly constitute genocide.'[297]

Some authors engage in further 'legal' analysis to bolster their claim, even if they sometimes do disservice to the legal definition of genocide. In his book, *The Great Game of Genocide*, Bloxham writes:

> The Armenian fate was composed of the two elements: ethnic cleansing, or forced collective displacement, and direct physical annihilation. Only because of the presence of both elements is the epithet genocide applicable, and I shall endeavour to show how both emerged and fused.[298]

If he wants to imply that 'direct physical annihilation' by itself would not constitute genocide, he is either applying an adaptation of the concept or simply using a tautology to emphasize the magnitude of atrocities.

Levon Chorbajian, in the introduction to an edited volume on *Studies in Comparative Genocide*, discusses various definitions of genocide ranging from the Genocide Convention to Genocide Studies, concluding that the Armenian case falls within 'what I call classic genocides', that is 'genocides initiated by

[293] See Chapter 2, n 13.

[294] See Marjorie Housepian Dobkin, 'What Genocide? What Holocaust? News from Turkey, 1915–1923. A Case Study' in Richard G. Hovannisian (ed), *The Armenian Genocide in Perspective* (Transaction Books 1986) 98–9.

[295] See Bloxham, 'The Armenian Genocide of 1915–1916: Cumulative Radicalization and the Development of a Destruction Policy' (ch 3, n 66) 189.

[296] Kuper, 'The Turkish Genocide of Armenians, 1915–1917' (ch 2, n 1) 44.

[297] Ibid.

[298] Bloxham, *The Great Game of Genocide. Imperialism, Nationalism, and the Destruction of the Ottoman Armenians* (ch 4, n 231) 69.

authoritarian states, premeditated, involving great cruelty, and bringing about large numbers of deaths in absolute terms and deaths as a percentage of target populations'.[299]

Tessa Hofmann, in a contribution on the persecution of Christians in Armenia, similarly highlights a number of elements relevant in her opinion under the heading 'Commission of a Genocide' ('Durchführung eines Genozids').[300] Alongside the 'fatal plans' of the Ottoman Ministry of Defence, she lists the disarmament of the Armenian population, the formation of death squads, forced labour, liquidation of the elite and, finally, the deportation of the remaining population.[301]

But all of this serves not to question but to emphasize the justification of the label. The atrocities committed against the Armenians under Ottoman rule stand almost undisputed as genocide today. 'Almost' due to the fact that the issue is still highly politicized. For Turkey, the unwillingness and inability to recognize the extent of atrocities or to attribute the label 'genocide' to the events remain the official governmental position.[302] Even 'basic facts are hotly disputed', and '[e]very small aspect of the Armenian genocide is the subject of heated disputation':[303]

> As the epithet 'genocide perpetrator' has become the major stigma under international law, the politico-legal battle between, crudely speaking, representatives of Turks and Armenians has raged around the applicability of the term, and specifically the key notion of intent to destroy.[304]

[299] Chorbajian, 'Introduction' (ch 2, n 184) xxi.
[300] See Hofmann, 'Christenverfolgung in Armenien (1894–1941). Die Synergie von nationalistischem Völkermord und stalinistischer Religionsunterdrückung' (ch 4, n 4) 169–75.
[301] Ibid 170–5.
[302] For the recent exchange of view in light of Joe Biden's acknowledgement of the Armenian genocide, see Humeyra Pamuk, 'In Historic Move, Biden Says 1915 Massacres of Armenians Constitute Genocide' *Reuters* (24 April 2021) <https://www.reuters.com/world/middle-east/biden-says-1915-massacres-armenians-constitute-genocide-2021-04-24/>; Ezgi Erkoyun and Tuvan Gumrukcu, 'Erdogan Urges Biden to Reverse "Wrong Step" on Armenian Declaration' *Reuters* (26 April 2021) <https://www.reuters.com/world/us/erdogan-calls-biden-reverse-wrong-step-armenian-declaration-2021-04-26/>.
[303] Beachler, *The Genocide Debate. Politicians, Academics, and Victims* (ch 3, n 42) 89 and 91.
[304] Bloxham, *The Great Game of Genocide. Imperialism, Nationalism, and the Destruction of the Ottoman Armenians* (ch 4, n 231) 95.

A public debate in Turkey appears impossible today,[305] where the repression of (Christian) minorities continues by other means.[306] Even the slightest acknowledgement or discussion of the Armenian genocide – as in this book – could lead to serious repercussions.

In scholarship, however, the fate of the Armenians of Asia Minor is written firmly into the canon of twentieth-century genocides. William Rubinstein, in his book *Genocide*, sees it 'generally regarded as the earliest and one of the most harrowing of modern genocides'.[307] Niall Ferguson, invoking the definition of the Genocide Convention in the foreword of his book *The War of the World. History's Age of Hatred*,[308] writes 'that it is now widely acknowledged to have been the first true genocide'.[309] For Donald Bloxham, '[t]he Armenian Genocide was a – perhaps *the* – archetypical example of a nationalist genocide'.[310]

What makes the process of atrocity labelling in the case of the Armenian genocide particularly interesting for the purposes of this book is not necessarily the ongoing Turkish soliloquy over whether the events of 1915 were, in fact, genocide. It is that it was preceded by a number of atrocities that usually only serve as an introductory overture to the 'actual' genocide of 1915, although they were already so massive in scale – a fact that usually invites the use of the word 'genocide', as could be seen in the case of the Congo Free State.

The events prior to 1915, be it the 'Hamidian massacres' of the 1890s or the massacres in Cilicia in 1909, are considered a mere prelude. Perhaps this narrative can be traced to Arnold Toynbee, who found a rise in complexity from the early atrocities to the Armenian genocide and, finally, the Holocaust.[311] Leo Kuper writes that '[t]he massacres of between one hundred and two hundred thousand Armenians in 1895-1896 were a sort of ambassadorial note by the Sultan to the European powers to refrain from intervention in the domestic

[305] See Raffi Sarkissian, 'The Armenian Genocide; A Contextual View of the Crime and Politics of Denial' in Ralph Henham and Paul Behrens (eds), *The Criminal Law of Genocide. International, Comparative and Contextual Aspects* (Ashgate 2007).

[306] As the recent example of the Hagia Sophia being turned into a mosque exemplifies. See UNESCO, Statement on Hagia Sophia, Istanbul, 10 July 2020 <https://en.unesco.org/news/unesco-statement-hagia-sophia-istanbul>.

[307] Rubinstein, *Genocide: A History* (ch 1, n 40) 127.

[308] See Ferguson, *The War of the World. History's Age of Hatred* (ch 4, n 26) xl.

[309] Ibid 177.

[310] Donald Bloxham, 'Determinants of the Armenian Genocide' in Richard G. Hovannisian (ed), *Looking Backward, Moving Forward. Confronting the Armenian Genocide* (Transaction Publishers 2003) 44.

[311] See Kuper, 'Types of Genocide and Mass Murder' (ch 1, n 25) 36.

affairs of Turkey, and a most bloody warning to the Armenians themselves'.[312] The same narrative is spun by Hovannisian in his contribution 'The Historical Dimensions of the Armenian Question, 1878-1923':

> In the following months, systematic pogroms swept over every district of Turkish Armenia. The slaughter of between 100,000 and 200,000 Armenians, the forced religious conversion of the population of cores of villages, the looting and burning of hundreds of other settlements, and the coerced flight into exile of countless Armenians were Abdul-Hamid's actual response to European meddling.[313]

As opposed to the 1915 genocide, the previous atrocities committed against the Armenian population are commonly referred to 'only' as 'slaughter',[314] 'pogroms',[315] 'murder',[316] 'massacre(s)'[317] or 'extirpation'.[318] Kuper calls the 1894 atrocities committed in Sasun 'an old-style city massacre'.[319] Equally, Boris Barth speaks of 'traditional forms of violence' ('traditionelle Formen von

[312] Ibid.

[313] Hovannisian, 'The Historical Dimensions of the Armenian Question, 1878–1923' (ch 4, n 231) 25.

[314] Bloxham, *The Great Game of Genocide. Imperialism, Nationalism, and the Destruction of the Ottoman Armenians* (ch 4, n 231) 51; Hovannisian, 'The Historical Dimensions of the Armenian Question, 1878–1923' (ch 4, n 231) 25. See also Hesemann, *Völkermord an den Armeniern. Mit unveröffentlichten Dokumenten aus dem Geheimarchiv des Vatikans über das größte Verbrechen des Ersten Weltkriegs* (ch 4, n 239) 78, who speaks in German of a 'butchery' ('Gemetzel').

[315] Kaiser, 'Genocide at the Twilight of the Ottoman Empire' (ch 4, n 231) 368; Segesser, *Recht statt Rache oder Rache durch Recht? Die Ahndung von Kriegsverbrechen in der internationalen wissenschaftlichen Debatte 1872–1945* (ch 2, n 5) 203. When speaking of 'pogroms', it is equally hard to differentiate between the nature of events and the legal definition. Whereas '[a] pogrom is defined as "an organized massacre in Russia for the destruction or annihilation of any body or class," but used in the English-speaking world since 1905–6 "chiefly" to apply "to those directed against the Jews."', it is also the case that 'the term pogrom has also come to connote "official planning or collusion"'. See Brass, 'Introduction: Discourses of Ethnicity, Communialism, and Violence' (ch 1, n 79) 33. He continues: 'Pogroms might indeed best be defined as attacks upon the persons and property of a particular ethnic, racial, or communal group in which the state and/or its agents are implicated to a significant degree, but which are given the appearance, by design of the authorities or otherwise, of a riot.' See ibid.

[316] Bloxham, *The Great Game of Genocide. Imperialism, Nationalism, and the Destruction of the Ottoman Armenians* (ch 4, n 231) 60.

[317] See, *inter alia*, ibid 4 and 51; Fein, *Accounting for Genocide. National Responses and Jewish Victimization During the Holocaust* (ch 1, n 8) 6; Hesemann, *Völkermord an den Armeniern. Mit unveröffentlichten Dokumenten aus dem Geheimarchiv des Vatikans über das größte Verbrechen des Ersten Weltkriegs* (ch 4, n 239) 78; Hofmann, 'Christenverfolgung in Armenien (1894–1941). Die Synergie von nationalistischem Völkermord und stalinistischer Religionsunterdrückung' (ch 4, n 4) 161–5; Kaiser, 'Genocide at the Twilight of the Ottoman Empire' (ch 4, n 231) 368; Kuper, *Genocide. Its Political Use in the Twentieth Century* (ch 1, n 34) 106; Rubinstein, *Genocide: A History* (ch 1, n 40) 129; Segesser, *Recht statt Rache oder Rache durch Recht? Die Ahndung von Kriegsverbrechen in der internationalen wissenschaftlichen Debatte 1872–1945* (ch 2, n 5) 204; Ternon, *L'État Criminel. Les Génocides au XXe Siècle* (ch 1, n 36) 182; Weitz, *A Century of Genocide. Utopias of Race and Nation* (ch 1, n 34) 4.

[318] Kuper, *Genocide. Its Political Use in the Twentieth Century* (ch 1, n 34) 106.

[319] Kuper, 'The Turkish Genocide of Armenians, 1915–1917' (ch 2, n 1) 54.

Gewalt'), comparing these with the anti-Jewish pogroms of Tsarist Russia.[320] This is echoed by Eric Weitz:

> Already in the 1890s, massacres had erupted with the connivance of the authorities and had resulted in the killing of hundreds of thousands of Armenians. While horrific and tragic, these were still largely traditional forms of violence, much like pogroms against Jews in the Russian Empire, though on a vastly greater scale.[321]

The reader might be left puzzled: What constitutes 'traditional violence'? Recalling some of the thoughts expressed at the very beginning of this book: Why – think Rwanda – would or should it influence the process of atrocity labelling? Equally, scale is invoked as a distinguishing characteristic to what is supposedly otherwise understood as a perhaps less severe mere 'pogrom'.

Jay Winter, in a contribution in the edited volume *The Specter of Genocide. Mass Murder in Historical Perspective*, makes the earlier events sound like measures taken against looming insurgency when he writes that 'Armenian separatism had been suppressed with widespread loss of life in 1894 and 1896'.[322] These arguments – combatting insurgency[323] or false victimhood[324] – still feature in publications today,[325] as well as in the official Turkish position.

Mark Levene, in *Genocide in the Age of the Nation-State*, is one of few authors to discuss the events prior to 1915 under the heading of 'genocide' but only sees these atrocities as building blocks in a progressive narrative:

> All this points to a consciously and systematically organised campaign, aimed at eroding the Armenian social and institutional base to such a point that it could no longer effectively function within a broader *political* equation. That this did not succeed – at least not in the Ottoman state mind – rather suggests that the 1894-6 massacres should be treated, albeit retrospectively, as a transitional phase in an evolution towards total genocide.[326]

[320] Barth, *Genozid. Völkermord Im 20. Jahrhundert. Geschichte, Theorien, Kontroversen* (ch 2, n 174) 63.
[321] Weitz, *A Century of Genocide. Utopias of Race and Nation* (ch 1, n 34) 4.
[322] Winter, 'Under Cover of War: The Armenian Genocide in the Context of Total War' (ch 4, n 249) 207.
[323] See Sadi Cayci, 'Armenian Genocide Claims: A Contextual Version of the 1915 Incidents' in Ralph Henham and Paul Behrens (eds), *The Criminal Law of Genocide. International, Comparative and Contextual Aspects* (Ashgate 2007) 22–5.
[324] See ibid 25.
[325] See Cayci, 'Armenian Genocide Claims: A Contextual Version of the 1915 Incidents' (ch 4, n 323).
[326] Levene, *Genocide in the Age of the Nation-State. Volume II: The Rise of the West and the Coming of Genocide* (ch 4, n 13) 309.

Had an 'erosion of the Armenian social and institutional base' taken place, it would have been genocide. Without it, it can only be seen as a prelude to genocide.

Bloxham, in a journal article on 'The Armenian Genocide of 1915-1916', writes that it was 'not a genocide, since the victims were generally adult males and the killings had a regional pattern' but 'this was an attack on the Armenians as a whole, combining elements of pogrom against a minority and calculated use of force against a protonational group – a sort of "cull"'.[327] How is 'culling' applied to an ethnic group of human beings not suggestive of genocide? One is left to wonder.

Only in 1915 does Bloxham find it fit to apply the term, 'when the policy of oppression broadened across the empire and increased to genocidal proportions'.[328] While he does not (directly) make the argument along the scale of atrocities by numbers of victims, his focus appears to be on the geographical scope. What before was only regional and dispersed now spanned across the entire Ottoman Empire.

Similar lines of argument can be found, relying on what might be considered the contextual elements of crimes against humanity: in line with the subtitle of his book *Genocide – Its Use in the 20th Century*, Leo Kuper sees what he calls the 'genocidal process' as centring on the level of state organization.[329]

Tessa Hofmann, in her contribution on the persecution of Christians in Armenia, distinguishes between the events before 1915 as 'panislamic massacres of Christians' ('panislamischen Christenmassaker') and after as 'nationalist genocide of Christians' ('nationalistischen Völkermord an Christen').[330] Both categories could potentially fall under the legal definition, depending on the analysis of relevant legal elements present in each event. It is not conceivable how the notions of 'panislamic' or 'nationalist' as such determine the categorization as genocide unless one reads 'nationalist' as state-organized in an appropriation of contextual elements of crimes against humanity.

[327] Bloxham, 'The Armenian Genocide of 1915–1916: Cumulative Radicalization and the Development of a Destruction Policy' (ch 3, n 66) 149.
[328] Ibid 157.
[329] Kuper, *Genocide. Its Political Use in the Twentieth Century* (ch 1, n 34) 101–19.
[330] Hofmann, 'Christenverfolgung in Armenien (1894–1941). Die Synergie von nationalistischem Völkermord und stalinistischer Religionsunterdrückung' (ch 4, n 4) 163.

There are also voices in the literature that sow doubt on the supposed 'primitive' nature of massacres committed in the 1890s and beyond. Already Kuper had argued that these atrocities 'do not appear to have been all that amateurish and ineffective'.[331] Yves Ternon also finds that the 'massacres' had a systematic character that took on a genocidal form.[332]

Similarly, Tessa Hofmann points out that the question of how to deal with the Armenian minority dates back to the 1880s and contemporaneous assessments suggest centrally organized character of the atrocities.[333] She also refers to a secret report of a provincial governor to Sultan Abdul Hamid II that praises the resulting majority Muslim population as a beneficial consequence of the massacres of 1895 to 1896.[334] Were one to look for 'conduct [. . .] pursuant to or in furtherance of a State or organizational policy to commit such attack', the requirement seems satisfied.

Another narrative distinguishes the events but acknowledges their interconnectedness and the role of the earlier events in paving the way to the Armenian genocide of 1915. Manus Midlarsky, in his book *The Killing Trap. Genocide in the Twentieth Century*, finds 'the massacre of approximately 200,000 Armenians by the Ottoman authorities in 1894-96' to be 'qualitatively distinct from that of the genocide of 1915-16',[335] although he concedes: 'It is likely that the precursors of the World War I genocides [. . .] enabled the later onset of the 1915-16 genocide.'[336] Equally, Levon Chorbajian writes: 'The 1915 Genocide was the culmination of decades of scapegoating, harassment, exploitations, persecution and terror.'[337]

Particularly, in the atrocities of 1909, the leading role of the Committee of Union and Progress was demonstrated in detail by Vahakn Dadrian.[338] For

[331] Kuper, *Genocide. Its Political Use in the Twentieth Century* (ch 1, n 34) 115; Kuper, 'The Turkish Genocide of Armenians, 1915–1917' (ch 2, n 1) 55.

[332] See Ternon, *L'État Criminel. Les Génocides au XXe Siècle* (ch 1, n 36) 182.

[333] See Hofmann, 'Christenverfolgung in Armenien (1894–1941). Die Synergie von nationalistischem Völkermord und stalinistischer Religionsunterdrückung' (ch 4, n 4) 164–5.

[334] See ibid 168.

[335] Midlarsky, *The Killing Trap. Genocide in the Twentieth Century* (ch 4, n 42) 5.

[336] Ibid 219.

[337] Chorbajian, 'Introduction' (ch 2, n 184) xxiii. See also Naimark, *Fires of Hatred. Ethnic Cleansing in Twentieth-Century Europe* (ch 4, n 4) 23.

[338] See Vahakn N. Dadrian, 'The Convergent Roles of the State and a Governmental Party in the Armenian Genocide' in Levon Chorbajian and George Shirinian (eds), *Studies in Comparative Genocide* (Palgrave Macmillan/St Martin's Press 1999) 95–103 et *passim*. See also Ternon, *L'État Criminel. Les Génocides au XXe Siècle* (ch 1, n 36) 183.

him, it 'served as a test case' for later events[339] – again a kind of 'blueprint argument' as in the case of German South-West Africa but within a single case study. As German imperialism and mentality evolved from colonial Germany to a system capable of the horrors of the Second World War and the Holocaust, so here are experiences collected that facilitate the decisions made just a few years later.

Others have taken the complete opposite view. Donald Bloxham, in *The Great Game of Genocide*, writes that

> there is no straight line connecting the massacres of the 1890s with the genocide of 1915, for the guiding ideologies of the perpetrators were different, and the earlier killings were not conducted under the same sort of close centralized authority as their later counterparts, both occurred in the key context of the empire's terminal decline.[340]

This also draws, once more, on the contextual elements of crimes against humanity when Bloxham writes that the earlier events 'had not the same scale of centralized systematization'[341] as in 1915, therefore not qualifying as 'a case of full-blown genocide'.[342]

Apart from the question of organization and continuity, scholars have offered further criteria for distinction. Norman Naimark, in *Fires of Hatred*, looks at the object and purpose of the measures, arguing that '[t]he goal was severe punishment, not extermination'.[343] Similarly, Yehuda Bauer, in a contribution on 'Comparison of Genocides', draws the line at intent, perhaps the only proper justification under the legal definition:

> The massacres that occurred in 1895-6, and then again early in the twentieth century were not concentrated attempts to eliminate the Armenian *ethnos*; but the events of 1915-17 undoubtedly were: the idea was that there should be no Armenians left in the Ottoman Empire.[344]

[339] Dadrian, 'The Convergent Roles of the State and a Governmental Party in the Armenian Genocide' (ch 4, n 338) 102. See also Ternon, *L'État Criminel. Les Génocides au XXe Siècle* (ch 1, n 36) 182.
[340] Bloxham, *The Great Game of Genocide. Imperialism, Nationalism, and the Destruction of the Ottoman Armenians* (ch 4, n 231) 4.
[341] Ibid 66.
[342] Ibid.
[343] Naimark, *Fires of Hatred. Ethnic Cleansing in Twentieth-Century Europe* (ch 4, n 4) 23. See also Barth, *Genozid. Völkermord Im 20. Jahrhundert. Geschichte, Theorien, Kontroversen* (ch 2, n 174) 64.
[344] Bauer, 'Comparison of Genocides' (ch 1, n 30) 36.

Richard Hovannisian finds,

> the major difference between Abdul-Hamid and his Young Turk successors was that he unleashed massacres in an effort to maintain a state structure in which the Armenians would be kept in their place without the right to resist corrupt and oppressive government, whereas the Young Turks were to employ the same tactic in 1915 on a grander scale to bring about fundamental and far-reaching changes in the status quo and to create an entirely new frame of reference that did not include the Armenians at all.[345]

Similarly, Niall Ferguson writes of the 1915 genocide that the events were 'qualitatively different, however; so much so that it is now widely acknowledged to have been the first true genocide'.[346]

Naimark also takes into account the severity and temporal scope of the massacres committed in the 1890s and beyond: 'Unlike genocidal schemes, the victims who were able could escape and return';[347] something he also reports, however, of the events of 1915.[348]

But a baser – or at least pragmatic – motive for the distinction between the 1915 genocide and earlier atrocities has also been suggested:

> Undoubtedly, an aspect of this revolves around an anxiety that 'elevating' the events of 1894-6 to the title will detract from the totality of the 1915 genocide, when this itself still remains contested in some quarters.[349]

Whichever is the proper explanation (or justification) for treating events differently, nowhere is a proper analysis conducted based on the definition of the Genocide Convention.

4.3.4 Holocaust

In defending the categorization as 'genocide', comparisons, convergences and parallels to the Holocaust are drawn,[350] oftentimes to bolster the moral

[345] Hovannisian, 'The Historical Dimensions of the Armenian Question, 1878–1923' (ch 4, n 231) 25–6.
[346] Ferguson, *The War of the World. History's Age of Hatred* (ch 4, n 26) 176–7.
[347] Naimark, *Fires of Hatred. Ethnic Cleansing in Twentieth-Century Europe* (ch 4, n 4) 23.
[348] See ibid 34–5.
[349] Levene, *Genocide in the Age of the Nation-State. Volume II: The Rise of the West and the Coming of Genocide* (ch 4, n 13) 308.
[350] For example, Robert Melson, *Revolution and Genocide: On the Origins of the Armenian Genocide and the Holocaust* (University of Chicago Press 1992); Robert Melson, 'Provocation or Nationalism: A Critical Inquiry into the Armenian Genocide of 1915' in Richard G. Hovannisian (ed), *The*

opprobrium of the Armenian genocide by placing both on equal footing.[351] Perhaps it is true that 'scholars and activists seemed to think that they had to prove that the Young Turks' annihilation of the Armenian population was "just like" the Holocaust in order for it to qualify as a genocide'.[352]

For sure, the Armenian genocide stands firmly today in the canon of twentieth-century genocides alongside the Holocaust, and it is often cited as the template in Hitler's mind drawn from a commonly attributed quote made in the context of the occupation of Poland:

> Who, after all, speaks today about the annihilation of the Armenians?[353]

Jay Winter seeks to 'locate the Holocaust of the Second World War within the history of the twentieth century" by drawing upon the idea of 'total war' in relation to the Armenian genocide[354] and 'refer[ring] to genocide as a feature of total war'.[355] Yves Ternon finds the case a prototype of twentieth-century genocides ('le prototype des génocides du XXe siècle')[356] and sees it as the most proximate and comparable with the Holocaust ('le génocide arménien est, dans ce siècle, le crime le plus proche du génocide juif, donc le plus comparable avec celui-ci').[357]

Armenian Genocide in Perspective (Transaction Books 1986) 79–81. See Kuper, 'The Turkish Genocide of Armenians, 1915–1917' (ch 2, n 1) 44; Schaller, 'Der Völkermord an den Armeniern im Osmanischen Reich, 1915–1917. Ereignis Historiographie und Vergleich' (ch 4, n 231) 272, fn 137 with further references.

351 See Schaller, 'Der Völkermord an den Armeniern im Osmanischen Reich, 1915–1917. Ereignis Historiographie und Vergleich' (ch 4, n 231) 255.

352 Weitz, *A Century of Genocide. Utopias of Race and Nation* (ch 1, n 34) xi. See also Shaw, *What Is Genocide?* (ch 1, n 36) 54.

353 Naimark, *Fires of Hatred. Ethnic Cleansing in Twentieth-Century Europe* (ch 4, n 4) 57. See also Kevork B. Bardakjian, *Hitler and the Armenian Genocide* (The Zoryan Institute 1985) 43; Sarkissian, 'The Armenian Genocide; A Contextual View of the Crime and Politics of Denial' (ch 4, n 305) 3. And for a discussion on the authenticity of the document Bardakjian 3–24. Cf further Hesemann, *Völkermord an den Armeniern. Mit unveröffentlichten Dokumenten aus dem Geheimarchiv des Vatikans über das größte Verbrechen des Ersten Weltkriegs* (ch 4, n 239) 16–21 and 28, who draws a line beyond Hitler to the atrocitites committed against Christians in the Middle East today; Power, *A Problem from Hell. America and the Age of Genocide* (ch 1, n 13) Chapter 2, fn 16, who simply attributes it to an 'August 22, 1939, meeting with military chiefs in Obersalzburg [*sic*]' and quotes it as 'Who today still speaks of the massacre of the Armenians'.

354 Winter, 'Under Cover of War: The Armenian Genocide in the Context of Total War' (ch 4, n 249) 189–90.

355 Ibid 206. Cf ibid 212.

356 Ternon, *L'État Criminel. Les Génocides au XXe Siècle* (ch 1, n 36) 179.

357 Ibid 199. Cf, however, also ibid: 'Pourtant, ces deux événements sont plus différents que semblables. Les deux États criminels n'avaient ni le même héritage culturel, ni le même degré de développement économique, ni les mêmes raisons de tuer. Les différences portent sur le mobile, la préméditation, la vision de la victime par le meurtrier, l'intention du crime et le comportement de l'État successeur.'

Accordingly, Levon Chorbajian called the Armenian genocide 'a twentieth-century model of commission',[358] and Irving Howoritz describes it as 'the essential prototype of genocide in the twentieth century'.[359] Jay Winter writes, '[t]he massacre of the Armenians was not the same as, but constituted a step on the way to, the industrialized murder of European Jewry by the Nazis.'[360] With the Syrian town of Deir ez-Zor, to where Armenians were driven in death marches and where the survivors were herded to starve in camps or massacred, there is also an 'Armenian Auschwitz'.[361]

All of this may lead to the conclusion – as in the continuity argument regarding German South-West Africa – that the Armenian genocide itself facilitated the commission of the Holocaust:

> The fact that the Armenian Genocide had been so readily forgotten contributed to the failure of the European Jewish Community to notice the early activities leading to Hitler's final solution.[362]

Parallels are further sought in both the historical context and the events themselves. For Dominik Schaller, the Armenian and Jewish genocides have been 'widely perceived as ideal types of genocide because of the perpetrators' alleged "irrational" motives: nationalism and racism'.[363] Chalk and Jonassohn consider the Armenian genocide 'the first of the modern ideologically-motivated genocides'.[364] Dadrian, in his typology of forms of genocide, has determined the Armenian genocide as the only 'optimal genocide' aside from the Holocaust.[365]

In analysing the Armenian case, Robert Melson finds the 'fateful convergence of a minority's renaissance and its connections to the outside world with the majority's disasters, fear of external aggression, and transformation of ideology and identity [. . .] to be at the core of both the Armenian and Jewish

[358] Chorbajian, 'Introduction' (ch 2, n 184) xxii. Cf, however, Rubinstein, *Genocide: A History* (ch 1, n 40) 140–6.
[359] Horowitz, *Taking Lives. Genocide and State Power* (ch 1, n 26) 159.
[360] Winter, 'Under Cover of War: The Armenian Genocide in the Context of Total War' (ch 4, n 249) 212.
[361] See Kieser, 'Einleitung: Der Völkermord an den Armeniern, die Türkei und Europa' (ch 4, n 244) 9.
[362] Sarkissian, 'The Armenian Genocide; A Contextual View of the Crime and Politics of Denial' (ch 4, n 305) 6.
[363] Schaller, 'Genocide and Mass Violence in "The Heart of Darkness": Africa in the Colonial Period' (ch 4, n 17) 346.
[364] Chalk and Jonassohn, *The History and Sociology of Genocide. Analyses and Case Studies* (ch 1, n 40) 249.
[365] Dadrian, 'A Typology of Genocide' (ch 1, n 34) 210–11. In this type of genocide 'the scale of casualties is maximum and victimization is optimal'. See ibid 210. Cf, however, Naimark, *Fires of Hatred. Ethnic Cleansing in Twentieth-Century Europe* (ch 4, n 4) 35.

genocides': 'In the grip of its new ideology the state radically redefines its identity and decides to eliminate the offending communal group from the social structure.'[366] Michael Hesemann argues a 'dual link' by emphasizing the religious background for both the Armenian genocide and the destruction of the European Jews,[367] and Hovannisian, in his contribution 'The Historical Dimensions of the Armenian Question, 1878-1923', offers multiple parallels between the Armenian genocide and the Holocaust:

> The similarities include the perpetration of genocide under cover of a major international conflict, thus minimizing the possibility of external intervention; conception of the plan by a monolithic and xenophobic clique; espousal of an ideology giving purpose and justification to chauvinism, racism, exclusivism, and intolerance toward elements resisting or deemed unworthy of assimilation; imposition of strict party discipline and secrecy during the period of preparation; formation of extralegal special armed forces to ensure the rigorous execution of the operation; provocation of public hostility toward the victim group and ascribing to it the very excesses to which it would be subjected; certainty of the vulnerability of the intended prey (demonstrated in the Armenian case by the previous general massacres of 1894-96 and 1909); exploitation of advances in mechanization and communication to achieve unprecedented means for control, coordination, and thoroughness; and use of sanctions such as promotions and the incentive to loot, plunder, and vent passions without restraint or, conversely, the dismissal and punishment of reluctant officials and the intimidation of persons who might consider harboring members of the victim group.[368]

Parallels are also drawn to counter the 'missing masterplan' anti-thesis to the proposition of intent, finding 'any claim that the murder of the Armenians when it unfolded was not a genocide, simply because there might not be unequivocal evidence of genocidal intent prior to May 1915, is as absurd as the suggestion that the Nazi "final solution" was not a genocide because it was

[366] Melson, 'Provocation or Nationalism: A Critical Inquiry into the Armenian Genocide of 1915' (ch 4, n 350) 80. See also Richard Hrair Dekmejian, 'Determinants of Genocide: Armenians and Jews as Case Studies' in Richard G. Hovannisian (ed), *The Armenian Genocide in Perspective* (Transaction Books 1986) 95.

[367] See Hesemann, *Völkermord an den Armeniern. Mit unveröffentlichten Dokumenten aus dem Geheimarchiv des Vatikans über das größte Verbrechen des Ersten Weltkriegs* (ch 4, n 239) 28–9. On the general link, see also ibid 308–13.

[368] Hovannisian, 'The Historical Dimensions of the Armenian Question, 1878–1923' (ch 4, n 231) 30.

not inscribed before the invasion of Poland or the USSR that every Jew was to be murdered.'[369]

Further, the bond of victimhood extends to alternate histories as Sarkissian proposes: 'The Armenian genocide could have easily been extended to include the Ottoman Jews'[370] – 'The Jewish population of Yishu were well aware they were next in line for a Turkish genocide.'[371]

Nevertheless, the suggestion of supposed parallels, convergences or even continuities – including the presences of German military during the Armenian genocide – with the Holocaust, has also been criticized.[372]

As regards the atrocities of the 1890s and beyond, Tessa Hofmann points out that the term 'holocaust' was used in contemporaneous US and European publications as a 'synonym for the mass destruction of Ottoman Christians' ('Synonym für die Massenvernichtung osmanischer Christen'), which often occurred in form of 'live immolations' ('Lebendverbrennung'), as in the case of Urfa in 1895, where 3,000 Armenians were burned alive after having fled into a church.[373]

Michael Hesemann writes that the description of an American missionary eyewitness of this event was the first time that this word was used in connection with an ethnic massacre.[374] He further speaks of the events of 1895–6 as the first 'Holocaust' (in parenthesis).[375] While this might be an allusion to the first use of the word, Hesemann points explicitly to the aim of killing the Armenian population 'in part'.[376]

[369] See Bloxham, 'The Armenian Genocide of 1915–1916: Cumulative Radicalization and the Development of a Destruction Policy' (ch 3, n 66) 189. See also Naimark, *Fires of Hatred. Ethnic Cleansing in Twentieth-Century Europe* (ch 4, n 4) 28.

[370] Sarkissian, 'The Armenian Genocide; A Contextual View of the Crime and Politics of Denial' (ch 4, n 305) 6.

[371] Ibid.

[372] See Ferguson, *The War of the World. History's Age of Hatred* (ch 4, n 26) 180.

[373] See Hofmann, 'Christenverfolgung in Armenien (1894–1941). Die Synergie von nationalistischem Völkermord und stalinistischer Religionsunterdrückung' (ch 4, n 4) 165. See also Schaller, 'Der Völkermord an den Armeniern im Osmanischen Reich, 1915–1917. Ereignis Historiographie und Vergleich' (ch 4, n 231) 272, fn 137.

[374] See Hesemann, *Völkermord an den Armeniern. Mit unveröffentlichten Dokumenten aus dem Geheimarchiv des Vatikans über das größte Verbrechen des Ersten Weltkriegs* (ch 4, n 239) 92.

[375] See ibid 87.

[376] Ibid 93: '"Und das sollen die christlichen Mächte ruhig mit ansehen?", hatte Kaiser Wilhelm II., bislang der treueste Freund des Sultans, am 11. November 1895 auf einem Bericht seines Botschafters in Konstantinopel über die Massaker notiert: "Schande über uns alle". In einem weiteren Bericht vom Dezember 1895 hieß es glasklar: "Es scheint wirklich an höchster Stelle die Absicht bestanden zu haben und noch zu bestehen, die Armenier numerisch so weit zu reduzieren, dass sie der Regierung in Zukunft keine ernsten Verlegenheiten mehr bereiten können." "Unerhört!", kommentierte der Kaiser.'

4.3.5 Assessment

Considering that the atrocities committed against the Armenians under Ottoman rule stand almost undisputed as genocide today – notwithstanding the formalistic argument of non-retroactivity of criminal law or Turkish denialism– contributions often focus more on individual aspects of state policy or the fate of the victims than on labelling.[377] The Armenian genocide is considered a prototype for genocide as such and for the Holocaust, with which it is seen comparable at both the meta- and micro-levels.

But patterns and tendencies in the process of labelling become apparent when comparing the Armenian genocide of 1915 with the atrocities of the 1890s and beyond. In seeking to distinguish events, several elements alien to the legal definition of genocide under the Genocide Convention are put forward, ranging from the underlying policy, to temporal and regional scope and to the contextual elements of crimes against humanity. As highlighted in the chapter on conceptualizing mass atrocities, only crimes against humanity require 'conduct [. . .] pursuant to or in furtherance of a State or organizational policy to commit such attack'. The international crime of genocide does not.

Overall, it is striking how little the nature of the atrocities committed during the 1890s and in 1909 are explored within the literature. Most of the time, they serve as mere preludes to the atrocities of 1915. From the call for the disarmament of February 1915 until 8 April 1915 when the first deportations commenced, or at the latest as of 24 April onwards, what has before been referred to as every imaginable label except genocide becomes exactly that: genocide in the very sense of the word,[378] irrespective even of a particular definition.

4.4 The famine in Ukraine between 1932 and 1933

4.4.1 Course of events

In 1932, excessively high grain quotas and subsequent procurement by the Soviet government led to a famine affecting large parts of modern-day

[377] For example, Kaiser, 'Genocide at the Twilight of the Ottoman Empire' (ch 4, n 231) 383–5.
[378] Cf Kuper, *Genocide. Its Political Use in the Twentieth Century* (ch 1, n 34) 106.

Ukraine.[379] This was accompanied by punitive measures for resistance against governmental measures and a restriction on the free movement from affected areas, largely exacerbating the crisis.[380] The famine lasted into the following year, leaving large parts of the Ukrainian population to succumb to sickness and starvation. Among the horrors experienced through the famine looms largest the need to resort even to cannibalism in order to survive.

As in all previous case studies, the events have been considered originally obscured by history: 'Ignored at the time it took place, the famine was so quickly forgotten that it ranks as history's most successful instance of the denial of genocide by the perpetrators.'[381] The Ukrainian famine was for a long time – and to some extent still is[382] – difficult to assess due to the inaccessibility of relevant Soviet archival material.[383] Still, as early as 1953, in his essay 'Soviet Genocide in Ukraine', Lemkin himself had called it 'the classic example of Soviet genocide'[384] and it is more than noteworthy that Russia in 2015 placed the essay on its Federal List of Extremist Materials.[385] The events have been

[379] See Snyder, *Bloodlands. Europe between Hitler and Stalin* (ch 2, n 107) vii–viii. Other areas hit by these measures included the Don, Kuban and Volga regions (but studies on these specific events are not part of the narrative analysis here, although they are usually discussed as a side issue to the events in what is now Ukraine). On the use of this term, see also Shaw, *What Is Genocide?* (ch 1, n 36) 189.

[380] See Olga Andriewsky, 'Towards a Decentred History: The Study of the Holodomor and Ukrainian Historiography' in Andrij Makuch and Frank E. Sysyn (eds), *Contextualising the Holodomor. The Impact of Thirty Years of Ukrainian Famine Studies* (Canadian Institute of Ukrainian Studies Press 2015) 25–7 and 30–1; Conquest, *The Harvest of Sorrow. Soviet Collectivization and the Terror-Famine* (ch 4, n 36) 327–9; Robert W. Davies and Stephen G. Wheatcroft, *The Years of Hunger: Soviet Agriculture 1931–1933* (Palgrave Macmillan 2004) 426–9; Andrea Graziosi, *The Great Soviet Peasant War. Bolsheviks and Peasants, 1917–1933* (Harvard University Press 1996) 67–8; James E. Mace, 'The Man-Made Famine of 1933 in the Soviet Ukraine: What Happened and Why?' in Israel W. Charny (ed), *Toward the Understanding and Prevention of Genocide. Proceedings of the International Conference on the Holocaust and Genocide* (Westview Press 1984) 74–5; Snyder, *Bloodlands. Europe Between Hitler and Stalin* (ch 2, n 107) 42–6; Françoise Thom, 'Reflections on Stalin and the Holodomor' in Andrij Makuch and Frank E. Sysyn (eds), *Contextualising the Holodomor. The Impact of Thirty Years of Ukrainian Famine Studies* (Canadian Institute of Ukrainian Studies Press 2015) 83; Nicolas Werth, 'Die große ukrainische Hungersnot von 1932/33' in Jörg Baberowski and Robert Kindler (eds), *Macht ohne Grenzen. Herrschaft und Terror im Stalinismus* (Campus Verlag 2014) 126–31.

[381] James E. Mace, 'The American Press and the Ukrainian Famine' in Helen Fein (ed), *Genocide Watch* (Yale University Press 1992) 117.

[382] See Werth, 'Die große ukrainische Hungersnot von 1932/33' (ch 4, n 380) 139.

[383] See Vincent Comerford, Lindsay Janssen and Christian Noack, 'Introduction' in Vincent Comerford, Lindsay Janssen and Christian Noack (eds), *Holodomor and Gorta Mór. Histories, Memories and Representations of Famine in Ukraine and Ireland* (Anthem Press 2012) 5–6; Werth, 'Die große ukrainische Hungersnot von 1932/33' (ch 4, n 380) 118.

[384] Reproduced in Serbyn, 'Lemkin on Genocide of Nations' (ch 4, n 31). See also Irvin-Erickson, *Raphaël Lemkin and the Concept of Genocide* (ch 2, n 19) 188–9.

[385] See Anton Weiss-Wendt, *Putin's Russia and the Falsification of History. Reasserting Control over Past* (Bloomsbury 2021) 20; Weiss-Wendt, *A Rhetorical Crime. Genocide in the Geopolitical Discourse of the Cold War* (ch 2, n 122) 171.

referred to as Stalin's 'greatest crime':[386] the Holodomor – a composite Ukrainian word roughly translating to 'killing by hunger'.[387]

As the common narrative of the history of the Holodomor goes, when Robert Conquest's *Harvest of Sorrow* was published in 1986, he had written the first[388] – or at least 'pioneering'[389] – history of the famine in Ukraine between 1932 and 1933, based largely on eyewitness accounts.[390] In it, Conquest characterizes the events as a 'terror-famine' and 'genocidal'.[391]

Reviews of the book immediately joined the discussion over whether the term 'genocide' applied to the events.[392] Since then, the question centres on the actual intent of Stalin's regime that Conquest had first argued in *Harvest*

[386] Rubinstein, *Genocide: A History* (ch 1, n 40) 202.

[387] See Barth, *Genozid. Völkermord Im 20. Jahrhundert. Geschichte, Theorien, Kontroversen* (ch 2, n 174) 136; Mace, 'Is the Ukrainian Genocide a Myth?' (ch 4, n 44) 57; Roman Serbyn, 'The Holodomor: Genocide Against the Ukrainians' in Lubomyr Y. Luciuk (ed), *Holodomor: Reflections on the Great Famine of 1932–1933 in Soviet Ukraine* (Kashtan Press 2008) 61; Nicolas Werth, 'The Crimes of the Stalin Regime: Outline for an Inventory and Classification' in Dan Stone (ed), *The Historiography of Genocide* (Palgrave Macmillan 2008) 414; Nicolas Werth, 'Mass Deportations, Ethnic Cleansing, and Genocidal Politics in the Later Russian Empire and the USSR' in Donald Bloxham and A. Dirk Moses (eds), *The Oxford Handbook of Genocide Studies* (Oxford University Press 2010) 396.

[388] This view is promoted by Conquest himself. See *The Harvest of Sorrow. Soviet Collectivization and the Terror-Famine* (ch 4, n 36) 4–5: 'It would not be true to say that there are no books on the collectivization and the terror-famine. Much has in fact been published, but it has almost all been either documentary or of a specialist nature (and I have been greatly indebted to both). But no history in the ordinary sense of the word has previously appeared.'

[389] Werth, 'The Crimes of the Stalin Regime: Outline for an Inventory and Classification' (ch 4, n 387) 406.

[390] See Andrea Graziosi, Lubomyr A. Hajda and Halyna Hryn, 'Introduction' in Andrea Graziosi, Lubomyr A. Hajda and Halyna Hryn (eds), *After the Holodomor. The Enduring Impact of the Great Famine on Ukraine* (Harvard University Press, 2013) xv; Lubomyr Hajda, 'Foreword' in Halyna Hryn (ed), *Hunger by Design. The Great Ukrainian Famine and Its Soviet Context* (Harvard University Press 2008) ix; Bohdan Klid and Alexander J. Motyl, 'Introduction' in Bohdan Klid and Alexander J. Motyl (eds), *The Holodomor Reader. A Sourcebook on the Famine of 1932–1933 in Ukraine* (Canadian Institute of Ukrainian Studies Press 2012) xxx; Naimark, 'How the Holodomor Can Be Integrated into Our Understanding of Genocide' (ch 1, n 43) 117; Frank Sysyn, 'Thirty Years of Research on the Holodomor: A Balance Sheet' in Andrij Makuch and Frank E. Sysyn (eds), *Contextualising the Holodomor. The Impact of Thirty Years of Ukrainian Famine Studies* (Canadian Institute of Ukrainian Studies Press 2015) 3–5. Others list Conquest's work alongside the documentary 'Harvest of Despair' and the institution of investigatory commissions. See Lubomyr Y. Luciuk, 'Foreword: What Was Sown Shall Be Reaped' in Lubomyr Y. Luciuk (ed), *Holodomor: Reflections on the Great Famine of 1932–1933 in Soviet Ukraine* (Kashtan Press 2008) iv; Marples, 'Ethnic Issues in the Famine of 1932–1933 in Ukraine' (ch 1, n 86) 36–7; Frank Sysyn, 'The Ukrainian Famine of 1932–3: The Role of the Ukrainian Diaspora in Research and Public Discussion' in Levon Chorbajian and George Shirinian (eds), *Studies in Comparative Genocide* (Palgrave Macmillan/St Martin's Press 1999) 189. For a bibliography of works published prior to 1990, see Chalk and Jonassohn, *The History and Sociology of Genocide. Analyses and Case Studies* (ch 1, n 40) 457–9.

[391] See Conquest, *The Harvest of Sorrow. Soviet Collectivization and the Terror-Famine* (ch 4, n 36) 306. See also ibid 272–3.

[392] See Sysyn, 'The Ukrainian Famine of 1932–3: The Role of the Ukrainian Diaspora in Research and Public Discussion' (ch 4, n 390) 191; Sysyn, 'Thirty Years of Research on the Holodomor: A Balance Sheet' (ch 4, n 390) 4 and 6–7.

of Sorrow[393] (but later relativized with some nuance).[394] Alongside a multitude of publications, including a large number of edited conference proceedings, partly initiated from within the Ukrainian émigré community in Canada and the United States, document collections have been published in English and other Western languages with the purpose of granting direct insight into the minds of the perpetrators.[395]

Still, as late as 2021, one finds the statement that publications in English language journals are either one-sided or scarce.[396] But already in 1986, the US government set up a commission to investigate the events, and the final report found that, indeed, genocide had taken place[397] (although in other instances the report refers to the events as crimes against humanity).[398] On 15 May 2003 and again on 28 November 2006, the Ukrainian parliament passed legislation recognizing the Holodomor as genocide.[399] According to a poll in 2013, two-thirds of the Ukrainian population considered the events to

[393] See Conquest, *The Harvest of Sorrow. Soviet Collectivization and the Terror-Famine* (ch 4, n 36) 326–9.

[394] See Jones, *Genocide. A Comprehensive Introduction* (ch 1, n 34) 302, fn 31; Stanislav V. Kulchytskyi, 'Holodomor in Ukraine 1932–1933: An Interpretation of Facts' in Vincent Comerford, Lindsay Janssen and Christian Noack (eds), *Holodomor and Gorta Mór. Histories, Memories and Representations of Famine in Ukraine and Ireland* (Anthem Press 2012) 22.

[395] For example, Ruslan Pyrih, *Holodomor of 1932–33 in Ukraine. Documents and Materials* (Kyiv Mohyla Academy 2008); Dmytro Zlepko (ed), *Der ukrainische Hunger-Holocaust. Stalins verschwiegener Völkermord 1932/33 an 7 Millionen ukrainischen Bauern im Spiegel geheimgehaltener Akten des deutschen Auswärtigen Amtes* (Verlag Helmut Wild 1988).

[396] See Marples, 'Ethnic Issues in the Famine of 1932–1933 in Ukraine' (ch 1, n 86) 41.

[397] See Commission on the Ukrainian Famine, *Investigation of the Ukrainian Famine 1932–1933. Report to Congress* (United States Government Printing Office 1988). See also Mace, 'Is the Ukrainian Genocide a Myth?' (ch 4, n 44) 49. On earlier activities and efforts of the Ukrainian *émigré* community in the United States leading up to this initiative, see Valeriy Vasylyev, 'The Holodomor through the Eyes of the Soviet Ukrainian Leadership, 1950–80' in Andrea Graziosi, Lubomyr A. Hajda and Halyna Hryn (eds), *After the Holodomor. The Enduring Impact of the Great Famine on Ukraine* (Harvard University Press 2013) 255–62.

[398] See Commission on the Ukrainian Famine, *Investigation of the Ukrainian Famine 1932–1933. Report to Congress* (ch 4, n 397) xxv.

[399] Both available online at <http://zakon2.rada.gov.ua/laws/show/789-15> and <http://zakon2.rada.gov.ua/laws/show/376-16>. The author is indebted to Nika Rassadina for assistance with the original texts. For an English translation of the law of 28 November 2006, see Embassy of Ukraine to Canada, 'Law of Ukraine No. 376–V "On Holodomor of 1932–33 in Ukraine"' <http://canada.mfa.gov.ua/en/ukraine-%D1%81%D0%B0/holodomor-remembrance/holodomor-remembrance-ukraine/holodomor-law-ukraine>. On memory politics in Ukraine, see Heorhiy Kasianov, 'Holodomor and the Politics of Memory in Ukraine After Independence' in Vincent Comerford, Lindsay Janssen and Christian Noack (eds), *Holodomor and Gorta Mór. Histories, Memories and Representations of Famine in Ukraine and Ireland* (Anthem Press 2012) 167–88. See also Kerstin S. Jobst, 'Der Umgang mit dem Erbe der Sowjetunion in der Ukraine – Integrative und desintegrative Maßnahmen der Regierung Kučma,' in Andreas Körber (ed), *Interkulturelles Geschichtslernen. Geschichtsunterricht unter den Bedingungen von Einwanderung und Globalisierung. Konzeptionelle Überlegungen und praktische Ansätze* (Waxmann 2001) 255.

constitute 'genocide'.[400] None of this has succeeded in bringing closure to the scholarly debate.

Without having to take recourse to Foucault's truism, the highly political nature of the history of the Ukrainian famine has been widely acknowledged.[401] German historian Kerstin Jobst has called the Holodomor a trauma that has attained the quality of a national myth and that plays a mythical role in the collective national memory of Ukraine.[402] Here, the process of atrocity labelling lays bare both motivations and consequences, as 'in the case of the Holodomor, scholars are presented with the perfect case study of the appropriation of memory on different levels; they observe, so to speak, the process of collective commemoration from below (now that the political taboo had been lifted) and its political exploitation from above, under laboratory conditions'.[403]

4.4.2 Numbers

As in the case of the Congo Free State, the victim estimates climb so high that they can be difficult to fathom. Israel Charny speaks of six million.[404] James Mace assumes 'an estimated five to seven million lives'.[405] Roman Serbyn writes that the 'famine has been estimated at between six and seven million'.[406] According to Wasyl Hryshko, '[b]y the most conservative estimate, based on an analysis of Soviet statistics, the casualties of the famine in the Ukrainian

[400] See Andriewsky, 'Towards a Decentred History: The Study of the Holodomor and Ukrainian Historiography' (ch 4, n 380) 18.

[401] See Kulchytskyi, 'Holodomor in Ukraine 1932–1933: An Interpretation of Facts' (ch 4, n 394) 19; Marples, 'Ethnic Issues in the Famine of 1932–1933 in Ukraine' (ch 1, n 86) 35; Snyder, *Bloodlands. Europe Between Hitler and Stalin* (ch 2, n 107) 404; Werth, 'Die große ukrainische Hungersnot von 1932/33' (ch 4, n 380) 138; Nicolas Werth, 'The Great Ukrainian Famine of 1932–33' (*Sciences Po, Mass Violence and Resistance – Research Network*) <https://www.sciencespo.fr/mass-violence-war-massacre-resistance/en/document/great-ukrainian-famine-1932-33>.

[402] See Jobst, *Geschichte Der Ukraine* (ch 4, n 40) 234.

[403] Comerford, Janssen and Noack, 'Introduction' (ch 4, n 382) 6. For a cursory overview of the debate, including in the political and public sphere, see Beachler, *The Genocide Debate. Politicians, Academics, and Victims* (ch 3, n 42) 147–50. See also Jobst, *Geschichte Der Ukraine* (ch 4, n 40) 248–50. And the Section on 'Commemoration and Controversy' in Lubomyr Y. Luciuk, *Holodomor: Reflections on the Great Famine of 1932–1933 in Soviet Ukraine* (Kashtan Press 2008) Chapters 17–33.

[404] See Israel W. Charny, 'The Study of Genocide' in Israel W. Charny (ed), *Genocide. A Critical Bibliographical Review* (Facts on File Publications 1988) 3.

[405] Mace, 'The Man-Made Famine of 1933 in the Soviet Ukraine: What Happened and Why?' (ch 4, n 380) 67. See also ibid 78.

[406] Roman Serbyn, 'Ukraine (Famine)' in Dinah L. Shelton (ed), *Encyclopedia of Genocide and Crimes Against Humanity. Vol. 3 [T-Z, Index]* (Thomson Gale 2005) 1058.

SSR totalled 7.5 million Ukrainians'.[407] Hiroaki Kuromiya writes of '7,8 million lives, the approximate number of actual deaths from the 1932-1933 famine'.[408] Walter Dushnyck writes that the 'figures fluctuate between 4 to 10 million victims in Ukraine alone'.[409]

At the 'lower' end of the spectrum, Serguei Adamets, France Meslé, Serhiy Pyrozhkov and Jacques Vallin arrive at 4.6 million 'total Ukrainian population losses strictly due to the *Holodomor*' of which '1.1 million were due to the crisis birth deficit, 0.9 to forced outward migration, and 2.6 to the excess mortality'.[410] Snyder sees it 'reasonable to propose a figure of approximately 3.3 million deaths by starvation and hunger-related disease in Soviet Ukraine in 1932-1933'.[411] Stanislav Kulchytskyi speaks of 'over'[412] and, in another instance, of '[a]t least' 3.5 million victims.[413] Andrea Graziosi sees 3.5–3.8 million deaths in Ukraine.[414] Jones estimates '[p]erhaps' 3.9 million.[415] Werth speaks of '[o]ver'[416] and Douglas Irvin-Erickson of 'more than' 4 million.[417]

Aygul Ashirova, in her work on Stalinism in Central Asia, portrays the Ukrainian famine as the bleaker comparison to the famine in Turkmenistan, writing that at least 4.5 million died.[418] Conquest assumed around 5 million

[407] Wasyl Hryshko, *The Ukrainian Holocaust of 1933* (Bahriany Foundation 1983) 107–8. He continues to cite additional estimates and numbers.

[408] Hiroaki Kuromiya, 'The Great Famine: The Issue of Intentionality' in Lubomyr Y. Luciuk (ed), *Holodomor: Reflections on the Great Famine of 1932–1933 in Soviet Ukraine* (Kashtan Press 2008) 118.

[409] Walter Dushnyck, *50 Years Ago: The Famine Holocaust in Ukraine. Terror and Human Misery as Instruments of Soviet Russian Imperialism* (World Congress of Free Ukrainians 1983) 31 with further estimates at 31–5. See also Serguei Adamets and others, 'The Great Famine: Population Losses in Ukraine' in Lubomyr Y. Luciuk (ed), *Holodomor: Reflections on the Great Famine of 1932–1933 in Soviet Ukraine* (Kashtan Press 2008) 46.

[410] Adamets and others, 'The Great Famine: Population Losses in Ukraine' (ch 4, n 409) 45–6.

[411] Snyder, *Bloodlands. Europe Between Hitler and Stalin* (ch 2, n 107) 53. See also ibid 411.

[412] Stanislav Kulchytsky, 'Defining the Holodomor as Genocide' in Lubomyr Y. Luciuk (ed), *Holodomor: Reflections on the Great Famine of 1932–1933 in Soviet Ukraine* (Kashtan Press 2008) 136.

[413] Kulchytskyi, 'Holodomor in Ukraine 1932–1933: An Interpretation of Facts' (ch 4, n 394) 24.

[414] See Andrea Graziosi, 'The Soviet 1931–1933 Famines and the Ukrainian Holodomor: Is a New Interpretation Possible, and What Would Its Consequences Be?' in Halyna Hryn (ed), *Hunger by Design. The Great Ukrainian Famine and Its Soviet Context* (Harvard University Press 2008) 6. See also already Andrea Graziosi, 'Les Famines Soviétiques de 1931–1933 et Le Holodomor Ukrainien. Une Nouvelle Interprétation Est-Elle Possible et Quelles En Seraient Les Conséquences?' (2005) 46 *Cahiers du Monde Russe* 453–72.

[415] Jones, *Genocide. A Comprehensive Introduction* (ch 1, n 34) 266.

[416] Irvin-Erickson, *Raphaël Lemkin and the Concept of Genocide* (ch 2, n 19) 188.

[417] Werth, 'The Great Ukrainian Famine of 1932–33' (ch 4, n 401). Cf, however, Werth, 'The Crimes of the Stalin Regime: Outline for an Inventory and Classification' (ch 4, n 387) 407, where he speaks of 'between 3.5 and 3.8 million deaths'.

[418] Aygul Ashirova, *Stalinismus und Stalin-Kult in Zentralasien. Turkmenistan 1924–1953* (ibidem-Verlag 2009) 129. Cf, however, with regard to Kasachstan by percentage of population Kuromiya, 'The Great Famine: The Issue of Intentionality' (ch 4, n 408) 121.

Table 4.6 Death Toll Estimates – Holodomor (from High to Low)

Author(s)	Number
Walter Dushnyck	4–10 million
David R. Marples	3–10 million (assessment of the literature)
Hiroaki Kuromiya	7.8 million
Wasyl Hryshko	7.5 million
Roman Serbyn	6–7 million
James Mace	5–7 million
Israel Charny	6 million
Robert Conquest	Around 5 million / 20–25%
Serguei Adamets et al.	4.6 million
Aygul Ashirova	4.5 million
Douglas Irvin-Erickson	More than 4 million
Nicolas Werth	Over 4 million
Adam Jones	3.9 million
Andrea Graziosi	3.5–3.8 million
Kerstin Jobst	3–3.5 million
Stanislav Kulchytskyi	3.5 million
Timothy Snyder	3.3 million
Lubomyr Luciuk	2.6 million
Olga Andriewsky	2.4–5 million (assessment of the literature)

deaths, 'a quarter to a fifth', as a result of the famine[419] with a total of 14.5 million deaths together with the effects of the general policy of dekulakization.[420]

David R. Marples finds estimates from three to ten million in the literature.[421] Olga Andriewsky writes that 'researchers have identified the names of some 882,510 victims of the Ukrainian Famine of 1932-1933'[422] and estimates 'are now beginning to settle on a range of 2.5 to 4 million excess deaths' during the famine.[423] Kerstin Jobst presents the number of 3–3.5 million deaths as the current historiographical consensus,[424] and Lubomyr Luciuk refers to the number of '"only" 2.6 million' as the low estimate.[425]

419 Conquest, *The Harvest of Sorrow. Soviet Collectivization and the Terror-Famine* (ch 4, n 36) 249 as well as 303 and 306 with further estimates from various sources at 303–4.

420 Ibid 301.

421 See Marples, 'Ethnic Issues in the Famine of 1932–1933 in Ukraine' (ch 1, n 86) 45. See on this also Rubinstein, *Genocide: A History* (ch 1, n 40) 203; Snyder, *Bloodlands. Europe between Hitler and Stalin* (ch 2, n 107) 404; Werth, 'Die große ukrainische Hungersnot von 1932/33' (ch 4, n 380) 118, fn 4.

422 Andriewsky, 'Towards a Decentred History: The Study of the Holodomor and Ukrainian Historiography' (ch 4, n 380) 18.

423 Ibid 24, with further references.

424 See Jobst, *Geschichte Der Ukraine* (ch 4, n 40) 244.

425 See Luciuk, 'Foreword: What Was Sown Shall Be Reaped' (ch 4, n 390) v.

4.4.3 Genocide

As opposed to actual events and numbers, the most controversial question surrounding the Holodomor remains the genocidal intent towards a specific victim group, the Ukrainians.[426] Following Conquest's publication and the ensuing debate, two competing narratives persist: the 'intent narrative' (or '"genocidal" interpretation'[427]) sees the Holodomor as a scheme to destroy the Ukrainian peasants or 'nation'[428] and the 'collateral narrative' sees it as a (willingly accepted) side-effect of Stalin's policy of collectivization[429] with very little blend between these two positions:[430]

> Some scholars flatly rejected the notion that the famine was genocide, others avoided the problem of classification by using descriptive terms such as 'great famine', 'artificial famine', or 'man-made famine'. Still others accepted the idea of genocide, *but saw its victims primarily as the kulaks, or peasants*; and, finally, some scholars recognized the famine as a genocide that was *specifically directed against the Ukrainian nation.*[431]

To follow Douglas Irvin-Erickson, in his book on Raphaël Lemkin and the Genocide Convention, the exclusion of political groups from the legal definition of genocide 'has led to strange contortions in how genocide is

[426] See Andriewsky, 'Towards a Decentred History: The Study of the Holodomor and Ukrainian Historiography' (ch 4, n 380) 28 and 32–4; Stanislav Kul'chyts'kyi, 'The Holodomor of 1932–1933: How and Why?' in Andrij Makuch and Frank E. Sysyn (eds), *Contextualising the Holodomor. The Impact of Thirty Years of Ukrainian Famine Studies* (Canadian Institute of Ukrainian Studies Press 2015) 92; Werth, 'The Crimes of the Stalin Regime: Outline for an Inventory and Classification' (ch 4, n 387) 407. Cf, however, Roman Serbyn, 'The Ukrainian Famine of 1932–1933 as Genocide in the Light of the UN Convention of 1948' (2006) LXII *The Ukrainian Quarterly* 181.

[427] Graziosi, Hajda and Hryn, 'Introduction' (ch 4, n 390) xx.

[428] See Marples, 'Ethnic Issues in the Famine of 1932–1933 in Ukraine' (ch 1, n 86) 35–6. Cf Kasianov, 'Holodomor and the Politics of Memory in Ukraine After Independence' (ch 4, n 399) 167. Cf also Dietsch, 'Holodomor: The 1932–1933 Ukrainian Famine-Genocide: Argumentum Ex Silentio' (ch 1, n 19) 181–7.

[429] See Andrea Graziosi, 'Why and in What Sense Was the Holodomor a Genocide?' in Lubomyr Y. Luciuk (ed), *Holodomor: Reflections on the Great Famine of 1932–1933 in Soviet Ukraine* (Kashtan Press 2008) 140–1.

[430] Cf Yaroslav Bilinsky, 'Was the Ukrainian Famine of 1932–1933 Genocide?' (1999) 1 *Journal of Genocide Research* 147, 147; Kulchytskyi, 'Holodomor in Ukraine 1932–1933: An Interpretation of Facts' (ch 4, n 394) 20; Stanislav Kul'chyts'kyi, 'The Holodomor and Its Consequences in the Ukrainian Countryside' in Andrea Graziosi, Lubomyr A. Hajda and Halyna Hryn (eds), *After the Holodomor. The Enduring Impact of the Great Famine on Ukraine* (Harvard University Press, 2013) 3; Marples, 'Ethnic Issues in the Famine of 1932–1933 in Ukraine' (ch 1, n 86) 38; Serbyn, 'Ukraine (Famine)' (ch 4, n 406) 1055; Werth, 'Die große ukrainische Hungersnot von 1932/33' (ch 4, n 380) 138.

[431] Serbyn, 'Ukraine (Famine)' (ch 4, n 406) 1059, emphasis in original.

conceptualized, legally and historically'.[432] This becomes visible in different emanations when it comes to academic discussions on the Holodomor.

Broader scholarly preoccupation with the famine in Ukraine began with its fiftieth anniversary in 1983. Walter Dushnyck's *50 Years Ago: The Famine Holocaust in Ukraine*, preceding Conquest's publication by three years, rests on the far end of the 'intent narrative'[433] (the author of the foreword distances herself from the argument).[434] The subtitle *Terror and Human Misery as Instruments of Soviet Russian Imperialism* already expresses the anti-Soviet and anti-Russian spirit of the pamphlet. The introduction begins:

> Fifty years ago Ukraine was ravaged and brought to the verge of virtual physical extinction not by some natural cause such as pestilence, drought, floods or an extremely poor harvest. In 1932 Ukraine was especially selected by the Kremlin to be punished for its aversion and overt opposition to the enforced collectivization of agriculture. Fifty years ago communist Russia deliberately committed a horrendous crime against the Ukrainian people which for the sheer magnitude of its victims has no equal in the history of mankind.[435]

Beyond comparisons with other genocides, Dushnyck instead implicitly elevates the Holodomor to an event of even greater magnitude than the Holocaust.

The pamphlet is strewn with pictures and newspaper clippings of victims of the famine and various accounts of the atrocities committed against the Ukrainians. The terms in which Dushnyck describes the famine are superlative and seek to invoke a multitude of connotations: 'genocide',[436] 'genocidal policy',[437] 'cruel and inhuman pogrom',[438] 'conscious and deliberate holocaust of the Ukrainian nation'[439] and 'mass genocide'.[440] His argument

[432] Irvin-Erickson, *Raphaël Lemkin and the Concept of Genocide* (ch 2, n 19) 188.
[433] See Dushnyck, *50 Years Ago: The Famine Holocaust in Ukraine. Terror and Human Misery as Instruments of Soviet Russian Imperialism* (ch 4, n 409).
[434] See Dana G. Dalrymple, 'Foreword' in Walter Dushnyck (ed), *50 Years Ago: The Famine Holocaust in Ukraine. Terror and Human Misery as Instruments of Soviet Russian Imperialism* (World Congress of Free Ukrainians 1983) 5.
[435] Dushnyck, *50 Years Ago: The Famine Holocaust in Ukraine. Terror and Human Misery as Instruments of Soviet Russian Imperialism* (ch 4, n 409) 10.
[436] Ibid.
[437] Ibid 12.
[438] Ibid 17.
[439] Ibid 26.
[440] Ibid 37.

juxtaposes the usual scholarly diligence and burden of proof: 'There have been no contradictions nor denials worthy of notice that the famine in Ukraine was man-made and politically motivated.'[441]

To substantiate the claim, Dushnyck cites a long list of authors to show that '[a] great number of scholars of all nationalities almost unanimously concur in their assessment that the famine in Ukraine was a deliberate and political program to destroy the Ukrainian people':[442] 'There is not the shadow of a doubt that the famine in Ukraine in 1932-1933 was deliberate genocide.'[443]

Written in the similar style of an anti-Soviet[444] and anti-Russian[445] polemic and published in the same anniversary year as Dushnyck's pamphlet, *The Ukrainian Holocaust of 1933* by Wasyl Hryshko goes even further in its assessment, calling the Holodomor 'the first instance of peacetime genocide in history' and 'unparalleled, for a time of peace, in the number of victims it claimed.'[446]

Talking about the 'Soviet genocide directed against Ukrainians as a nation within the borders of the Soviet Union', Hryshko invokes the definition of the Genocide Convention.[447] But he misrepresents the catalogue of included groups by adding 'any other group identified by certain common traits, including those of a socio-political nature': 'An act of genocide involved the *partial or complete extermination or an attempt at extermination applied to a group of people as a group regardless of the nature of the group*.'[448] It is precisely political groups that are excluded – by active Soviet intervention[449] – from the definition of the Genocide Convention.

Hryshko continues his trail of thought by making the crime of genocide an inherent feature of Soviet ideology:

> [A]ll of the above definitions of genocide, and especially those supplementary definitions offered by the Soviets, correspond precisely to those acts that typify the genocidal policies practiced by the totalitarian partocracy in the

441 Ibid 50.
442 Ibid 51.
443 Ibid.
444 See Hryshko, *The Ukrainian Holocaust of 1933* (ch 4, n 407) at 2–3 and 117–23 and repeatedly throughout the book.
445 See, for polemical references, ibid. 3–5, 105, 110–11, and 114.
446 Ibid 107.
447 Ibid 1.
448 Ibid 2, emphasis in original.
449 See Chapter 2, n 102.

> Soviet Union. Of course, the nature of the ideology and theory on which Communist political practice is based has made it possible for the Soviet rulers to camouflage their genocidal policy in such a way that it is not as obvious to external observers as the simple [*sic*!] Nazi genocide that was the concern of the authors of the United Nations Convention on genocide. A policy of genocide is implicit in the very goals proclaimed by the Communist ideological conception of 'building a new world of socialism and then communism' by means of revolutionary destruction of the 'old world'.[450]

Hryshko sees the famine only as the 'culmination' of a longstanding policy against the Ukrainian population, including the dekulakization.[451] In addition, he portrays Ukrainian communists as unwittingly falling for the scheming of 'Moscow', making final 'efforts to avoid the catastrophe and to stop Moscow from what struck them as simply a foolishly short-sighted plan'.[452]

In 1986, Robert Conquest's *Harvest of Sorrow* brought an intensification of the debate. Acknowledging that 'the term "genocide" is often used rhetorically', Conquest recalls the definition of the Genocide Convention.[453] He concludes that it applies to the actions of the Soviet Union in Ukraine and backs up his finding by referencing Lemkin's article on the famine of 1953: 'Such, at least, was the view of Professor Rafael [*sic*] Lemkin who drafted the Convention.'[454]

It seems important for Conquest to emphasize that atrocity labelling is a secondary exercise since 'a crime has been committed against the Ukrainian nation', making it irrelevant 'whether these events are to be formally defined as genocide'.[455] Still, *Harvest of Sorrow* features an entire chapter on the question of intent and goals of the measures with a view to the definition of the Genocide Convention.[456] And the conclusions affirm Conquest's previous assessment that, indeed, there was intent:

> Thus, the facts are established; the motives are consistent with all that is known of Stalinist attitudes; and the verdict of history cannot be other than one of criminal responsibility. Moreover, until there is a frank Soviet

[450] Hryshko, *The Ukrainian Holocaust of 1933* (ch 4, n 407) 2. See also ibid 109–12.
[451] Hryshko, *The Ukrainian Holocaust of 1933* (ch 4, n 407) 5 and 72–8.
[452] See ibid 81.
[453] See Conquest, *The Harvest of Sorrow. Soviet Collectivization and the Terror-Famine* (ch 4, n 36) 272.
[454] Ibid.
[455] Ibid.
[456] See ibid 322–30.

> investigation of these actions, the silence must surely be seen as the silence of complicity, or justification.

While Conquest does not provide a walkthrough of the definition of the Genocide Convention, his effort at establishing the intent of the Stalinist regime would suggest a categorization of his approach as an intentional full transplant.

With the success of the publication also came cementation of this 'intent narrative', and the Holodomor was inducted into the canon of Genocide Studies – even though Conquest later retracted some of his claims.[457]

Preceding Conquest's book, James Mace had also already come to the conclusion that the famine was provoked: 'The purpose [of the Holodomor], insofar as we may discern it, was to destroy the Ukrainian nation as a political factor and social organism.'[458] In a 1988 contribution on 'Genocide in the U.S.S.R.', Mace writes of the collectivization that 'its national and ethnic target (i.e. genocidal nature) must be inferred from the clarity with which it was geographically focused against areas containing target populations and from the particularly harsh policies of the Soviet authorities in the national sphere as applied to the main victimized group, the Ukrainians'.[459] In an article focussing on the coverage of the famine in US news outlets, Mace conjures an act both intentional and systematic: 'In 1932-1933 several million Soviet citizens, most of them Ukrainians, starved to death in a famine organized by Joseph Stalin and his closest collaborators.'[460]

Bohdan Klid and Alexander Motyl dedicated their book *The Holodomor Reader* as follows: 'To the memory of James Mace, whose pioneering work on the Holodomor brought the famine-genocide to the world's attention.'[461] In a sense, though published almost thirty years later, it closes the circle to Hryshko's contribution to the narrative of the Holodomor. In the introduction, the editors formulate their agenda of creating 'a thorough reference work on the Ukrainian genocide'.[462] Ultimately, they write, 'the view of the Holodomor as genocide' will 'gain the upper hand', though not just because the facts fit the

[457] See Davies and Wheatcroft, *The Years of Hunger: Soviet Agriculture 1931–1933* (ch 4, n 380) 441, fn 145.
[458] Mace, 'The Man-Made Famine of 1933 in the Soviet Ukraine: What Happened and Why?' (ch 4, n 380) 67.
[459] Mace, 'Genocide in the U.S.S.R.' (ch 2, n 185) 117.
[460] Mace, 'The American Press and the Ukrainian Famine' (ch 4, n 381) 113.
[461] Klid and Motyl, 'Introduction' (ch 4, n 390) xlvi.
[462] Ibid xxix.

definition but 'because expert opinion is formed on the basis of both evidence and the normative and political zeitgeist':[463]

> In sum, experts, like all people, are swayed by life – by the zeitgeist. And the Holodomor-as-genocide thesis is just such an example of a zeitgeist-in-the-making. The currently undisputed status of the Holodomor as a mass killing will set the norm for future scholars without political agendas. As the diehards exit, their place will be taken by scholars who view the famine from the perspective of today's norm – and of yesterday's. As a growing number of experts come to regard the Holodomor as genocide, a tipping point will be reached, and scholars, like all rational beings, will accept the genocide interpretation simply because it is the zeitgeist and makes sense.[464]

Thereby, they claim to base their 'personal view' on the 'interpretation of genocide by Raphael Lemkin, who first coined the term' and make reference to his 1953 article on the famine in Ukraine.[465] Even further, 'the roots of the genocide reach into the failed national-liberation struggles of 1917-22, when Bolshevik forces, centered in Russia, crushed the Ukrainian drive for independence, Stalin's genocidal campaign began in 1929, reached its apogee in 1932-33, and ended sometime in the 1930s, perhaps as late as the Great Terror of 1937-38'.[466] While the editors acknowledge the alternate narrative, they portray it as a backward emanation of Stalinism as opposed to the 'intent narrative', which they paint in both progressive and nationalist Ukrainian colours:

> While there are scholars and policy makers who still dispute Lemkin's interpretation, it is our belief that expert opinion has begun decisively to shift – and will continue to shift – toward viewing the Holodomor as genocide. The opening of Soviet archives, the contributions of Ukrainian and Western scholars, the abandonment of formerly popular revisionist views of Stalin and Stalinism, and the unceasing efforts of Ukrainians in Ukraine and throughout the world have combined to produce that shift.[467]

The dynamics of the debate are best illustrated by the publications of Italian historian Andrea Graziosi who let his view be shaped throughout his continued

[463] Ibid xxxi.
[464] Ibid.
[465] Ibid xxix.
[466] Ibid xxx.
[467] Ibid.

study of the Holodomor. In his 1996 work, *The Great Soviet Peasant War*, he still found that it was not 'a consciously pre-arranged famine' but that 'Stalin decided to use it to teach a lesson to the "esteemed grain-growers" called to pay the price of their "quiet" war against the Soviet power' and 'to uproot what he believed to be nationalism's natural breeding ground'.[468]

In a later article published around ten years later in the conference volume *Hunger by Design*, Graziosi asks, '*Was there also* a Ukrainian genocide?', and shares his line of thinking while seeking to apply different labels to the Ukrainian famine:

> The answer seems to be *no* if one thinks of a famine conceived by the regime, or – this being even more untenable – by Russia, to destroy the Ukrainian people. It is equally *no* if one adopts a restrictive definition of genocide as the planned will to exterminate *all* the members of a religious or ethnic group, in which case only the Holocaust would qualify. [. . .] Based on Lemkin's definition – if one thinks of the substantial difference in mortality rates in different republics; adds to the millions of Ukrainian victims, including the ones from Kuban, the millions of Ukrainians forcibly Russified after December 1932, as well as the scores of thousands of peasants who met a similar fate after evading the police roadblocks and taking refuge in the Russian republic; keeps in mind that one is therefore dealing with the loss of approximately 20 to 30 percent of the Ukrainian ethnic population; remembers that such a loss was caused by the decision, unquestionably a subjective act, to use the Famine in an anti-Ukrainian sense on the basis of the 'national interpretation' Stalin developed in the second half of 1932; reckons that without such a decision the death count would have been at the most in the hundreds of thousands (that is, less than in 1921-1922); and finally, if one adds to all of the above the destruction of large [*sic*] part of the republic's Ukrainian political and cultural elite, from village teachers to national leaders – I believe that the answer to our question, 'Was the Holodomor a genocide?' cannot but be positive.[469]

His main argument – and, in a sense, a rare fusion between the 'intent' and the 'collateral' camps[470] – is a change of mind that supposedly overcame

[468] Graziosi, *The Great Soviet Peasant War. Bolsheviks and Peasants, 1917–1933* (ch 4, n 380) 66–7.

[469] Graziosi, 'The Soviet 1931–1933 Famines and the Ukrainian Holodomor: Is a New Interpretation Possible, and What Would Its Consequences Be?' (ch 4, n 414) 10–11. See almost *verbatim* also Graziosi, 'Why and in What Sense Was the Holodomor a Genocide?' (ch 4, n 429) 153–4.

[470] See Werth, 'The Great Ukrainian Famine of 1932–33' (ch 4, n 401).

Stalin throughout the course of 1932, a period that saw both the failure of Soviet collectivization policies and the suicide of his second wife, Nadeschda Sergejewna Allilujewa.[471]

In the introduction to the 2013 conference volume *After the Holodomor* that Graziosi co-authored together with Lubomyr Hajda and Halyna Hryn, they speak of '[t]he presence of multiple genocides, or quasi-genocides, of which the Holodomor is the epitome'.[472] Graziosi's publications bear witness to an evolution from the rejection to the full application of a label.

Stanislav Kulchytskyi – considered as an important proponent of the 'intent interpretation'[473] – invokes the provisions of the Genocide Convention, finding the governmental policy that triggered the famine to fall within the required elements of the definition.[474] He cites a number of contemporary documents to prove intent,[475] even though these do not necessarily shed light on the particular victim group against which the measures were specifically directed. While Kulchytskyi sees the measures at 'the intersection between socio-economic and nationalities policies',[476] he has been criticized for misrepresenting the context of his sources.[477] At one point, he concedes:

> Supposedly, these repressions were not aimed at members of a particular nationality, but against all citizens of the Ukrainian republic. However, obviously the majority of these citizens were at the same time Ukrainians.[478]

In a later publication, while asserting that 'it is useful to examine the Kremlin's actions that caused the Ukrainian Holodomor in the context of the UN Convention on the Prevention and Punishment of Genocide, adopted on 9 December 1948', he leaves the final assessment for others:[479]

[471] Cf Terry Martin, *The Affirmative Action Empire. Nations and Nationalism in the Soviet Union, 1923–1939* (Cornell University Press 2001) 302–7.

[472] Graziosi, Hajda and Hryn, 'Introduction' (ch 4, n 390) xxiv.

[473] See Brian J. Boeck, 'Complicating the National Interpretation of the Famine: Reexamining the Case of Kuban' in Andrea Graziosi, Lubomyr A. Hajda and Halyna Hryn (eds), *After the Holodomor. The Enduring Impact of the Great Famine on Ukraine* (Harvard University Press, 2013) 33; Werth, 'Die große ukrainische Hungersnot von 1932/33' (ch 4, n 380) 138, fn 4.

[474] See Kulchytsky, 'Defining the Holodomor as Genocide' (ch 4, n 412) 132–3; Kulchytskyi, 'Holodomor in Ukraine 1932–1933: An Interpretation of Facts' (ch 4, n 394) 24.

[475] See Kulchytskyi, 'Holodomor in Ukraine 1932–1933: An Interpretation of Facts' (ch 4, n 394) 29–30.

[476] Ibid 24.

[477] See Boeck, 'Complicating the National Interpretation of the Famine: Reexamining the Case of Kuban' (ch 4, n 473) 33–4.

[478] Kulchytskyi, 'Holodomor in Ukraine 1932–1933: An Interpretation of Facts' (ch 4, n 394) 29.

[479] Kul'chyts'kyi, 'The Holodomor of 1932–1933: How and Why?' (ch 4, n 426) 91.

> Sooner or later, thanks to the force of irrefutable facts, the international community will issue a legal assessment of the Stalinist terror-famine, which by its very nature was genocidal. Perhaps the UN Convention on Genocide will be amended.[480]

Yaroslav Bilinsky, in the *Journal of Genocide Research*, argues that the Holodomor 'clearly fits the somewhat loose UN Genocide Convention'.[481] But it also fits an even 'narrower definition', namely 'any act that puts the very existence of a group in jeopardy'.[482] Similarly, in an article in *The Ukrainian Quarterly*, Roman Serbyn specifically makes this claim 'on the basis of the UN Convention'.[483] He also attempts to interpret the word 'nation' in the definition of the Genocide Convention in a political sense.[484] Following an opinionated account of (mis)conceptions of the historical evidence by a number of authors, he concludes that the intent element can be derived from the 'nexus joining the Ukrainian national group in the Ukrainian SSR (whether taken in its civic or ethnic sense) and the Ukrainian ethnic group in Kuban': 'their Ukrainianness'.[485]

The volume *Holodomor: Reflections on the Great Famine of 1932-1933 in Soviet Ukraine* unites a number of different positions. Donald Rayfield, after finding that the Holodomor constitutes both a 'man-made catastrophe' and 'mass murder', recalls the definition of genocide under '[t]he Conventions [*sic*!] on genocide'.[486] He then finds that it is, indeed, genocide, having addressed counterarguments by recalling the higher number of Ukrainian casualties in relation to other groups within the Soviet Union and 'clear documentary evidence of at least reckless determination to go ahead regardless of mortality'.[487] David Saunders wants to see 'the onus [placed] on those who deny the case for undue severity to work harder at making their case',[488] thereby implying that

480 Ibid 92.
481 Bilinsky, 'Was the Ukrainian Famine of 1932–1933 Genocide?' (ch 4, n 430) 152.
482 Ibid.
483 Serbyn, 'The Ukrainian Famine of 1932–1933 as Genocide in the Light of the UN Convention of 1948' (ch 4, n 426) 184. See also Serbyn, 'The Holodomor: Genocide Against the Ukrainians' (ch 4, n 387) 68.
484 See Serbyn, 'The Ukrainian Famine of 1932–1933 as Genocide in the Light of the UN Convention of 1948' (ch 4, n 426) 186–7 and 200.
485 Ibid 203.
486 Donald Rayfield, 'The Ukrainian Famine of 1933: Man-Made Catastrophe, Mass Murder, or Genocide?' in Lubomyr Y. Luciuk (ed), *Holodomor: Reflections on the Great Famine of 1932–1933 in Soviet Ukraine* (Kashtan Press 2008) 91.
487 Ibid 92–3.
488 David Saunders, 'The Starvation of Ukrainians in 1933: By-Product or Genocide?' in Lubomyr Y. Luciuk (ed), *Holodomor: Reflections on the Great Famine of 1932–1933 in Soviet Ukraine* (Kashtan Press 2008) 101.

labelling an atrocity anything other than 'genocide' equals trivialization. The contribution by Hiroaki Kuromiya argues that there is still insufficient evidence to determine the character of the Holodomor as genocide.[489] According to Steven Jacobs: 'The ongoing consensus of the academic-scholarly community is that [it] [. . .] was indeed genocide.'[490]

Outside of specialist literature on the Holodomor itself, a number of prominent historians and 'genocide scholars' have dealt with the question within a broader context. Yves Ternon devotes an entire chapter of his book on crimes committed by states to the question of whether there was, indeed, genocide in the Soviet Union.[491] Looking at the multitude of Stalinist persecutions and atrocities, he concludes – as Naimark later would – that the Holodomor is the only instance.[492] Ternon reaches his conclusion on the basis of an intent to destroy the Ukrainians for the very reasons of being Ukrainian but leaves the question of final (archival) proof to others.[493]

In *Stalin's Genocides*,[494] Norman Naimark argues that not one single instance but the totality of atrocities committed by and under Stalin should be considered as amounting to the crime of genocide. In his assessment, the Holodomor is the only instance of all of Stalin's crimes actually qualifying as genocide in the legal sense.[495] Graziosi has also endorsed Naimark's cumulative view of events as relevant for the process of atrocity labelling:

> Norman Naimark has recently and correctly reminded us of its [genocide's] crucial importance [. . .], stressing Stalin's personal role in Soviet genocides to which only his death put a sudden stop. [. . .] In the case of the Holodomor, the trigger was Stalin's previously discussed combination of the social, i.e. the peasant, and the national factors. These pushed him in late fall 1932 to escalate what would have in due course become, by the spring of 1933, a serious but limited famine, caused by his own policies, into a Holodomor intended not to eradicate, but to emasculate the Ukrainian nation by

489 Kuromiya, 'The Great Famine: The Issue of Intentionality' (ch 4, n 408) 126.

490 Steven Jacobs, 'Raphael Lemkin and the Holodomor: Was It Genocide?' in Lubomyr Y. Luciuk (ed), *Holodomor: Reflections on the Great Famine of 1932–1933 in Soviet Ukraine* (Kashtan Press 2008) 161.

491 See Ternon, *L'État Criminel. Les Génocides au XXe Siècle* (ch 1, n 36) 234–60.

492 See ibid 260.

493 See ibid 248.

494 Some of the following remarks have already been published within the context of a book review. See Markus P. Beham, 'Norman M. Naimark, Stalin's Genocides (Princeton University Press, 2010)' (2011) 16 *Austrian Review of International and European Law* 539.

495 Naimark, *Stalin's Genocides* (ch 3, n 13) 136.

> breaking its peasantry and crippling its intellectual and political elite. [. . .] The Ukrainian peasants and intelligentsia and Ukrainian language and culture were thus subjected in 1932-34 to policies that, taken together, fully satisfy the definition of 'genocide' as adopted by the United Nations.[496]

With regard to the definition of the Genocide Convention, Naimark calls for a 'broader and more flexible' approach[497] and interprets the definition of Articles II and III of the Convention against the background of its drafting history.[498] He concludes: 'The origins of the term "genocide" in the writings of Raphael Lemkin and the development of the 1948 U.N. convention on the prevention and punishment of genocide do not preclude using the term to identify political and social groups as victims of genocide.'[499]

In a later contribution, 'How the Holodomor Can Be Integrated into Our Understanding of Genocide', Naimark holds that 'a consensus has evolved among a substantial group of scholars that the Holodomor fits the general template of genocide'[500] and that 'there are many aspects of the study of genocide that are illuminated by an understanding of the Holodomor'.[501] As Conquest and Graziosi before him, Naimark invokes the authority of Lemkin:

> Lemkin is a real hero of the genocide story, and it is certainly an admirable part of his lasting legacy that he understood the genocidal essence of the 1932-33 killer famine in Ukraine. [. . .] [S]ince the mid-1990s the work of the courts – the indictments, the arguments, the witness testimonies, the sentencing – have added measurably to the sophistication of scholarship about genocide, demonstrating again the validity of Lemkin's approach of combining international legal scholarship with historical case studies. Scholars, too, have published increasingly detailed studies about diverse prototypes of genocide that have opened up Lemkin's concept to many previously marginalized cases, including the Holodomor.[502]

Naimark categorizes the Holodomor as a 'Communist genocide', as 'took place in the Soviet Union in the 1930s, in Maoist China during the Great Leap

[496] Andrea Graziosi, 'The Impact of Holodomor Studies on the Understanding of the USSR' in Andrij Makuch and Frank E. Sysyn (eds), *Contextualising the Holodomor. The Impact of Thirty Years of Ukrainian Famine Studies* (Canadian Institute of Ukrainian Studies Press 2015) 68–9.

[497] Naimark, *Stalin's Genocides* (ch 3, n 13) 8.

[498] Ibid 15.

[499] Ibid 132.

[500] Naimark, 'How the Holodomor Can Be Integrated into Our Understanding of Genocide' (ch 1, n 43) 112.

[501] Ibid 118.

[502] Ibid 116–7.

Forward at the end of the 1950s, and in Cambodia, during the horror years of Khmer Rouge rule from 1965 to the beginning of 1969', and, more specifically, as one of 'Stalin's genocides',[503] considering the genocide definition under the Genocide Convention and its commission of political groups insufficient with regard to group complexities.[504] In *Genocide – A World History*, Naimark writes: 'The horrors that ensued in the Ukrainian countryside, the Holodomor, should be considered genocide.'[505]

In *Bloodlands*, Timothy Snyder assumes intent by seeing '[h]unger as a form of aggression [. . .] for Stalin in a Ukrainian national struggle, against which starvation was the only defense'[506] and references Lemkin's depiction of the Holodomor as 'the classical example of Soviet genocide'.[507] Only in one of the final chapters on 'Numbers and Terms' does he offer his personal assessment of whether the events constituted genocide. While asserting that he 'prefer[s] *mass killing* to *genocide* for a number of reasons',[508] he concludes: 'In each of the cases discussed in this book, the question "Was it genocide?" can be answered: yes, it was.'[509]

Niall Ferguson, in *The War of the Worlds*, raises the question of intent when he writes that 'it is not too much to say that the man-made famine caused by collectivization in the Ukraine was Stalin's brutal answer to what he regarded as the "Ukrainian question"'.[510] He recounts the victims of Stalinist terror to conclude that 'genocide predated totalitarianism' and points to the Armenian genocide.[511] Ferguson also makes an interesting conceptual argument to counter the exclusion of political groups from the Genocide Convention:

> We tend to think of class as a category quite distinct from race, since in Western societies today the former can be more readily changed than the latter. Yet the dividing line is not always so clear-cut. In most medieval and early modern European societies, class was a hereditary attribute; in India

[503] Ibid 118.
[504] Ibid 121–2.
[505] See Naimark, *Genocide. A World History* (ch 1, n 40) 90.
[506] Snyder, *Bloodlands. Europe Between Hitler and Stalin* (ch 2, n 107) 42.
[507] Ibid 53.
[508] Ibid 412, emphasis in original.
[509] Ibid 413.
[510] Barth, *Genozid. Völkermord Im 20. Jahrhundert. Geschichte, Theorien, Kontroversen* (ch 2, n 174) 216.
[511] Ferguson, *The War of the World. History's Age of Hatred* (ch 4, n 26) xl.

> today it remains difficult to shed one's caste origins. In 1930s Russia, too, class was treated as an inheritable trait.[512]

On the opposite side stand Robert Davies and Stephen Wheatcroft, who in their study of Soviet agricultural policy counter the 'intent narrative' by concluding that their investigation shows 'a Soviet leadership which was struggling with a famine crisis which had been caused partly by their wrongheaded policies, but was unexpected and undesirable'.[513] Consequently, they do not enter the discussion of labelling the events as genocide at all.

Michael Ellman, in response to Davies and Wheatcroft,[514] specifically deals with the question of the legal qualification of events.[515] Whereas he finds that 'a crime (or series of crimes) for which Team-Stalin was clearly guilty in 1930-1934 is crimes against humanity', he concludes: 'Whether or not Team-Stalin was guilty of genocide in 1932-33 depends on how "genocide" is defined.'[516] Although he sees the possibility that the events meet the elements required under the definition of the Genocide Convention, his personal assessment is that the evidence is insufficient for the purpose of proving a specific intent.[517] Kerstin Jobst, in her book on the history of Ukraine, takes an equally agnostic position and writes that while the famine cannot be reduced to bad harvests and natural disasters,[518] it is simply not yet possible today to fully evaluate whether the events constitute a 'hunger genocide'.[519]

Others are more direct in rejecting the 'intent narrative'. William Rubinstein, in his book *Genocide*, concludes that there is simply no such proof:

> There is, of course, no evidence that Stalin wished to exterminate the Ukrainian people, as opposed to cowing them into obedience. The Soviet famines were the entirely unnecessary byproduct of an ideologically driven social planning on a grand scale, not of deliberate mass murder. This is of small comfort to the millions of its victims, but it is important that historians distinguish accurately among these categories of horrors.[520]

[512] Ibid 213.
[513] Davies and Wheatcroft, *The Years of Hunger: Soviet Agriculture 1931–1933* (ch 4, n 380) 441.
[514] See ibid 841; Robert W. Davies and Stephen G. Wheatcroft, 'Stalin and the Soviet Famine of 1932–33: A Reply to Ellman' (2006) 58 *Europe-Asia Studies* 625, 625–33.
[515] Ellman, 'Stalin and the Soviet Famine of 1932–33 Revisited' (ch 1, n 75) 680–8.
[516] Ibid 690.
[517] See ibid.
[518] See Jobst, *Geschichte Der Ukraine* (ch 4, n 40) 245.
[519] Ibid 248: 'Hungergenozid'.
[520] Rubinstein, *Genocide: A History* (ch 1, n 40) 204.

Boris Barth, who claims to base his analysis on the Genocide Convention definition,[521] writes that the genocide theory does not hold closer scrutiny since at no point in time did the Stalinist regime attempt to destroy the Ukrainians as a people.[522]

4.4.4 Holocaust

Intentional or not (a different question of 'intent' here), the word 'Holodomor' phonetically evokes the connotation of the Holocaust, and the term 'Holocaust' itself has repeatedly been used for publications on the Ukrainian famine.[523] Conquest's best-seller *Harvest of Sorrow* has been hailed precisely for 'breaking the taboo and daring to compare Nazi crimes and the Great Soviet famines'.[524] The book begins as follows:

> Fifty years ago as I write these words, the Ukraine and the Ukrainian, Cossack and other areas to its east – a great stretch of territory with some forty million inhabitants – was like one vast Belsen. A quarter of the rural population, men, women and children, lay dead or dying, the rest in various stages of debilitation with no strength to bury their families or neighbours. At the same time, (as at Belsen), well-fed squads of police or party officials supervised the victims.[525]

Recalling this passage at a Holodomor conference in 2003, Lubomyr Hajda argued that it 'captured the essence of the tragedy with searingly memorable imagery'.[526] During a keynote address at a Holodomor conference at the Ukrainian Research Institute at Harvard University in 2008, Nicolas Werth

[521] See Barth, *Genozid. Völkermord Im 20. Jahrhundert. Geschichte, Theorien, Kontroversen* (ch 2, n 174) 62.
[522] Ibid 144.
[523] For example, Miron Dolot, *Execution by Hunger. The Hidden Holocaust* (WW Norton & Company 1985); Dushnyck, *50 Years Ago: The Famine Holocaust in Ukraine. Terror and Human Misery as Instruments of Soviet Russian Imperialism* (ch 4, n 409); Hryshko, *The Ukrainian Holocaust of 1933* (ch 4, n 407). See on this also Kul'chyts'kyi, 'The Holodomor of 1932–1933: How and Why?' (ch 4, n 426) 92; Zlepko, *Der ukrainische Hunger-Holocaust. Stalins verschwiegener Völkermord 1932/33 an 7 Millionen ukrainischen Bauern im Spiegel geheimgehaltener Akten des deutschen Auswärtigen Amtes* (ch 4, n 395). See also Dietsch, 'Holodomor: The 1932–1933 Ukrainian Famine-Genocide: Argumentum Ex Silentio' (ch 1, n 19) 184; Kulchytskyi, 'Holodomor in Ukraine 1932–1933: An Interpretation of Facts' (ch 4, n 394) 22; Rubinstein, *Genocide: A History* (ch 1, n 40) 202.
[524] Nicolas Werth, 'Keynote Address for the Holodomor Conference, Harvard Ukrainian Research Institute, 17–18 November 2008' in Andrea Graziosi, Lubomyr A. Hajda and Halyna Hryn (eds), *After the Holodomor. The Enduring Impact of the Great Famine on Ukraine* (Harvard University Press 2013) ixxx.
[525] See Conquest, *The Harvest of Sorrow. Soviet Collectivization and the Terror-Famine* (ch 4, n 36) 3.
[526] Hajda, 'Foreword' (ch 4, n 390) ix.

equally found Conquest's imagery 'to capture the essence of the 1932-33 Famine'[527] and places the events under the definition of the Genocide Convention.[528] Similarly, Yuri Shapoval invokes the symbolism of the Holocaust:

> The writer Vasily Grossman placed the death by starvation of a Ukrainian child, 'in the middle of the broad steppe', side by side with the death by starvation of a Jewish child in a Nazi concentration camp. Some still fear such comparisons, and well they should, because it represents a truth.[529]

In another publication, he writes that the Holodomor has at least 'the character of a genocide'.[530] In analysing the debate, Kerstin Jobst finds that the famine as genocide and as a comparable event to the Holocaust has become a mainstream position in Ukraine.[531]

Graziosi originally takes an intermediate position,[532] writing that 'though one cannot speak of a famine intentionally created to wipe out the Ukrainian nation, it cannot be denied that [. . .] the scale and concentration of hunger-related deaths in Ukraine, and the policies then adopted by the regime, make the 1932-1933 famine a phenomenon which, at least in Europe, can be compared only to later Nazi crimes'.[533]

For Hryshko, actions against Ukrainians 'correspond exactly to those forms of genocide as defined in the United Nations convention':[534]

> Thus, we have a clear case of 'classical' genocide which in terms of the number of victims, counted in the millions, and in its magnitude can be

[527] Werth, 'Keynote Address for the Holodomor Conference, Harvard Ukrainian Research Institute, 17–18 November 2008' (ch 4, n 524) ixxx.

[528] See ibid xxxvi–xxxvii.

[529] Yuri Shapoval, 'The Struggle for History: Recognizing the Holodomor' in Lubomyr Y. Luciuk (ed), *Holodomor: Reflections on the Great Famine of 1932–1933 in Soviet Ukraine* (Kashtan Press 2008) 86.

[530] Yurii Shapoval, 'Understanding the Causes and Consequences of the Famine-Genocide of 1932–1933 in Ukraine: The Significance of Newly Discovered Archival Documents' <http://faminegenocide.com/print/resources/shapoval.htm>. On file with the author since the source is no longer available except through the Wayback Machine, this is a revised version of a contribution originally printed in Taras Hunczak and Roman Serbyn (eds), *Famine in Ukraine, 1932–1933: Genocide by Other Means* (Shevchenko Scientific Society 2007).

[531] See Jobst, *Geschichte Der Ukraine* (ch 4, n 40) 251.

[532] See Werth, 'The Crimes of the Stalin Regime: Outline for an Inventory and Classification' (ch 4, n 387) 414–5; Werth, 'Mass Deportations, Ethnic Cleansing, and Genocidal Politics in the Later Russian Empire and the USSR' (ch 4, n 387) 396–8.

[533] Graziosi, *The Great Soviet Peasant War. Bolsheviks and Peasants, 1917–1933* (ch 4, n 380) 65, fn 134. See also Graziosi, 'The Soviet 1931–1933 Famines and the Ukrainian Holodomor: Is a New Interpretation Possible, and What Would Its Consequences Be?' (ch 4, n 414) 10.

[534] Hryshko, *The Ukrainian Holocaust of 1933* (ch 4, n 407) 6.

compared to Hitler's attempt to destroy the Jewish nationality in Europe during World War II.[535]

As already suggested by the title of his book, *The Ukrainian Holocaust of 1933*, he states that 'the fateful chain of tragic events in Ukraine in 1933 has come to be called the "Ukrainian Holocaust"'.[536] This is echoed by James Mace, who concludes: 'Purely in terms of mortality, it was thus of the same order of magnitude as the Jewish Holocaust.'[537] In a later conference paper, he holds that 'the Ukrainian famine was a deliberate act of genocide of roughly the same order of magnitude as the Jewish Holocaust'[538] (a comparative approach he himself criticizes later on).[539]

Françoise Thom, in his contribution to the volume *Contextualising the Holodomor*, speaks of the procurement of grain as 'Stalin's most draconian genocidal measures'[540] and relates the famine to 'the Jewish genocide organized by Himmler' since, equally, 'the starvation of Ukraine was surrounded by the deepest secrecy'.[541] Alexander Motyl, in the edited volume *Holodomor: Reflections on the Great Famine of 1932-1933 in Soviet Ukraine*, adds an analytical angle: 'Looking closely at the Holocaust is the best way of understanding just why the Ukrainian Famine of 1932-1933 was genocide.'[542]

As in the previous two cases, the fate of the Herero and Nama in German South-West Africa and the Armenians in Asia Minor, continuity is sown as a red thread into the narrative of twentieth-century genocides alongside the Holocaust. Dmytro Zlepko, in a later German-language materials collection, invoking the definition of the Genocide Convention, puts the Holodomor on a level with the atrocities committed against the Armenians in Asia Minor and the Holocaust as one of three genocides committed during the twentieth century.[543] Equally, Mace compares the Holodomor with both the Armenian genocide and the Holocaust:

535 Ibid. See also ibid 108–9, 115, and 143.
536 Hryshko, *The Ukrainian Holocaust of 1933* (ch 4, n 407) 6.
537 Mace, 'The Man-Made Famine of 1933 in the Soviet Ukraine: What Happened and Why?' (ch 4, n 380) 67.
538 James E. Mace, 'The Man-Made Famine of 1933 in Soviet Ukraine' in Bohdan Krawchenko and Roman Serbyn (eds), *Famine in Ukraine 1932–1933* (University of Toronto Press 1986) 11.
539 Mace, 'Is the Ukrainian Genocide a Myth?' (ch 4, n 44) 56–7.
540 Thom, 'Reflections on Stalin and the Holodomor' (ch 4, n 380) 83.
541 Ibid 84.
542 Motyl, 'Looking at the Holodomor Through the Lens of the Holocaust' (ch 4, n 6) 171.
543 See Dmytro Zlepko, 'Einführung' in Dmytro Zlepko (ed), *Der ukrainische Hunger-Holocaust. Stalins verschwiegener Völkermord 1932/33 an 7 Millionen ukrainischen Bauern im Spiegel geheimgehaltener Akten des deutschen Auswärtigen Amtes* (Verlag Helmut Wild 1988) 14. This idea is also picked up by

> When will we recognize that truly massive destruction is always accompanied by fervently held political ideals? After all, the Young Turks did it for the salvation of the Ottoman Empire, the Nazis for a new Germany and purified Aryan race, the Stalinists for a world without classes or exploitation.[544]

Others take this 'canon' of twentieth-century genocides to elevate the events above the Holocaust even. Federigo Argentieri finds that '[o]f the three genocides that happened in Europe and the near East between 1915 and 1945 [the Armenian genocide, the Holodomor, and the Holocaust] [. . .] the Ukrainian *Holodomor* holds a special place, because it was the only one to happen in times of international peace'.[545]

4.4.5 Assessment

In the case of the Holodomor, intent and group definition become the elements with which the label sticks or drops. The preoccupation of scholarship with this question suggests an attempt to place the events under the legal definition of the Genocide Convention, which is almost surprisingly often invoked. But what seems to be full transplants turns out to be misrepresentations or adaptations, bolstered by scope. Others simply make it a question of time before the Holodomor is recognized – under whichever definition – as genocide.

Comparisons with the Holocaust appropriate different connotations with different degrees of historical validity and success. The creation of a canon of twentieth-century genocides incorporating the Holodomor – and within which it even stands unique, perhaps above the Holocaust in scale – serves as an argumentative bolster to the process of atrocity labelling. However, the widely different mortality estimates might also be explained through poor archival access and insufficient documentation, with the very high ranges to be found mostly in the earlier literature of the 1980s.

Werth, 'The Crimes of the Stalin Regime: Outline for an Inventory and Classification' (ch 4, n 387) 415: ' [I]n the number of its victims, the Holodomor, when seen in context, is the only twentieth-century European event that can be compared to the two other generally recognized instances of genocide: the Armenian genocide and the Holocaust.'

544 Mace, 'The American Press and the Ukrainian Famine' (ch 4, n 381) 132.

545 Federigo Argentieri, 'Holodomor, 75 Years On' in Lubomyr Y. Luciuk (ed), *Holodomor: Reflections on the Great Famine of 1932–1933 in Soviet Ukraine* (Kashtan Press 2008) 107.

5

Conclusion

The Genocide Convention introduced to international law and helped popularize a legal concept which is understood across the world today. It might not appear overly bold to argue that it has probably not only had a more popular and interdisciplinary impact than any other idea put forward in international law to date. But it has also created a separate, perhaps now even primary, social reality. As unbelievably horrific as the events described in this book are, the imagination of atrocities apparently depends upon the outcome of atrocity labelling. This might equally constitute the reason to engage in the process in the first place.

The machinery of discourse and the construction of reality within each narrative follows several patterns: numbers and scale, supposed genocidal elements and comparative proximity to the collective memory of the Holocaust. Clearly, the latter takes on a hegemonic role within the process of atrocity labelling as it saturates the term 'genocide' with symbolic capital.

While the Genocide Convention features prominently in the literature on the four case studies discussed in this book, its definition of the crime does not, other than by implication. Nor are any substantive attempts made to instrumentalize other international crimes such as war crimes or crimes against humanity. It is a genocide, or it is not. Where scholars strive for comparative compilations, they offer alternative definitions of the term to throw a broader net or simply rely on its vulgarization.

Throughout the four case studies, atrocity labelling oftentimes sees the inverted application of Charny's 'Templates for Denial of a Known Genocide':[1] acknowledgement as genocide, redress to official statements, emphasis on the

[1] Cf Israel W Charny, 'The Psychology of Denial of Known Genocides' in Israel W Charny (ed), *Genocide. A Critical Bibliographical Review. Volume Two* (Facts on File Publications 1991) 13–4.

facts required to subsume them under the legal definition and arrive at a certain number of victims, and using a particularly gruesome aspect of horror as a symbol for an event to emotionalize the analysis with a view to convince the reader – the latter easily found in the sad accounts of atrocities: the mutilations in the Congo Free State, the closely guarded exit from an inhospitable desert in German South-West Africa and the windswept camps for those who made it back, the endless death treks forced upon Armenians and the dying at Deir ez-Zor, as well as the frantic acts of cannibalism during the Holodomor.

Is it possible to find further commonalities in the four case studies to closer delineate the process of atrocity labelling? By way of induction, a number of common patterns and tendencies appear to take precedence over the legal elements of the crime as defined by Article II of the Genocide Convention:

(1) **Scale implies genocide.** The discussions surrounding the labelling process – whether an event is genocide or not – ultimately revolve around scale, referred to by Eric Weitz as 'history by body count'.[2] While Timothy Snyder has emphasized the necessity of viewing the numbers of atrocity victims as individual fates in all discussions about the extent of mass atrocities,[3] authors who speak of 'genocidal proportions' usually refer to the number of victims, not to the killing of individuals for their membership within a group. While reasons for varying estimates differ, the higher the number of victims, the greater authority for attribution or at least the more justified appears a comparison. Extent, although irrelevant from the perspective of the definition of the Genocide Convention, plays a central role in atrocity labelling. This also resonates with the six million deaths in the collective memory of the Holocaust.

(2) **The contextual elements of crimes against humanity imply genocide.** The fact that an act 'is committed in the context of a widespread or systematic attack against the civilian population and with knowledge of the attack [. . .] pursuant to or in furtherance of a State or organizational policy to commit such attack', as required by the *lege artis* definition of crimes against humanity, is used as a legitimizing and differentiating criterion for assessing events as genocide. Even more so than a

[2] Weitz, *A Century of Genocide. Utopias of Race and Nation* (ch 1, n 34) x.

[3] See Snyder, *Bloodlands. Europe Between Hitler and Stalin* (ch 2, n 107) 407–8.

'widespread or systematic attack', a 'master plan' of governmental policy implies genocide. Against the background of dissatisfaction with the legal definition of genocide, it demonstrates the thirst for legal arguments as an authoritative gloss. However, the genocide label is only legally justified if any of the acts listed in Article II of the Genocide Convention were committed 'with intent to destroy, in whole or in part, a national, ethnical, racial or religious group'.

(3) **Continuity implies genocide.** Suggesting an event is a precursor of the Holocaust or serves as a kind of 'blueprint' reaches into the future to claim a label. While certain historical continuities can surely be identified, as in individual biographies of German soldiers or officers, a supposed 'genocidal mentality' of the German population, for example, can only be understood as (rhetorical) hyperboles within the labelling process. This is not to say, of course, that imperialist fantasies did not exist within the military elite, but it should be necessary to equally consider discontinuities and ruptures to actually contribute to the bigger picture of understanding atrocities if that is the goal. The aspect of continuity is also sometimes accompanied by and connected to the attempt to establish a 'canon' of recognized genocides which circulate around the Holocaust and to which individual cases can be attributed: Armenia, Ukraine, Cambodia, Rwanda and so on.[4]

(4) **Representations of the Holocaust imply genocide.** Connotations awakening the collective memory of the destruction of the European Jews – the 'symbolic capital' of the term – have become an essential element in applying the term 'genocide' to other situations: the already mentioned number of six million deaths, the furnaces of Auschwitz or the medical experiments conducted in the concentration camps and elsewhere. Sometimes, the Holocaust apparently does not even appear in its evocation of incredulity magnanimous enough, requiring an elevation

[4] For example, Charny, 'The Study of Genocide' (ch 4, n 404) 7; Leo Kuper, 'Foreword' in Israel W Charny (ed), *Genocide. A Critical Bibliographical Review. Volume Two* (Facts on File Publication 1991) xii; Midlarsky, *The Killing Trap. Genocide in the Twentieth Century* (ch 4, n 42) 7. Cf also Bloxham and Moses, 'Editor's Introduction: Changing Themes in the Study of Genocide' (ch 1, n 21) 4; Douglas Irvin-Erickson, Alexander Laban Hinton and Thomas La Pointe, 'Introduction' in Douglas Irvin-Erickson, Alexander Laban Hinton and Thomas La Pointe (eds), *Hidden Genocides. Power, Knowledge, Memory* (Rutgers University Press 2014) 6; Shaw, *What Is Genocide?* (ch 1, n 36) viii; Stone, 'Introduction' (ch 1, n 35) 1.

of events above and beyond in scale, scope or scenario, although there are hardly any explicit examples provided to justify comparative and superlative adjectives. Holocaust comparisons appear to serve as labelling catalysts, not as an instrument of comparative methodology.

(5) **Only 'genocide, the noun' implies genocide.** Use of the word 'genocidal' appears prominently where an event cannot clearly be labelled as genocide. In the case of the Congo, this is so done in order to illustrate the extent and moral gravity of the atrocities committed. In the case of the Armenians, 'genocidal' is used to contrast the repeated 'small-scale' commission of atrocities against the exceptional character of the later events during the First World War. This equally dilutes the understanding of genocide and suggests that other labels such as 'crimes against humanity' or 'war crimes' express insufficient moral opprobrium.

(6) **Genocide Studies implies genocide.** This somewhat banal statement is perhaps the most important for the field as it pertains not to questions of law but to the comparative study of atrocities. Genocide Studies includes the study of events that are not accepted as genocide under any possible definition but are added to a chain of knowledge of atrocities committed throughout the twentieth century, throughout the nineteenth century and throughout the whole of history. Accordingly, the attribution seems to be due less to a qualitative assessment or analytical investigation than explorative curiosity: the more events that can be added to the collection, ranging from the biblical annihilation of the Amalekites and Canaanites to Carthage or Genghis Khan, the better. But while 'history is full of horrible events that also should be studied', 'no light will be shed on them by lumping together what should be kept apart'.[5] But in light of the reduced limelight produced by discussing events under any other label in the humanities or the political and social sciences, Genocide Studies is perhaps the only haven for the discussion of mass atrocities there currently is.

Peeking over the shoulders of 'genocide scholars', the observations made within the four case studies reveal patterns and tendencies that appear to guide the process of atrocity labelling. These can be contrasted with the legal parameters

[5] Chalk and Jonassohn, 'Conceptualizations of Genocide and Ethnocide' (ch 1, n 34) 182.

of the Genocide Convention definition: with the 'intent to destroy, in whole or in part, a national, ethnical, racial or religious group', with 'killing members of a group' or other acts falling within the definition of the Genocide Convention. They could also serve to increasingly take recourse to other international crimes such as 'crimes against humanity' or 'war crimes' that could either be more inclusive or, as in the case of 'ethnic cleansing', more specific.

Instead of rallying for the application of the term 'genocide', the study of atrocities could benefit from harnessing the complexities of other international crimes that are equally grounded in the effort to address factual circumstances of atrocities. Simply diluting concepts for the sake of greater inclusivity will surely not add analytical clarity to understanding events from either the historian's or the political or social scientist's perspective. Additionally, one should be wary of the consequences, be they an unwillingness to apply particular terms or welcome proxy arguments to avoid humanitarian action.

So, when we talk of genocide, can 'such a polemically-loaded term be operationalised for serious academic investigation?'[6] Wherever the process of atrocity labelling is uncovered and opened for discussion, probably yes. But the discourse must be unchained from the label of genocide alone. For wherever the process of atrocity labelling follows the pull of symbolic capital and is appropriated with intentions of activism and accusation, the answer in any serious scholarly enquiry should be: 'probably not'.

[6] See Moses, 'Introduction: The Field of Genocide Studies' (ch 1, n 30) 1.

Table of documents

'Preliminary Treaty of Peace between Russia and Turkey: Signed at San Stefano, February 9/ March 3, 1878' (1908) 2 *American Journal of International Law* 387, 396.

'Treaty between Great Britain, Germany, Austria, France, Italy, Russia, and Turkey for the Settlement of Affairs in the East: Signed at Berlin, July 13, 1878' (1908) 2 *American Journal of International Law* 401, 422.

Joint Declaration of France, Great Britain and Russia, 24 May 1915 <http://www.armenian-genocide.org/Affirmation.160/current_category.7/affirmation_detail.html>

Treaty of Versailles, 28 June 1919.

Treaty of Sèvres, 10 August 1920.

Charter of the International Military Tribunal, Annex to the Agreement by the Government of the United Kingdom of Great Britain and Northern Ireland, the Government of the United States of America, the Provisional Government of the French Republic and the Government of the Union of Soviet Socialist Republics for the Prosecution and Punishment of the Major War Criminals of the European Axis, 8 August 1945, 82 United Nations Treaty Series 280.

Statute of the International Court of Justice, 26 June 1945.

United Nations General Assembly, 'The Crime of Genocide (Request from the Delegations for Cuba, India and Panama for the Inclusion of an Additional Item in the Agenda)', 2 November 1946, A/BUR/50.

United Nations General Assembly Resolution 95 (I), 'Affirmation of the Principles of International Law Recognized by the Charter of the Nürnberg Tribunal', 11 December 1946, A/64/Add 1.

United Nations General Assembly Resolution 96 (I), 'The Crime of Genocide', 11 December 1946, A/64/Add 1.

Convention for the Prevention and Punishment of the Crime of Genocide, 9 December 1948, 78 UNTS 277.

Yearbook of the International Law Commission, 1966, Vol. II.

Convention on the Non-Applicability of Statutory Limitations to War Crimes and Crimes against Humanity, 26 November 1968, 754 United Nations Treaty Series 73.

International Convention on the Suppression and Punishment of the Crime of Apartheid, 30 November 1973, 1015 United Nations Treaty Series 243.

United Nations Economic and Social Council, Commission on Human Rights, Sub-Commission on Prevention of Discrimination and Protection of Minorities, 'Study of the Question of the Prevention and Punishment of the Crime of Genocide', 4 July 1978, E/CN.4/Sub.2/416.

Convention against Torture and Other Cruel, Inhuman or Degrading Treatment or Punishment, New York, 10 December 1984, 1465 United Nations Treaty Series 85.

United Nations Economic and Social Council, Commission on Human Rights, Sub-Commission on Prevention of Discrimination and Protection of Minorities, 'Revised and Updated Report on the Question of the Prevention and Punishment of the Crime of Genocide', 2 July 1985, E/CN.4/Sub.2/1985/6.

United Nations Office of Legal Affairs, Treaty Section, Depositary Notification, Convention on the Prevention and Punishment of the Crime of Genocide, Ratification by the United States of America, 29 December 1988, C.N.281.1988. TREATIES-2.

Report of the Secretary General Pursuant to Paragraph 2 of Security Council Resolution 808 (1993), 3 May 1993, S/25704.

Summary Records of the Meetings of the Committee of the Whole, 3rd Meeting of the Committee of the Whole, 17 June 1998, A/CONF.183/C.1/SR.3, in United Nations Diplomatic Conference of Plenipotentiaries on the Establishment of an International Criminal Court, Rome, 15 June–17 July 1998, Volume 2, A/CONF.183/13 (Vol. II).

Rome Statute of the International Criminal Court, 17 July 1998, 2187 United Nations Treaty Series 3.

International Criminal Court, Elements of Crimes, ICC-ASP/1/3(part II-B), 9 September 2002 <https://www.icc-cpi.int/NR/rdonlyres/336923D8-A6AD-40EC-AD7B-45BF9DE73D56/0/ElementsOfCrimesEng.pdf>

Law on the Establishment of the Extraordinary Chambers, with inclusion of amendments as promulgated on 27 October 2004 (NS/RKM/1004/006) <http://www.eccc.gov.kh/sites/default/files/legal-documents/KR_Law_as_amended_27_Oct_2004_Eng.pdf>

Report of the International Commission of Inquiry on Darfur to the United Nations Secretary-General, Pursuant to Security Council Resolution 1564 of 18 September 2004, 25 January 2005, S/2005/60.

United Nations General Assembly Resolution 60/1, '2005 World Summit Outcome', 24 October 2005, A/RES/60/1.

Updated Statute of the International Criminal Tribunal for the former Yugoslavia as of September 2009 <http://www.icty.org/x/file/Legal%20Library/Statute/statute_sept09_en.pdf>

Statute of the International Criminal Tribunal for Rwanda as of 31 January 2010 <http://www.unictr.org/Portals/0/English%5CLegal%5CStatute%5C2010.pdf>

Whitney R. Harris World Law Institute, Washington University School of Law, Crimes Against Humanity Initiative, Proposed International Convention on the Prevention and Punishment of Crimes Against Humanity, August 2010 <https://sites.law.wustl.edu/docs/harris/cah/EnglishTreatyFinal.pdf>

International Law Commission, Report on the Work of its Sixty-fifth Session (6 May to 7 June and 8 July to 9 August 2013), 68 UNGAOR, Supplement No. 10 (A/68/10).

United Nations, Framework of Analysis for Atrocity Crimes. A Tool for Prevention, October 2014 <https://www.un.org/en/genocideprevention/documents/about-us/Doc.3_Framework%20of%20Analysis%20for%20Atrocity%20Crimes_EN.pdf>

UNESCO, Statement on Hagia Sophia, Istanbul, 10 July 2020 <https://en.unesco.org/news/unesco-statement-hagia-sophia-istanbul>

United Nations Human Rights Office of the High Commissioner, Global Action Against Mass Atrocity Crimes Platform for Prevention, High Level Dialogue on Atrocity Prevention, Statement by Michelle Bachelet, UN High Commissioner for Human Rights, 16 November 2020 <https://www.ohchr.org/EN/NewsEvents/Pages/DisplayNews.aspx?NewsID=26507&LangID=E>

Permanent Mission of the Russian Federation to the United Nations, Statement by Permanent Representative Vassily Nebenzia at the Eleventh Emergency Special Session of the General Assembly, 28 February 2022 <https://russiaun.ru/en/news/ga_ess2802>

Table of cases

International Court of Justice, *Reservations to the Convention on the Prevention and Punishment of the Crime of Genocide*, Advisory Opinion of 28 May 1951 (1951) ICJ Reports 15.

International Court of Justice, *Barcelona Traction, Light and Power Company, Limited (New Application: 1962)* (Belgium *v.* Spain), Judgement of 5 February 1970 (1970) ICJ Reports 3.

ICTY, *Prosecutor v. Duško Tadić aka 'Dule'*, Judgement of 7 May 1997, Case No. IT-94-1-T.

ICTY, *Prosecutor v. Duško Tadić aka 'Dule'*, Decision on the Defence Motion for Interlocutory Appeal on Jurisdiction of 2 October 1995, Case No. IT-94-1-AR72.

ICTR, *Prosecutor v. Jean-Paul Akayesu*, Judgement of 2 September 1998, Case No. ICTR-96-4-T.

ICTR, *Prosecutor v. Jean Kambanda*, Judgement and Sentence of 4 September 1998, Case No. ICTR-97-23-S.

ICTR, *Prosecutor v. Clément Kayishema and Obed Ruzindana*, Judgement of 21 May 1999, Case No. ICTR-95-1.

ICTR, *Prosecutor v. Clément Kayishema and Obed Ruzindana*, Separate and Dissenting Opinion of Judge Tafazzal Hossain Khan Regarding the Verdicts Under the Charges of Crimes Against Humanity/Murder and Crimes Against Humanity/Extermination of 21 May 1999, Case No. ICTR-95-1-T.

ICTR, *Prosecutor v. Georges Anderson Nderubumwe Rutaganda*, Judgement of 6 December 1999, Case No. ICTR-96-3-T.

ICTY, *Prosecutor v. Tihomir Blaškić*, Judgement, Case No. IT-95-14-T, Judgement of 3 March 2000.

International Court of Justice, *Armed Activities on the Territory of the Congo (New Application: 2002)* (Democratic Republic of the Congo *v.* Rwanda), Judgement of 3 February 2006 (Jurisdiction and Admissibility) (2006) ICJ Reports 6.

International Court of Justice, *Application of the Convention on the Prevention and Punishment of the Crime of Genocide* (Bosnia and Herzegovina *v.* Serbia and Montenegro), Judgement of 26 February 2007 (2007) ICJ Reports 43.

International Criminal Court, Pre-Trial Chamber I, Warrant of Arrest for Omar Hassan Ahmad al-Bashir of 4 March 2009, ICC-02/05-01/09-1.

German Constitutional Court, Decision of 20 February 2009, 1 BvR 2266/04, 1 BvR 2620/05.

International Court of Justice, *Allegations of Genocide under the Convention on the Prevention and Punishment of the Crime of Genocid*e (Ukraine *v.* Russian Federation), Application for the Institution of Proceedings of 26 February 2022.

International Court of Justice, *Allegations of Genocide under the Convention on the Prevention and Punishment of the Crime of Genocid*e (Ukraine *v.* Russian Federation), Declaration of Judge Bennouna to the Order of 16 March 2022.

Bibliography

Adamets S and others, 'The Great Famine: Population Losses in Ukraine' in Lubomyr Y Luciuk (ed), *Holodomor: Reflections on the Great Famine of 1932–1933 in Soviet Ukraine* (Kashtan Press 2008).

Adami M, 'Germany Recognizes Herero and Nama Genocide' *Politico* (28 May 2021) <https://www.politico.eu/article/germany-recognizes-colonial-herero-nama-genocide/>

Akçam T, 'The Genocide of the Armenians and the Silence of the Turks' in Levon Chorbajian and George Shirinian (eds), *Studies in Comparative Genocide* (Palgrave Macmillan/St Martin's Press 1999).

Akçam T, *The Young Turks' Crime Against Humanity. The Armenian Genocide and Ethnic Cleansing in the Ottoman Empire* (Princeton University Press 2012).

Akhavan P, 'Proliferation of Terminology and the Illusion of Progress' (2007) 2 *Genocide Studies and Prevention: An International Journal* 73.

Akhavan P, 'Preventing Genocide: Measuring Success by What Does Not Happen' (2011) 22 *Criminal Law Forum* 1.

Akhavan P, 'The Universal Repression of Crimes Against Humanity before National Jurisdictions: The Need for a Treaty-Based Obligation to Prosecute' in Leila Nadya Sadat (ed), *Forging a Convention for Crimes Against Humanity* (Cambridge University Press 2011).

Akhavan P, 'Cultural Genocide: Legal Label of Mourning Metaphor?' (2016) 61 *McGill Law Journal / Revue de droit de McGill* 243.

Alvarez A, *Native America and the Question of Genocide* (Rowman & Littlefield 2014).

American Society of International Law, 'Signature Topics – Atrocity Prevention' <https://www.asil.org/related-terms-vocabulary/signature-topics-atrocity-prevention>

Andriewsky O, 'Towards a Decentred History: The Study of the Holodomor and Ukrainian Historiography' in Andrij Makuch and Frank E Sysyn (eds), *Contextualising the Holodomor. The Impact of Thirty Years of Ukrainian Famine Studies* (Canadian Institute of Ukrainian Studies Press 2015).

Apter DE, 'Political Violence in Analytical Perspective' in David E Apter (ed), *The Legitimization of Violence* (Macmillan 1997).

Arendt H, *The Origins of Totalitarianism* (Harcourt, Brace and Company 1951).

Argentieri F, 'Holodomor, 75 Years On' in Lubomyr Y Luciuk (ed), *Holodomor: Reflections on the Great Famine of 1932–1933 in Soviet Ukraine* (Kashtan Press 2008).

Ascherson N, *The King Incorporated. Leopold the Second and the Congo* (Granta Books 1999).

Ashirova A, *Stalinismus und Stalin-Kult in Zentralasien. Turkmenistan 1924–1953* (ibidem-Verlag 2009).

Asuncion AC, 'Pulling the Stops on Genocide: The State or the Individual?' (2009) 20 *European Journal of International Law* 1195.

Auswärtiges Amt, 'Außenminister Maas zum Abschluss der Verhandlungen mit Namibia' (28 May 2021) <https://www.auswaertiges-amt.de/de/newsroom/-/2463396>

Balakian P, 'Raphael Lemkin, Cultural Destruction, and the Armenian Genocide' (2013) 27 *Holocaust and Genocide Studies* 57.

Balint J, 'The Ottoman State Special Military Tribunal for the Genocide of the Armenians: "Doing Government Business"' in Kevin Jon Heller and Gerry Simpson (eds), *The Hidden Histories of War Crimes Trials* (Oxford University Press 2013).

Bardakjian KB, *Hitler and the Armenian Genocide* (The Zoryan Institute 1985).

Barkan E, 'Genocides of Indigenous Peoples. Rhetoric of Human Rights' in Robert Gellately and Ben Kiernan (eds), *The Specter of Genocide. Mass Murder in Historical Perspective* (Cambridge University Press 2003).

Barrett JQ, 'Raphael Lemkin and "Genocide" at Nuremberg, 1945–1946' in Eckart Conze and Christoph Safferling (eds), *The Genocide Convention Sixty Years After its Adoption* (TMC Asser Press 2010).

Barth B, *Genozid. Völkermord Im 20. Jahrhundert. Geschichte, Theorien, Kontroversen* (Beck 2006).

Bartov O, 'Seeking the Roots of Modern Genocide. On the Macro- and Microhistory of Mass Murder' in Robert Gellately and Ben Kiernan (eds), *The Specter of Genocide. Mass Murder in Historical Perspective* (Cambridge University Press 2003).

Bassiouni MC, 'Revisiting the Architecture of Crimes Against Humanity. Almost a Century in the Making, with Gaps and Ambiguities Remaining – the Need for a Specialized Convention' in Leila Nadya Sadat (ed), *Forging a Convention for Crimes Against Humanity* (Cambridge University Press 2011).

Bauer Y, 'Comparison of Genocides' in Levon Chorbajian and George Shirinian (eds), *Studies in Comparative Genocide* (Palgrave Macmillan/St Martin's Press 1999).

Bauman Z, *Modernity and the Holocaust* (Polity Press 1989).

Bazyler M, *Holocaust, Genocide, and the Law. A Quest for Justice in a Post-Holocaust World* (Oxford University Press 2016).

Beachler D, *The Genocide Debate. Politicians, Academics, and Victims* (Palgrave Macmillan 2011).

Beham MP, 'Norman M. Naimark, Stalin's Genocides (Princeton University Press, 2010)' (2011) 16 *Austrian Review of International and European Law* 539.

Beham MP, 'Bardo Fassbender and Anne Peters (Eds.), Oxford Handbook of the History of International Law (Oxford University Press 2012)' (2013) 18 *Austrian Review of International and European Law* 392.

Beham MP, '"Borrowed" Concepts: The Pitfalls of "Atrocity Labelling" in Contemporary Historiography' in Markus P Beham and Marija Wakounig (eds), *Transgressing Boundaries: Humanities in Flux* (Lit Verlag 2013).

Beham MP, 'Genocide and Collective Memory in International Relations' in Nicolas Maslowski (ed), *Collective Memory and International Relations. Conference Proceedings* (TROAS 2013).

Beham MP, 'Genocide and Crimes Against Humanity: Siamese Twins or Separated at Birth?' in Markus P Beham and Marija Wakounig (eds), *Mind and Memory in Discourse: Critical Concepts and Constructions* (Lit Verlag 2014).

Beham MP, *State Interest and the Sources of International Law. Doctrine, Morality, and Non-Treaty Law* (Routledge 2018).

Beham MP, 'The 1948 Genocide Convention: Origins, Impact, Legacy' (2018) 23 *Austrian Review of International and European Law* 85.

Benvenuto J, Hinton AL and Woolford A (eds), *Colonial Genocide in Indigenous North America* (Duke University Press 2014).

Beres LR, 'Reason and Realpolitik: International Law and the Prevention of Genocide' in Israel W Charny (ed), *Toward the Understanding and Prevention of Genocide. Proceedings of the International Conference on the Holocaust and Genocide* (Westview Press 1984).

Bettwy DS, 'The Genocide Convention and Unprotected Groups: Is the Scope of Protection Expanding under Customary International Law?' (2011) 2 *Notre Dame Journal of International & Comparative Law* 167.

Bilinsky Y, 'Was the Ukrainian Famine of 1932–1933 Genocide?' (1999) 1 *Journal of Genocide Research* 147.

Bley H, *Kolonialherrschaft und Sozialstruktur in Deutsch-Südwestafrika 1894–1914* (Leibniz-Verlag 1968).

Bloxham D, 'Determinants of the Armenian Genocide' in Richard G Hovannisian (ed), *Looking Backward, Moving Forward. Confronting the Armenian Genocide* (Transaction Publishers 2003).

Bloxham D, 'The Armenian Genocide of 1915–1916: Cumulative Radicalization and the Development of a Destruction Policy' (2003) 181 *Past & Present* 141.

Bloxham D, *The Great Game of Genocide. Imperialism, Nationalism, and the Destruction of the Ottoman Armenians* (Oxford University Press 2005).

Bloxham D, 'Internal Colonization, Inter-Imperial Conflict and the Armenian Genocide' in A Dirk Moses (ed), *Empire, Colony Genocide. Conquest, Occupation, and Subaltern Resistance in World History* (Berghahn Books 2008).

Bloxham D and Göçek FM, 'The Armenian Genocide' in Dan Stone (ed), *The Historiography of Genocide* (Palgrave Macmillan 2008).

Bloxham D and Moses AD, 'Editor's Introduction: Changing Themes in the Study of Genocide' in Donald Bloxham and A Dirk Moses (eds), *The Oxford Handbook of Genocide Studies* (Oxford University Press 2010).

Bloxham D and Moses AD (eds), *The Oxford Handbook of Genocide Studies* (Oxford University Press 2010).

Boeck BJ, 'Complicating the National Interpretation of the Famine: Reexamining the Case of Kuban' in Andrea Graziosi, Lubomyr A Hajda and Halyna Hryn (eds), *After the Holodomor. The Enduring Impact of the Great Famine on Ukraine* (Harvard University Press 2013).

Böttcher K and others, *Geflügelte Worte. Zitate, Sentenzen und Begriffe in ihrem geschichtlichen Zusammenhang* (VEB Bibliographisches Institut Leipzig 1981).

Brannigan A, *Beyond the Banality of Evil: Criminology and Genocide* (Oxford University Press 2013).

Brass PR, 'Introduction: Discourses of Ethnicity, Communialism, and Violence' in Paul R Brass (ed), *Riots and Pogroms* (Macmillan 1996).

Bridgman JM, *The Revolt of the Hereros* (University of California Press 1981).

Brown Scott J (ed), *The Hague Conventions and Declarations of 1899 and 1907, Accompanied by Tables of Signatures, Ratifications and Adhesions of the Various Powers, and Texts of Reservations* (Oxford University Press 1915).

Bryce J, *'The Armenian Massacres', Arnold J. Toynbee, Armenian Atrocities. The Murder of a Nation* (Hodder & Stoughton 1915).

Bublitz H, *Diskurs* (Transcript 2003).

Busse D, *Historische Semantik. Analyse eines Programms* (Klett-Cotta 1987).

Busse D, 'Architekturen des Wissens. Zum Verhältnis von Semantik und Epistemologie' in Ernst Müller (ed), *Begriffsgeschichte im Umbruch?* (Felix Meiner Verlag 2004).

Busse D, 'Juristisches Wissen als institutionelle Begriffsstrukturen. Analyseansätze aus Kognitionswissenschaften und wissensanalytischer Semantik (am Beispiel von Gesetzes-Begriffen)' (2015) 101 *Archiv für Rechts- und Sozialphilosophie* 354.

'Campaign Angers Holocaust Survivors' *BBC News* (1 March 2003) <http://news.bbc.co.uk/2/hi/europe/2810031.stm>

Carmichael C, *Genocide before the Holocaust* (Yale University Press 2009).

Cassese A, 'The Policy Element in Genocide: When Is It Required by International Rules?' in Eckart Conze and Christoph Safferling (eds), *The Genocide Convention Sixty Years After its Adoption* (TMC Asser Press 2010).

Cayci S, 'Armenian Genocide Claims: A Contextual Version of the 1915 Incidents' in Ralph Henham and Paul Behrens (eds), *The Criminal Law of Genocide. International, Comparative and Contextual Aspects* (Ashgate 2007).

Chalk F and Jonassohn K, 'Conceptualizations of Genocide and Ethnocide' in Bohdan Krawchenko and Roman Serbyn (eds), *Famine in Ukraine 1932–1933* (University of Toronto Press 1986).

Chalk F and Jonassohn K, 'The History and Sociology of Genocidal Killings' in Israel W Charny (ed), *Genocide. A Critical Bibliographical Review* (Facts on File Publications 1988).

Chalk F and Jonassohn K, *The History and Sociology of Genocide. Analyses and Case Studies* (Yale University Press 1990).

Charny I, 'Intervention and Prevention of Genocide' in Israel Charny (ed), *Genocide. A Critical Bibliographical Review* (Facts on File Publications 1988).

Charny IW, 'Editor's Preface' in Israel W Charny (ed), *Toward the Understanding and Prevention of Genocide. Proceedings of the International Conference on the Holocaust and Genocide* (Westview Press 1984).

Charny IW, 'Introduction' in Israel W Charny (ed), *Genocide. A Critical Bibliographical Review* (Facts on File Publications 1988).

Charny IW, 'The Study of Genocide' in Israel W Charny (ed), *Genocide. A Critical Bibliographical Review* (Facts on File Publications 1988).

Charny IW, 'The Psychology of Denial of Known Genocides' in Israel W Charny (ed), *Genocide. A Critical Bibliographical Review. Volume Two* (Facts on File Publications 1991).

Chorbajian L, 'Introduction' in Levon Chorbajian and George Shirinian (eds), *Studies in Comparative Genocide* (Palgrave Macmillan/St Martin's Press 1999).

Clark RS, 'History of Efforts to Codify Crimes Against Humanity. From the Charter of Nuremberg to the Statute of Rome' in Leila Nadya Sadat (ed), *Forging a Convention for Crimes Against Humanity* (Cambridge University Press 2011).

Clavero B, *Genocide or Ethnocide 1933–2007. How to Make, Unmake, and Remake Law With Words* (Giuffrè Editore 2008).

Cocker M, *Rivers of Blood, Rivers of Gold* (Pimlico 1999).

Comerford V, Janssen L and Noack C, 'Introduction' in Vincent Comerford, Lindsay Janssen and Christian Noack (eds), *Holodomor and Gorta Mór. Histories, Memories and Representations of Famine in Ukraine and Ireland* (Anthem Press 2012).

Commission on the Ukrainian Famine, *Investigation of the Ukrainian Famine 1932–1933. Report to Congress* (United States Government Printing Office 1988).

Conquest R, *The Harvest of Sorrow. Soviet Collectivization and the Terror-Famine* (Oxford University Press 1986).

Conrad J, *Heart of Darkness* (Blackwood's Magazine 1899).

Conze E and Safferling C (eds), *The Genocide Convention Sixty Years After Its Adoption* (TMC Asser Press 2010).

Conze E and Safferling C, 'The Genocide Convention Sixty Years After Its Adoption' in Eckart Conze and Christoph Safferling (eds), *The Genocide Convention Sixty Years After its Adoption* (TMC Asser Press 2010).

Cooper J, *Raphael Lemkin and the Struggle for the Genocide Convention* (Palgrave Macmillan 2015).

Cornevin R, 'The Germans in Africa Before 1918' in Peter Duignan and Lewis H Gann (eds), *Colonialism in Africa 1870–1960. Volume 1. The History and Politics of Colonialism 1870–1914* (Cambridge University Press 1969).

Curthoys A and Docker J, 'Defining Genocide' in Dan Stone (ed), *The Historiography of Genocide* (Palgrave Macmillan 2008).

Dadrian VN, 'A Typology of Genocide' (1975) 5 *International Review of Modern Sociology* 201.

Dadrian VN, 'Documentation of the Armenian Genocide in Turkish Sources' in Israel W Charny (ed), *Genocide. A Critical Bibliographical Review. Volume Two* (Facts on File Publications 1991).

Dadrian VN, 'The Convergent Roles of the State and a Governmental Party in the Armenian Genocide' in Levon Chorbajian and George Shirinian (eds), *Studies in Comparative Genocide* (Palgrave Macmillan/St Martin's Press 1999).

Dadrian VN, 'Stalin and the Soviet Famine of 1932–33: A Reply to Ellman' (2006) 58 *Europe-Asia Studies* 625.

Dalrymple DG, 'Foreword' in Walter Dushnyck (ed), *50 Years Ago: The Famine Holocaust in Ukraine. Terror and Human Misery as Instruments of Soviet Russian Imperialism* (World Congress of Free Ukrainians 1983).

Das Bundesarchiv, 'Der Krieg Gegen Die Herero 1904' <https://www.bundesarchiv.de/DE/Content/Virtuelle-Ausstellungen/Der-Krieg-Gegen-Die-Herero-1904/der-krieg-gegen-die-herero-1904.html>

Davies RW and Wheatcroft SG, *The Years of Hunger: Soviet Agriculture 1931–1933* (Palgrave Macmillan 2004).

de Vries GM, 'Genocide: An Agenda for Action' in Richard G Hovannisian (ed), *Looking Backward, Moving Forward. Confronting the Armenian Genocide* (Transaction Publishers 2003).

Dekmejian RH, 'Determinants of Genocide: Armenians and Jews as Case Studies' in Richard G Hovannisian (ed), *The Armenian Genocide in Perspective* (Transaction Books 1986).

Depelchin J, *From the Congo Free State to Zaire: How Belgium Privatized the Economy. A History of Belgian Stock Companies in Congo-Zaïre from 1885 to 1974* (Codesria Book Series 1992).

Dietsch J, 'Holodomor: The 1932–1933 Ukrainian Famine-Genocide: Argumentum Ex Silentio' in Lubomyr Y Luciuk (ed), *Holodomor: Reflections on the Great Famine of 1932–1933 in Soviet Ukraine* (Kashtan Press 2008).

Dolot M, *Execution by Hunger. The Hidden Holocaust* (WW Norton & Company 1985).

Drechsler H, *Südwestafrika unter Deutscher Kolonialherrschaft. Der Kampf der Herero und Nama gegen den deutschen Imperialismus* (2nd edn, Akademie Verlag 1984).

Drost PN, *The Crime of State. Penal Protection for Fundamental Freedoms of Persons and Peoples. Book I. Humanicide. International Governmental Crime Against Individual Human Rights* (AW Sythoff 1959).

Drost PN, *The Crime of State. Penal Protection for Fundamental Freedoms of Persons and Peoples. Book II. Genocide. United Nations Legislation on International Criminal Law* (AW Sythoff 1959).

Duignan P and Gann LH, 'Introduction' in Peter Duignan and Lewis H Gann (eds), *Colonialism in Africa 1870–1960. Volume 1. The History and Politics of Colonialism 1870–1914* (Cambridge University Press 1969).

Dülffer J, 'The United Nations and the Origins of the Genocide Convention 1946–1948' in Eckart Conze and Christoph Safferling (eds), *The Genocide Convention Sixty Years After its Adoption* (TMC Asser Press 2010).

Dumoulin M, *Léopold II un Roi Génocidaire?* (Académie Royale de Belgique 2005).

Dunant H, *Un Souvenir de Solférino* (Imprimerie Jules-Guillaume Fick 1862).

Durkheim É, *Les Règles de La Méthode Sociologique* (Ancienne Librairie Germer Baillière et Cie 1895).

Dushnyck W, *50 Years Ago: The Famine Holocaust in Ukraine. Terror and Human Misery as Instruments of Soviet Russian Imperialism* (World Congress of Free Ukrainians 1983).

Eckert A, 'Namibia - ein deutscher Sonderweg in Afrika? Anmerkungen zur internationalen Diskussion' in Joachim Zeller and Jürgen Zimmerer (eds), *Völkermord in Deutsch-Südwestafrika. Der Kolonialkrieg (1904–1908) in Namibia und seine Folgen* (Ch Links 2003).

Eide A, 'Famine' in Dinah L Shelton (ed), *Encyclopedia of Genocide and Crimes Against Humanity. Vol. 1 [A-H]* (Thomson Gale 2005).

Ellman M, 'Stalin and the Soviet Famine of 1932–33 Revisited' (2007) 59 *Europe-Asia Studies* 663.

El-Tayeb F, *Schwarze Deutsche. Der Diskurs um 'Rasse' und nationale Identität 1890–1933* (Campus 2001).

Emerson B, *Leopold II of the Belgians. King of Colonialism* (Weidenfeld and Nicolson 1979).

Erichsen CW and Olusoga D, *The Kaiser's Holocaust. Germany's Forgotten Genocide and the Colonial Roots of Nazism* (Faber and Faber 2010).

Erkoyun E and Gumrukcu T, 'Erdogan Urges Biden to Reverse "wrong Step" on Armenian Declaration' *Reuters* (26 April 2021) <https://www.reuters.com/world/us/erdogan-calls-biden-reverse-wrong-step-armenian-declaration-2021-04-26/>

Esterhuyse JH, *South West Africa 1880–1894. The Establishment of German Authority in South West Africa* (C Struik 1968).

Evans G, 'Crimes Against Humanity and the Responsibility to Protect' in Leila Nadya Sadat (ed), *Forging a Convention for Crimes Against Humanity* (Cambridge University Press 2011).

Ewans M, *European Atrocity, African Catastrophe. Leopold II, the Congo Free State and Its Aftermath* (Routledge Curzon 2002).

Fein H, *Accounting for Genocide. National Responses and Jewish Victimization During the Holocaust* (Free Press 1979).

Fein H, 'Scenarios of Genocide: Models of Genocide and Critical Responses' in Israel W Charny (ed), *Toward the Understanding and Prevention of Genocide. Proceedings of the International Conference on the Holocaust and Genocide* (Westview Press 1984).

Fein H, 'Introduction' in Helen Fein (ed), *Genocide Watch* (Yale University Press 1992).

Fein H, 'Definition and Discontent: Labelling, Detecting, and Explaining Genocide in the Twentieth Century' in Stig Förster and Gerhard Hirschfeld (eds), *Genozid in der modernen Geschichte* (Lit Verlag 1999).

Ferguson N, *The War of the World. History's Age of Hatred* (Penguin Books 2007).

First R, *South West Africa* (Penguin Books 1963).

Förster S and Hirschfeld G, 'Einleitung' in Stig Förster and Gerhard Hirschfeld (eds), *Genozid in der modernen Geschichte* (Lit Verlag 1999).

Foucault M, *L'Archéologie Du Savoir* (Éditions Gallimard 1969).

Gellately R and Kiernan B, 'Investigating Genocide' in Robert Gellately and Ben Kiernan (eds), *The Specter of Genocide. Mass Murder in Historical Perspective* (Cambridge University Press 2003).

Gellately R and Kiernan B, 'The Study of Mass Murder and Genocide' in Robert Gellately and Ben Kiernan (eds), *The Specter of Genocide. Mass Murder in Historical Perspective* (Cambridge University Press 2003).

'Genocide' *Washington Post* (3 December 1944) 4.

Genocide Prevention Task Force, *Preventing Genocide. A Blueprint for U.S. Policymakers* (United States Holocaust Memorial Museum, The American Academy of Diplomacy, and the Endowment of the United States Institute of Peace 2008).

Gerlach C, 'Extremely Violent Societies. An Alternative to the Concept of Genocide' in A Dirk Moses (ed), *Genocide. Critical Concepts in Historical Studies. Volume I. The Discipline of Genocide Studies* (Routledge 2010).

Gerson OH, 'Wahrnehmungslenkende Funktion der Sprache im Strafprozess - Verfahrensbalance durch kommunikative Autonomie' in Günter Köhnken and Rüdiger Deckers (eds), *Die Erhebung und Bewertung von Zeugenaussagen im Strafprozess. Juristische, aussagepsychologische und psychiatrische Aspekte. 3. Band* (Berliner Wissenschafts-Verlag 2018).

Gessler M and Segesser DM, 'Raphael Lemkin and the International Debate on the Punishment of War Crimes (1919–1948)' in A Dirk Moses (ed), *Genocide. Critical Concepts in Historical Studies. Volume I. The Discipline of Genocide Studies* (Routledge 2010).

Gewald J-B, *Herero Heroes. A Socio-Political History of the Herero of Namibia, 1890–1923* (Boydell & Brewer 1999).

Gilbert M, 'Twentieth Century Genocides' in Jay Winter (ed), *America and the Armenian Genocide of 1915* (Cambridge University Press 2003).

Goldblatt I, *History of South West Africa. From the Beginning of the Nineteenth Century* (Juta & Company Limited 1971).

Goltz G, 'Das Jahr 2005: ein Meilenstein in der Debatte in der Türkei über das Schicksal der Armenier im Osmanischen Reich 1915/1916' in Hans-Lukas Kieser and Elmar Plozza (eds), *Der Völkermord an den Armeniern, die Türkei und Europa / The Armenian Genocide, Turkey and Europe* (Chronos 2006).

Gordon GS, 'The Trial of Peter von Hagenbach: Reconciling History, Historiography and International Criminal Law' in Kevin Jon Heller and Gerry Simpson (eds), *The Hidden Histories of War Crimes Trials* (Oxford University Press 2013).

Graziosi A, *The Great Soviet Peasant War. Bolsheviks and Peasants, 1917–1933* (Harvard University Press 1996).

Graziosi A, 'Les Famines Soviétiques de 1931–1933 et Le Holodomor Ukrainien. Une Nouvelle Interprétation Est-Elle Possible et Quelles En Seraient Les Conséquences?' (2005) 46 *Cahiers du Monde Russe* 453.

Graziosi A, 'The Soviet 1931–1933 Famines and the Ukrainian Holodomor: Is a New Interpretation Possible, and What Would Its Consequences Be?' in Halyna Hryn (ed), *Hunger by Design. The Great Ukrainian Famine and Its Soviet Context* (Harvard University Press 2008).

Graziosi A, 'Why and in What Sense Was the Holodomor a Genocide?' in Lubomyr Y Luciuk (ed), *Holodomor: Reflections on the Great Famine of 1932–1933 in Soviet Ukraine* (Kashtan Press 2008).

Graziosi A, 'The Impact of Holodomor Studies on the Understanding of the USSR' in Andrij Makuch and Frank E Sysyn (eds), *Contextualising the Holodomor.*

The Impact of Thirty Years of Ukrainian Famine Studies (Canadian Institute of Ukrainian Studies Press 2015).

Graziosi A, Hajda LA and Hryn H, 'Introduction' in Andrea Graziosi, Lubomyr A Hajda and Halyna Hryn (eds), *After the Holodomor. The Enduring Impact of the Great Famine on Ukraine* (Harvard University Press 2013).

Guroian V, 'Collective Responsibility and Official Excuse Making: The Case of the Turkish Genocide of the Armenians' in Richard G Hovannisian (ed), *The Armenian Genocide in Perspective* (Transaction Books 1986).

Hajda L, 'Foreword' in Halyna Hryn (ed), *Hunger by Design. The Great Ukrainian Famine and Its Soviet Context* (Harvard University Press 2008).

Hankel G, *The Leipzig Trials: German War Crimes and Their Legal Consequences after World War I* (Republic of Letters 2014).

Harff B, 'Recognizing Genocides and Politicides' in Helen Fein (ed), *Genocide Watch* (Yale University Press 1992).

Harff B, 'No Lessons Learned from the Holocaust? Assessing Risks of Genocide and Political Mass Murder since 1955' (2003) 97 *American Political Science Review* 57.

Hasian M, *Restorative Justice, Humanitarian Rhetorics, and Public Memories of Colonial Camp Cultures* (Palgrave Macmillan 2014).

Heine M, 'Völkermord – Eine deutsche Erfindung' *Welt* (22 April 2015) <https://www.welt.de/kultur/article139894880/Voelkermord-eine-deutsche-Erfindung.html>

Hesemann M, *Völkermord an den Armeniern. Mit unveröffentlichten Dokumenten aus dem Geheimarchiv des Vatikans über das größte Verbrechen des Ersten Weltkriegs* (HERBiG 2015).

Higgins R, 'The Identity of International Law' in Bin Cheng (ed), *International Law: Teaching and Practice* (Stevens & Sons 1982).

Hinton AL, 'Introduction. Genocide and Anthropology' in Alexander Laban Hinton (ed), *Genocide. An Anthropological Reader* (Blackwell 2002).

Hitchcock RK and Totten S, 'Introduction. The Genocide of Indigenous Peoples' in Robert K Hitchcock and Samuel Totten (eds), *Genocide of Indigenous Peoples. A Critical Bibliographic Review* (Transaction Publishers 2011).

Hochschild A, *Les Fantômes du Roi Léopold. Un Holocauste Oublié* (Belfond 1998).

Hochschild A, *King Leopold's Ghost. A Story of Greed, Terror and Heroism in Colonial Africa* (Pan Books 2012).

Hofmann T, 'Christenverfolgung in Armenien (1894–1941). Die Synergie von nationalistischem Völkermord und stalinistischer Religionsunterdrückung' in Georg Plasger and Heinz-Günther Stobbe (eds), *Gewalt Gegen Christen. Formen, Gründe, Hintergründe* (Evangelische Verlagsanstalt 2014).

Hoffmann T, 'The Crime of Genocide in Its (Nearly) Infinite Domestic Variety' in Marco Odello and Piotr Łubiński (eds), *The Concept of Genocide in International Criminal Law - Developments after Lemkin* (Routledge 2020).

Horowitz IL, 'Science, Modernity and Authorized Terror: Reconsidering the Genocidal State' in Levon Chorbajian and George Shirinian (eds), *Studies in Comparative Genocide* (Palgrave Macmillan/St Martin's Press 1999).

Horowitz IL, *Taking Lives. Genocide and State Power* (5th edn, Transaction Publishers 2002).

Housepian Dobkin M, 'What Genocide? What Holocaust? News from Turkey, 1915–1923. A Case Study' in Richard G Hovannisian (ed), *The Armenian Genocide in Perspective* (Transaction Books 1986).

Houwink ten Cate J and van der Wilt H, 'Foreword' in Harmen G van der Wilt and others (eds), *The Genocide Convention: The Legacy of 60 Years* (Martinus Nijhoff 2012).

Hovanissian A, 'Turkey: A Cultural Genocide' in Levon Chorbajian and George Shirinian (eds), *Studies in Comparative Genocide* (Palgrave Macmillan/St Martin's Press 1999).

Hovannisian RG, *Armenia on the Road to Independence 1918* (University of California Press 1967).

Hovannisian RG, 'Genocide and Denial: The Armenian Case' in Israel W Charny (ed), *Toward the Understanding and Prevention of Genocide. Proceedings of the International Conference on the Holocaust and Genocide* (Westview Press 1984).

Hovannisian RG, 'Foreword' in Richard G Hovannisian (ed), *The Armenian Genocide in Perspective* (Transaction Books 1986).

Hovannisian RG, 'The Armenian Genocide and Patterns of Denial' in Richard G Hovannisian (ed), *The Armenian Genocide in Perspective* (Transaction Books 1986).

Hovannisian RG, 'The Historical Dimensions of the Armenian Question, 1878–1923' in Richard G Hovannisian (ed), *The Armenian Genocide in Perspective* (Transaction Books 1986).

Hovannisian RG, 'The Armenian Genocide' in Israel W Charny (ed), *Genocide. A Critical Bibliographical Review* (Facts on File Publications 1988).

Hryshko W, *The Ukrainian Holocaust of 1933* (Bahriany Foundation 1983).

Hull IV, 'Military Culture and the Production of "Final Solutions" in the Colonies' in Robert Gellately and Ben Kiernan (eds), *The Specter of Genocide. Mass Murder in Historical Perspective* (Cambridge University Press 2003).

Hunczak T and Serbyn R (eds), *Famine in Ukraine, 1932–1933: Genocide by Other Means* (Shevchenko Scientific Society 2007).

Huttenbach HR, 'The Psychology and Politics of Genocide Denial: A Comparison of Four Case Studies' in Levon Chorbajian and George Shirinian (eds), *Studies in Comparative Genocide* (Palgrave Macmillan/St Martin's Press 1999).

Irvin-Erickson D, *Raphaël Lemkin and the Concept of Genocide* (University of Pennsylvania Press 2017).

Irvin-Erickson D, Hinton AL and La Pointe T, 'Introduction' in Douglas Irvin-Erickson, Alexander Laban Hinton and Thomas La Pointe (eds), *Hidden Genocides. Power, Knowledge, Memory* (Rutgers University Press 2014).

'Israel Furious as Poland's President Signs Bill to Limit Property Claims' *Reuters* (14 August 2021) <https://www.reuters.com/world/europe/polands-president-signs-bill-limit-ww2-property-restitution-claims-2021-08-14/>

Jabri V, *Discourses on Violence. Conflict Analysis Reconsidered* (Manchester University Press 1996).

Jackson J, *The Thief at the End of the World. Rubber, Power, and the Seeds of Empire* (Viking 2008).

Jacobs S, 'Raphael Lemkin and the Holodomor: Was It Genocide?' in Lubomyr Y Luciuk (ed), *Holodomor: Reflections on the Great Famine of 1932–1933 in Soviet Ukraine* (Kashtan Press 2008).

Jäger S, *Kritische Diskursanalyse. Eine Einführung* (6th edn, UNRAST-Verlag 2012).

Jansen JC and Osterhammel J, *Kolonialismus. Geschichte, Formen, Folgen* (7th edn, CH Beck 2012).

Jobst K, *Geschichte Der Ukraine* (2nd edn, Reclam 2015).

Jobst KS, 'Der Umgang mit dem Erbe der Sowjetunion in der Ukraine – Integrative und desintegrative Maßnahmen der Regierung Kučma' in Andreas Körber (ed), *Interkulturelles Geschichtslernen. Geschichtsunterricht unter den Bedingungen von Einwanderung und Globalisierung. Konzeptionelle Überlegungen und praktische Ansätze* (Waxmann 2001).

Jokic A, 'Genocidalism' (2004) 8 *The Journal of Ethics* 251.

Jonassohn K, 'What Is Genocide?' in Helen Fein (ed), *Genocide Watch* (Yale University Press 1992).

Jones A, *Crimes Against Humanity: A Beginner's Guide* (Oneworld 2008).

Jones A, *Genocide. A Comprehensive Introduction* (3rd edn, Routledge 2017).

Kader D, 'Progress and Limitations in Basic Genocide Law' in Israel W Charny (ed), *Genocide. A Critical Bibliographical Review. Volume Two* (Facts on File Publications 1991).

Kaiser H, 'Genocide at the Twilight of the Ottoman Empire' in Donald Bloxham and A Dirk Moses (eds), *The Oxford Handbook of Genocide Studies* (Oxford University Press 2010).

Kasianov H, 'Holodomor and the Politics of Memory in Ukraine After Independence' in Vincent Comerford, Lindsay Janssen and Christian Noack (eds), *Holodomor and Gorta Mór. Histories, Memories and Representations of Famine in Ukraine and Ireland* (Anthem Press 2012).

Kaul H-P, 'The International Criminal Court and the Crime of Genocide' in Eckart Conze and Christoph Safferling (eds), *The Genocide Convention Sixty Years After its Adoption* (TMC Asser Press 2010).

Kelly MJ, 'Genocide - The Power of a Label' (2007) 40 *Case Western Reserve Journal of International Law* 147.

Kiernan B, 'Genocide and "Ethnic Cleansing"' in Stig Förster and Gerhard Hirschfeld (eds), *Genozid in der modernen Geschichte* (Lit Verlag 1999).

Kiernan B, 'Twentieth-Century Genocides. Underlying Ideological Themes from Armenia to East Timor' in Robert Gellately and Ben Kiernan (eds), *The Specter of Genocide. Mass Murder in Historical Perspective* (Cambridge University Press 2003).

Kiernan B, *Blood and Soil. A World History of Genocide and Extermination from Sparta to Darfur* (Yale University Press 2007).

Kieser H-L, 'Einleitung: Der Völkermord an den Armeniern, die Türkei und Europa' in Hans-Lukas Kieser and Elmar Plozza (eds), *Der Völkermord an den Armeniern, die Türkei und Europa / The Armenian Genocide, Turkey and Europe* (Chronos 2006).

King Jr. HT, 'Genocide and Nuremberg' in Paul Behrens and Ralph Henham (eds), *The Criminal Law of Genocide. International, Comparative and Contextual Aspects* (Ashgate 2007).

Kirsch S, 'The Two Notions of Genocide: Distinguishing Macro Phenomena and Individual Misconduct' in Eckart Conze and Christoph Safferling (eds), *The Genocide Convention Sixty Years After its Adoption* (TMC Asser Press 2010).

Klid B and Motyl AJ, 'Introduction' in Bohdan Klid and Alexander J Motyl (eds), *The Holodomor Reader. A Sourcebook on the Famine of 1932–1933 in Ukraine* (Canadian Institute of Ukrainian Studies Press 2012).

Klose F, '"A War of Justice and Humanity": Abolition and Establishing Humanity as an International Norm' in Fabian Klose and Mirjam Thulin (eds), *Humanity A History of European Concepts in Practice From the Sixteenth Century to the Present* (Vandenhoeck & Ruprecht 2016).

Kraft C, 'Nationalisierende Transnationalisierung. (Inter)nationale Strafrechtswissenschaft in der Zwischenkriegszeit' in Dietmar Müller and Adamantios Skordos (eds), *Leipziger Zugänge zur rechtlichen, politischen und kulturellen Verflechtungsgeschichte Ostmitteleuropas* (Leipziger Universitätsverlag 2015).

Kühne H, 'Die Ausrottungsfeldzüge der Kaiserlichen Schutztruppen in Afrika' in Commission Internationale d'Histoire Militaire (ed), *Actes du 4. Colloque International d'Historie Militaire (Ottawa, 23–25 VIII 1978)* (Ministère de la Défense nationale du Canada 1979).

Kulchytsky S, 'Defining the Holodomor as Genocide' in Lubomyr Y Luciuk (ed), *Holodomor: Reflections on the Great Famine of 1932–1933 in Soviet Ukraine* (Kashtan Press 2008).

Kul'chyts'kyi S, 'The Holodomor and Its Consequences in the Ukrainian Countryside' in Andrea Graziosi, Lubomyr A Hajda and Halyna Hryn (eds), *After the Holodomor. The Enduring Impact of the Great Famine on Ukraine* (Harvard University Press 2013).

Kul'chyts'kyi S, 'The Holodomor of 1932–1933: How and Why?' in Andrij Makuch and Frank E Sysyn (eds), *Contextualising the Holodomor. The Impact of Thirty Years of Ukrainian Famine Studies* (Canadian Institute of Ukrainian Studies Press 2015).

Kulchytskyi SV, 'Holodomor in Ukraine 1932–1933: An Interpretation of Facts' in Vincent Comerford, Lindsay Janssen and Christian Noack (eds), *Holodomor and Gorta Mór. Histories, Memories and Representations of Famine in Ukraine and Ireland* (Anthem Press 2012).

Kuper L, *Genocide. Its Political Use in the Twentieth Century* (Yale University Press 1982).

Kuper L, 'Types of Genocide and Mass Murder' in Israel W Charny (ed), *Toward the Understanding and Prevention of Genocide. Proceedings of the International Conference on the Holocaust and Genocide* (Westview Press 1984).

Kuper L, 'The Turkish Genocide of Armenians, 1915–1917' in Richard G Hovannisian (ed), *The Armenian Genocide in Perspective* (Transaction Books 1986).

Kuper L, 'Other Selected Cases of Genocide and Genocidal Massacres: Types of Genocide' in Israel W Charny (ed), *Genocide. A Critical Bibliographical Review* (Facts on File Publications 1988).

Kuper L, 'Foreword' in Israel W Charny (ed), *Genocide. A Critical Bibliographical Review. Volume Two* (Facts on File Publication 1991).

Kuromiya H, 'The Great Famine: The Issue of Intentionality' in Lubomyr Y Luciuk (ed), *Holodomor: Reflections on the Great Famine of 1932–1933 in Soviet Ukraine* (Kashtan Press 2008).

Landwehr A, *Geschichte Des Sagbaren. Einführung in Die Historische Diskursanalyse* (2nd edn, Edition Diskord 2004).

Landwehr A, *Historische Diskursanalyse* (Campus 2009).

Lang B, 'The Concept of Genocide' in A Dirk Moses (ed), *Genocide. Critical Concepts in Historical Studies. Volume I. The Discipline of Genocide Studies* (Routledge 2010).

LeBlanc L, 'The United States and the Genocide Convention: The Sovereignty Package in Perspective' in Harmen G van der Wilt and others (eds), *The Genocide Convention: The Legacy of 60 Years* (Martinus Nijhoff 2012).

Lemkin R, *Axis Rule in Occupied Europe. Laws of Occupation, Analysis of Government, Proposals for Redress* (Carnegie Endowment for International Peace 1944).

Lemkin R, 'Genocide. A Modern Crime' (1945) 4 *Free World* 39.

Lemkin R, 'Genocide' (1946) XV *American Scholar* 227.

Lemkin R, 'Genocide as a Crime under International Law' (1947) 41 *American Journal of International Law* 145.

Levene M, *Genocide in the Age of the Nation-State. Volume I: The Meaning of Genocide* (I.B. Tauris 2005).

Levene M, *Genocide in the Age of the Nation-State. Volume II: The Rise of the West and the Coming of Genocide* (I.B. Tauris 2005).

Lewis DL, *The Race to Fashoda. European Colonialism and African Resistance in the Scramble for Africa* (Bloomsbury 1988).

Lindqvist S, *Exterminate All the Brutes* (Granta Books 1996).

Linke A, 'Kulturelles Gedächtnis. Linguistische Perspektiven auf ein kulturwissenschaftliches Forschungsfeld' in Dietrich Busse, Thomas Niehr and Martin Wengeler (eds), *Brisante Semantik. Neuere Konzepte und Forschungsergebnisse einer kulturwissenschaftlichen Linguistik* (Max Niemeyer 2005).

Lippman M, 'The Convention on the Prevention and Punishment of the Crime of Genocide: Fifty Years Later' (1998) 15 *Arizona Journal of International and Comparative Law* 415.

Louis WR and Stengers J (eds), *E.D. Morel's History of the Congo Reform Movement* (Clarendon Press 1968).

Luciuk LY, 'Foreword: What Was Sown Shall Be Reaped' in Lubomyr Y Luciuk (ed), *Holodomor: Reflections on the Great Famine of 1932–1933 in Soviet Ukraine* (Kashtan Press 2008).

Luciuk LY, *Holodomor: Reflections on the Great Famine of 1932–1933 in Soviet Ukraine* (Kashtan Press 2008).

Mace JE, 'The Man-Made Famine of 1933 in the Soviet Ukraine: What Happened and Why?' in Israel W Charny (ed), *Toward the Understanding and Prevention of Genocide. Proceedings of the International Conference on the Holocaust and Genocide* (Westview Press 1984).

Mace JE, 'The Man-Made Famine of 1933 in Soviet Ukraine' in Bohdan Krawchenko and Roman Serbyn (eds), *Famine in Ukraine 1932–1933* (University of Toronto Press 1986).

Mace JE, 'Genocide in the U.S.S.R.' in Israel W Charny (ed), *Genocide. A Critical Bibliographical Review* (Facts on File Publications 1988).

Mace JE, 'The American Press and the Ukrainian Famine' in Helen Fein (ed), *Genocide Watch* (Yale University Press 1992).

Mace JE, 'Is the Ukrainian Genocide a Myth?' in Lubomyr Y Luciuk (ed), *Holodomor: Reflections on the Great Famine of 1932–1933 in Soviet Ukraine* (Kashtan Press 2008).

Mamdani M, 'The Politics of Naming. Genocide, Civil War, Insurgency' in A Dirk Moses (ed), *Genocide. Critical Concepts in Historical Studies. Volume I. The Discipline of Genocide Studies* (Routledge 2010).

Marples DR, 'Ethnic Issues in the Famine of 1932–1933 in Ukraine' in Vincent Comerford, Lindsay Janssen and Christian Noack (eds), *Holodomor and Gorta Mór. Histories, Memories and Representations of Famine in Ukraine and Ireland* (Anthem Press 2012).

Martin T, *The Affirmative Action Empire. Nations and Nationalism in the Soviet Union, 1923–1939* (Cornell University Press 2001).

McConnell-Ginet S, 'Words in the World: How and Why Meanings Can Matter' (2008) 84 *Language* 497.

Meiches B, *The Politics of Annihilation. A Genealogy of Genocide* (University of Minnesota Press 2019).

Melson R, 'Provocation or Nationalism: A Critical Inquiry into the Armenian Genocide of 1915' in Richard G Hovannisian (ed), *The Armenian Genocide in Perspective* (Transaction Books 1986).

Melson R, *Revolution and Genocide: On the Origins of the Armenian Genocide and the Holocaust* (University of Chicago Press 1992).

Melson R, 'Problems in the Comparison of the Armenian Genocide and the Holocaust: Definitions, Typologies, Theories, and Fallacies' in Stig Förster and Gerhard Hirschfeld (eds), *Genozid in der modernen Geschichte* (Lit Verlag 1999).

Méndez JE, 'The United Nations and the Prevention of Genocide' in Ralph Henham and Paul Behrens (eds), *The Criminal Law of Genocide. International, Comparative and Contextual Aspects* (Ashgate 2007).

Midlarsky MI, *The Killing Trap. Genocide in the Twentieth Century* (Cambridge University Press 2005).

Morel ED, *Red Rubber. The Story of the Rubber Slave Trade Flourishing on the Congo in the Year of Grace 1906* (The Nassau Print 1906).

Moses AD (ed), *Genocide and Settler Society. Frontier Violence and Stolen Indigenous Children in Australian History* (Berghahn Books 2004).

Moses AD, 'Genocide and Settler Society in Australian History' in A Dirk Moses (ed), *Genocide and Settler Society. Frontier Violence and Stolen Indigenous Children in Australian History* (Berghahn Books 2004).

Moses AD, 'Preface' in A Dirk Moses (ed), *Genocide and Settler Society. Frontier Violence and Stolen Indigenous Children in Australian History* (Berghahn Books 2004).

Moses AD (ed), *Empire, Colony Genocide. Conquest, Occupation, and Subaltern Resistance in World History* (Berghahn Books 2008).

Moses AD, 'Introduction: The Field of Genocide Studies' in A Dirk Moses (ed), *Genocide. Critical Concepts in Historical Studies. Volume I. The Discipline of Genocide Studies* (Routledge 2010).

Moses AD, 'Raphael Lemkin, Culture, and the Concept of Genocide' in Donald Bloxham and A Dirk Moses (eds), *The Oxford Handbook of Genocide Studies* (Oxford University Press 2010).

Moses AD and Stone D, 'Introduction', in A. Dirk Moses and Dan Stone (eds), *Colonialism and Genocide* (Routledge 2007).

Motyl AJ, 'Looking at the Holodomor Through the Lens of the Holocaust' in Lubomyr Y Luciuk (ed), *Holodomor: Reflections on the Great Famine of 1932–1933 in Soviet Ukraine* (Kashtan Press 2008).

Moyn S, *The Last Utopia. Human Rights in History* (Belknap Press of Harvard University Press 2010).

Müller D, 'Zu den Anfängen des Völkerstrafrechts. Vespasian Pella und Raphael Lemkin' in Dietmar Müller and Adamantios Skordos (eds), *Leipziger Zugänge zur rechtlichen, politischen und kulturellen Verflechtungsgeschichte Ostmitteleuropas* (Leipziger Universitätsverlag 2015).

Naimark NM, *Fires of Hatred. Ethnic Cleansing in Twentieth-Century Europe* (Harvard University Press 2001).

Naimark NM, *Stalin's Genocides* (Princeton University Press 2010).

Naimark NM, 'How the Holodomor Can Be Integrated into Our Understanding of Genocide' in Andrij Makuch and Frank E Sysyn (eds), *Contextualising the Holodomor. The Impact of Thirty Years of Ukrainian Famine Studies* (Canadian Institute of Ukrainian Studies Press 2015).

Naimark NM, *Genocide. A World History* (Oxford University Press 2017).

Nordbruch C, *Völkermord an den Herero in Deutsch-Südwestafrika? Widerlegung einer Lüge* (Grabert 2004).

Nuhn W, *Sturm Über Südwest. Der Hereroaufstand von 1904 - Ein Düsteres Kapitel Der Deutschen Kolonialen Vergangenheit Namibias* (Bernard & Graefe Verlag 1989).

Nzongola-Ntalaja G, *The Congo. From Leopold to Kabila. A People's History* (Zed Books 2002).

Oermann NO, *Mission, Church and State Relations in South West Africa Under German Rule (1884–1915)* (Franz Steiner Verlag 1999).

Ohandjanian A, *1915. Irrefutable Evidence. The Austrian Documents on the Armenian Genocide* (Republic of Armenia National Academy of Sciences Museum-Institute of the Armenian Genocide 2006).

O'Neill KL, 'Anthropology and Genocide' in Donald Bloxham and A Dirk Moses (eds), *The Oxford Handbook of Genocide Studies* (Oxford University Press 2010).

Osiel M, *Mass Atrocity, Collective Memory, and the Law* (Transaction Publishers 1997).

Ostler J, *Surviving Genocide. Native Nations and the United States from the American Revolution to Bleeding Kansas* (Yale University Press 2019).

Pakenham T, *The Scramble for Africa. White Man's Conquest of the Dark Continent From 1876 to 1912* (Avon Books 1992).

Pamuk H, 'In Historic Move, Biden Says 1915 Massacres of Armenians Constitute Genocide' *Reuters* (24 April 2021) <https://www.reuters.com/world/middle-east/biden-says-1915-massacres-armenians-constitute-genocide-2021-04-24/>

Parsons WS and Totten S, 'Introduction' in William S Parsons and Samuel Totten (eds), *Century of Genocide. Critical Essays and Eyewitness Accounts* (3rd edn, Routledge 2009).

Paulus AL and Simma B, 'The Responsibility of Individuals for Human Rights Abuses in Internal Conflicts: A Positivist View' (1999) 93 *American Journal of International Law* 302.

Poewe K, *The Namibian Herero. A History of Their Psychosocial Disintegration and Survival* (Edwin Mellen Press 1985).

Power S, *A Problem from Hell. America and the Age of Genocide* (Basic Books 2013).

Pyrih R, *Holodomor of 1932–33 in Ukraine. Documents and Materials* (Kyiv Mohyla Academy 2008).

Quigley J, *The Genocide Convention. An International Law Analysis* (Ashgate 2006).

Radbruch G, 'Gesetzliches Unrecht und übergesetzliches Recht' (1946) 1 *Süddeutsche Juristenzeitung* 105.

Ratner SR, 'Labeling Mass Atrocity: Does and Should International Criminal Law Rank Evil?' (2008) 54 *Wayne Law Review* 569.

Rayfield D, 'The Ukrainian Famine of 1933: Man-Made Catastrophe, Mass Murder, or Genocide?' in Lubomyr Y Luciuk (ed), *Holodomor: Reflections on the Great Famine of 1932–1933 in Soviet Ukraine* (Kashtan Press 2008).

Renton D, Seddon D and Zeilig L, *The Congo. Plunder & Resistance* (Zed Books 2007).

Ringrose ME, 'The Politicization of the Genocide Label: Genocide Rhetoric in the UN Security Council' (2020) 14 *Genocide Studies and Prevention: An International Journal* 124.

Robinson D, 'Defining "Crimes Against Humanity" at the Rome Conference' (1999) 93 *American Journal of International Law* 43.

Rubin AP, *Ethics and Authority in International Law* (Cambridge University Press 1997).

Rubinstein WD, *Genocide: A History* (Pearson Longman 2004).

Rudnyckyj JB, 'Linguicide: Concept and Definition' in Israel W Charny (ed), *Toward the Understanding and Prevention of Genocide. Proceedings of the International Conference on the Holocaust and Genocide* (Westview Press 1984).

Rummel RJ, *Statistics of Democide. Genocide and Mass Murder since 1900* (Lit Verlag 1998).

Sadat LN, 'A Comprehensive History of the Proposed International Convention on the Prevention and Punishment of Crimes Against Humanity' in Leila Nadya Sadat (ed), *Forging a Convention for Crimes Against Humanity* (Cambridge University Press 2011).

Sadat LN, *Forging a Convention for Crimes Against Humanity* (Cambridge University Press 2011).

Sadat LN, 'Preface and Acknowledgments' in Leila Nadya Sadat (ed), *Forging a Convention for Crimes Against Humanity* (Cambridge University Press 2011).

Samuel M, 'From Aggression to Atrocity: Rethinking the History of International Criminal Law' in Kevin Jon Heller and others (eds), *The Oxford Handbook of International Criminal Law* (Oxford University Press 2020).

Sands P, *East West Street. On the Origins of Genocide and Crimes Against Humanity* (Weidenfeld & Nicolson 2017).

Sarkin J, *Germany's Genocide of the Herero: Kaiser Wilhelm II, His General, His Settlers, His Soldiers* (UCT Press / James Currey 2011).

Sarkissian R, 'The Armenian Genocide; A Contextual View of the Crime and Politics of Denial' in Ralph Henham and Paul Behrens (eds), *The Criminal Law of Genocide. International, Comparative and Contextual Aspects* (Ashgate 2007).

Sartre J-P, 'On Genocide' (1968) VI *Ramparts* 35.

Saul B, 'The Implementation of the Genocide Convention at the National Level' in Paola Gaeta (ed), *The UN Genocide Convention: A Commentary* (Oxford University Press 2009).

Saunders D, 'The Starvation of Ukrainians in 1933: By-Product or Genocide?' in Lubomyr Y Luciuk (ed), *Holodomor: Reflections on the Great Famine of 1932–1933 in Soviet Ukraine* (Kashtan Press 2008).

Schabas WA, 'Crimes Against Humanity' in Dinah L Shelton (ed), *Encyclopedia of Genocide and Crimes Against Humanity. Vol. 1 [A-H]* (Thomson Gale 2005).

Schabas WA, 'Semantics or Substance? David Scheffer's Welcome Proposal to Strengthen Criminal Accountability for Atrocities' (2007) 2 *Genocide Studies and Prevention: An International Journal* 31.

Schabas WA, *Genocide in International Law. The Crime of Crimes* (2nd edn, Cambridge University Press 2009).

Schabas WA, 'Genocide in International Law and International Relations Prior to 1948' in Eckart Conze and Christoph Safferling (eds), *The Genocide Convention Sixty Years After its Adoption* (TMC Asser Press 2010).

Schabas WA, 'The Law and Genocide' in Donald Bloxham and A Dirk Moses (eds), *The Oxford Handbook of Genocide Studies* (Oxford University Press 2010).

Schabas WA, 'Genocide and Crimes against Humanity: Clarifying the Relationship' in Harmen G van der Wilt and others (eds), *The Genocide Convention: The Legacy of 60 Years* (Martinus Nijhoff 2012).

Schabas WA, *Unimaginable Atrocities. Justice, Politics, and Rights at the War Crimes Tribunals* (Oxford University Press 2012).

Schaller DJ, 'Der Völkermord an den Armeniern im Osmanischen Reich, 1915–1917. Ereignis Historiographie und Vergleich' in Vivianne Berg and others (eds), *Enteignet – Vertrieben – Ermordet. Beiträge zur Genozidforschung* (Chronos 2004).

Schaller DJ, 'Genozidforschung: Begriffe und Debatten. Einleitung' in Vivianne Berg and others (eds), *Enteignet – Vertrieben – Ermordet. Beiträge zur Genozidforschung* (Chronos 2004).

Schaller DJ, 'Kolonialkrieg, Völkermord und Zwangsarbeit in "Deutsch-Südwestafrika"' in Vivianne Berg and others (eds), *Enteignet – Vertrieben – Ermordet. Beiträge zur Genozidforschung* (Chronos 2004).

Schaller DJ, 'Raphael Lemkin's View of European Colonial Rule in Africa: Between Condemnation and Admiration' (2005) 7 *Journal of Genocide Research* 531.

Schaller DJ, 'From Conquest to Genocide. Colonial Rule in German Southwest Africa and German East Africa' in A Dirk Moses (ed), *Empire, Colony Genocide. Conquest, Occupation, and Subaltern Resistance in World History* (Berghahn Books 2008).

Schaller DJ, 'Genocide and Mass Violence in "The Heart of Darkness": Africa in the Colonial Period' in Donald Bloxham and A Dirk Moses (eds), *The Oxford Handbook of Genocide* (Oxford University Press 2010).

Schaller DJ, 'Genocide in Colonial South-West Africa: The German War against the Herero and Nama, 1904–1907' in Robert K Hitchcock and Samuel Totten (eds), *Genocide of Indigenous Peoples. A Critical Bibliographic Review* (Routledge 2011).

Scheffer D, 'Genocide and Atrocity Crimes' (2006) 1 *Genocide Studies and Prevention: An International Journal* 229.

Scheffer D, 'Atrocity Crimes Framing the Responsibility to Protect' (2007) 40 *Case Western Reserve Journal of International Law* 111.

Scheffer D, 'The Merits of Unifying Terms: "Atrocity Crimes" and "Atrocity Law"' (2007) 2 *Genocide Studies and Prevention: An International Journal* 91.

Scheffer D, 'The Future of Atrocity Law' (2001-2002) 25 *Suffolk Transnational Law Review* 389.

Schrank GI, 'German South West Africa: Social and Economic Aspects of Its History, 1884–1915' (PhD, New York University 1974).

Schwelb E, 'Crimes Against Humanity' (1946) 178 *British Year Book of International Law* 178.

Segesser DM, *Recht statt Rache oder Rache durch Recht? Die Ahndung von Kriegsverbrechen in der internationalen wissenschaftlichen Debatte 1872–1945* (Ferdinand Schöningh 2010).

Sémelin J, *Säubern und Vernichten. Die politische Dimension von Massakern und Völkermorden* (Hamburger Edition 2007).

Serbyn R, 'Ukraine (Famine)' in Dinah L Shelton (ed), *Encyclopedia of Genocide and Crimes Against Humanity. Vol. 3 [T-Z, Index]* (Thomson Gale 2005).

Serbyn R, 'The Ukrainian Famine of 1932–1933 as Genocide in the Light of the UN Convention of 1948' (2006) LXII *The Ukrainian Quarterly* 181.

Serbyn R, 'The Holodomor: Genocide Against the Ukrainians' in Lubomyr Y Luciuk (ed), *Holodomor: Reflections on the Great Famine of 1932–1933 in Soviet Ukraine* (Kashtan Press 2008).

Serbyn R, 'Lemkin on Genocide of Nations' (2009) 7 *Journal of International Criminal Justice* 123.

Shany Y, 'The Road to the Genocide Convention and Beyond' in Paola Gaeta (ed), *The UN Genocide Convention: A Commentary* (Oxford University Press 2009).

Shapoval Y, 'The Struggle for History: Recognizing the Holodomor' in Lubomyr Y Luciuk (ed), *Holodomor: Reflections on the Great Famine of 1932–1933 in Soviet Ukraine* (Kashtan Press 2008).

Shapoval Y, 'Understanding the Causes and Consequences of the Famine-Genocide of 1932–1933 in Ukraine: The Significance of Newly Discovered Archival Documents' <http://faminegenocide.com/print/resources/shapoval.htm>

Shaw M, 'Sociology and Genocide' in Donald Bloxham and A Dirk Moses (eds), *The Oxford Handbook of Genocide Studies* (Oxford University Press 2010).

Shaw M, *What Is Genocide?* (2nd edn, Polity Press 2015).

Shelton DL (ed), *Encyclopedia of Genocide and Crimes Against Humanity* (Thomson Gale 2005).

Siegelberg ML, 'Unofficial Men, Efficient Civil Servants: Raphael Lemkin in the History of International Law' (2013) 15 *Journal of Genocide Research* 297.

Simpson G, 'History of Histories' in Kevin Jon Heller and Gerry Simpson (eds), *The Hidden Histories of War Crimes Trials* (Oxford University Press 2013).

Slade R, *King Leopold's Congo. Aspects of the Development of Race Relations in the Congo Independent State* (Greenwood Press 1962).

Sloan J, 'Civilized Nations' *Max Planck Encyclopedia of Public International Law* <http://opil.ouplaw.com/home/EPIL>

Sluiter G, '"Chapeau Elements" of Crimes Against Humanity in the Jurisprudence of the UN Ad Hoc Tribunals' in Leila Nadya Sadat (ed), *Forging a Convention for Crimes Against Humanity* (Cambridge University Press 2011).

Smith RW, 'Denial of the Armenian Genocide' in Israel W Charny (ed), *Genocide. A Critical Bibliographical Review. Volume Two* (Facts on File Publications 1991).

Smith RW, 'State Power and Genocidal Intent: On the Uses of Genocide in the Twentieth Century' in Levon Chorbajian and George Shirinian (eds), *Studies in Comparative Genocide* (Palgrave Macmillan/St Martin's Press 1999).

Snyder T, *Bloodlands. Europe Between Hitler and Stalin* (The Bodley Head 2010).

Stanard MG, *Selling the Congo. A History of European Pro-Empire Propaganda and the Making of Belgian Imperialism* (University of Nebraska Press 2011).

Stannard DE, *American Holocaust. The Conquest of the New World* (Oxford University Press 1992).

Stapleton TJ, *A Military History of Africa. Volume 2. The Colonial Period: From the Scramble for Africa to the Algerian Independence War (ca. 1870–1963)* (Praeger 2013).

Stapleton TJ, 'Herero and Nama Genocide (1904–1907)' in Timothy J Stapleton (ed), *Encyclopedia of African Colonial Conflicts. Volume I: A-H* (ABC-CLIO 2017).

Stengers J, 'Morel and Belgium' in William Roger Louis and Jean Stengers (eds), *E.D. Morel's History of the Congo Reform Movement* (Clarendon Press 1968).

Stengers J, 'The Congo Free State and the Belgian Congo Before 1914' in Peter Duignan and Lewis H Gann (eds), *Colonialism in Africa 1870–1960. Volume 1. The History and Politics of Colonialism 1870–1914* (Cambridge University Press 1969).

Stolleis M, 'Der Historiker als Richter – der Richter als Historiker' in Norbert Frei, Dirk van Laak and Michael Stolleis (eds), *Geschichte vor Gericht. Historiker, Richter und die Suche nach Gerechtigkeit* (CH Beck 2000).

Stone D, 'Introduction' in Dan Stone (ed), *The Historiography of Genocide* (Palgrave Macmillan 2008).

Stone D (ed), *Historiography of Genocide* (Palgrave Macmillan 2010).

Sudholt G, *Die deutsche Eingeborenenpolitik in Südwestafrika. Von den Anfängen bis 1904* (Georg Olms Verlag 1975).

Sysyn F, 'The Ukrainian Famine of 1932–3: The Role of the Ukrainian Diaspora in Research and Public Discussion' in Levon Chorbajian and George Shirinian (eds), *Studies in Comparative Genocide* (Palgrave Macmillan/St Martin's Press 1999).

Sysyn F, 'Thirty Years of Research on the Holodomor: A Balance Sheet' in Andrij Makuch and Frank E Sysyn (eds), *Contextualising the Holodomor. The Impact of Thirty Years of Ukrainian Famine Studies* (Canadian Institute of Ukrainian Studies Press 2015).

Szawłowski R, 'Raphael Lemkin (1900–1959). The Polish Lawyer Who Created the Concept of "Genocide"' (2005) 2 *The Polish Quarterly of International Affairs* 98.

Tams CJ, Berster L and Schiffbauer B, 'General Introduction' in Christian J Tams, Lars Berster and Björn Schiffbauer (eds), *Convention on the Prevention and Punishment of the Crime of Genocide: A Commentary* (CH Beck/Hart/Nomos 2014).

Tanner J, 'Der Historiker und der Richter. Der Genozid an den Armeniern und die Genozidforschung aus rechtlicher und geschichtswissenschaftlicher Sicht' in Hans-Lukas Kieser and Elmar Plozza (eds), *Der Völkermord an den Armeniern, die Türkei und Europa / The Armenian Genocide, Turkey and Europe* (Chronos 2006).

Ternon Y, *L'État Criminel. Les Génocides au XXe Siècle* (Seuil 1995).

Theriault HC, 'Genocidal Mutation and the Challenge of Definition' (2010) 41 *Metaphilosophy* 481.

Theriault HC and Totten S, *The United Nations Genocide Convention. An Introduction* (University of Toronto Press 2020).

Thom F, 'Reflections on Stalin and the Holodomor' in Andrij Makuch and Frank E Sysyn (eds), *Contextualising the Holodomor. The Impact of Thirty Years of Ukrainian Famine Studies* (Canadian Institute of Ukrainian Studies Press 2015).

Time (17 August 1992).

Totten S (ed), *Advancing Genocide Studies. Personal Accounts and Insights from Scholars in the Field* (Transaction Publishers 2015).

Toynbee AJ, *Armenian Atrocities. The Murder of a Nation* (Hodder & Stoughton 1915).

Troebst S, 'Eastern Europe's Imprint on Modern International Law' in Annalisa Ciampi (ed), *History and International Law* (Edward Elgar Publishing 2019).

'U.N. Assembly Vote Outlaws Genocide' *Washington Post* (10 December 1948).

Üngör UÜ, *The Making of Modern Turkey. Nation and State in Eastern Anatolia, 1913–1950* (Oxford University Press 2012).

van der Wilt HG and others (eds), *The Genocide Convention: The Legacy of 60 Years* (Martinus Nijhoff 2012).

van Laak D, 'Widerstand gegen die Geschichtsgewalt. Zur Kritik an der "Vergangenheitsbewältigung"' in Norbert Frei, Dirk van Laak and Michael Stolleis (eds), *Geschichte vor Gericht. Historiker, Richter und die Suche nach Gerechtigkeit* (CH Beck 2000).

Van Schaack B, 'The Crime of Political Genocide: Repairing the Genocide Convention's Blind Spot' (1996) 106 *Yale Law Journal* 2259.

Van Schaack B, 'The Definition of Crimes against Humanity: Resolving the Incoherence' (1999) 37 *Columbia Journal of Transnational Law* 787.

Vanthemsche G, *Belgium and the Congo, 1885–1980* (Cambridge University Press 2012).

Vasylyev V, 'The Holodomor Through the Eyes of the Soviet Ukrainian Leadership, 1950–80' in Andrea Graziosi, Lubomyr A Hajda and Halyna Hryn (eds), *After the Holodomor. The Enduring Impact of the Great Famine on Ukraine* (Harvard University Press 2013).

Vervliet J, 'Raphael Lemkin (1900–1959) and the Genocide Convention of 1948. Brief Biographical and Bibliographical Notes' in Harmen van der Wilt and others (eds), *The Genocide Convention: The Legacy of 60 Years* (Martinus Nijhoff 2012).

von Hagen M, 'Wartime Occupation and Peacetime Alien Rule: "Notes and Materials" Toward a(n) (Anti-) (Post-) Colonial History of Ukraine' (2015) 34 *Harvard Ukrainian Studies* 153.

von Lingen K, 'Fulfilling the Martens Clause: Debating "Crimes Against Humanity", 1899–1945' in Fabian Klose and Mirjam Thulin (eds), *Humanity. A History of European Concepts in Practice From the Sixteenth Century to the Present* (Vandenhoeck & Ruprecht 2016).

Vrdoljak AF, 'Human Rights and Genocide: The Work of Lauterpacht and Lemkin in Modern International Law' (2009) 20 *European Journal of International Law* 1163.

Watkins JC and Weber JP (eds), *War Crimes and War Crime Trials: From Leipzig to the ICC and Beyond. Cases, Materials and Comments* (Carolina Academic Press 2006).

Watson A, *Legal Transplants. An Approach to Comparative Law* (2nd edn, University of Georgia Press 1993).

Weisbord RG, 'The King, the Cardinal and the Pope: Leopold II's Genocide in the Congo and the Vatican' (2003) 5 *Journal of Genocide Research* 35.

Weiss-Wendt A, 'Problems in Comparative Genocide Scholarship' in Dan Stone (ed), *The Historiography of Genocide* (Palgrave Macmillan 2008).

Weiss-Wendt A, 'The Soviet Perspective on the Drafting of the UN Genocide Convention' in Harmen G van der Wilt and others (eds), *The Genocide Convention: The Legacy of 60 Years* (Martinus Nijhoff 2012).

Weiss-Wendt A, *A Rhetorical Crime. Genocide in the Geopolitical Discourse of the Cold War* (Rutgers University Press 2018).

Weiss-Wendt A, *Putin's Russia and the Falsification of History. Reasserting Control over Past* (Bloomsbury 2021).

Weitz ED, *A Century of Genocide. Utopias of Race and Nation* (Princeton University Press 2003).

Wellington JH, *South West Africa and Its Human Issues* (The Clarendon Press 1967).

Werfel F, *Die vierzig Tage des Musa Dagh* (Paul Zsolnay 1933).

Werth N, 'The Crimes of the Stalin Regime: Outline for an Inventory and Classification' in Dan Stone (ed), *The Historiography of Genocide* (Palgrave Macmillan 2008).

Werth N, 'Mass Deportations, Ethnic Cleansing, and Genocidal Politics in the Later Russian Empire and the USSR' in Donald Bloxham and A Dirk Moses (eds), *The Oxford Handbook of Genocide Studies* (Oxford University Press 2010).

Werth N, 'Keynote Address for the Holodomor Conference, Harvard Ukrainian Research Institute, 17–18 November 2008' in Andrea Graziosi, Lubomyr A Hajda and Halyna Hryn (eds), *After the Holodomor. The Enduring Impact of the Great Famine on Ukraine* (Harvard University Press 2013).

Werth N, 'Die große ukrainische Hungersnot von 1932/3' in Jörg Baberowski and Robert Kindler (eds), *Macht ohne Grenzen. Herrschaft und Terror im Stalinismus* (Campus Verlag 2014).

Werth N, 'The Great Ukrainian Famine of 1932–33' (*Sciences Po, Mass Violence and Resistance – Research Network*) <https://www.sciencespo.fr/mass-violence-war-massacre-resistance/en/document/great-ukrainian-famine-1932-33>

Winter J, 'Under Cover of War: The Armenian Genocide in the Context of Total War' in Robert Gellately and Ben Kiernan (eds), *The Specter of Genocide. Mass Murder in Historical Perspective* (Cambridge University Press 2003).

Zeller J, '"Ombepera i koza – Die Kälte tötet mich". Zur Geschichte des Konzentrationslagers in Swakopmund (1904–1908)' in Joachim Zeller and Jürgen Zimmerer (eds), *Völkermord in Deutsch-Südwestafrika. Der Kolonialkrieg (1904–1908) in Namibia und seine Folgen* (Ch Links 2003).

Zeller J and Zimmerer J, 'Vorwort' in Joachim Zeller and Jürgen Zimmerer (eds), *Völkermord in Deutsch-Südwestafrika. Der Kolonialkrieg (1904–1908) in Namibia und seine Folgen* (Ch Links 2003).

Zimmerer J, *Deutsche Herrschaft über Afrikaner. Staatlicher Machtanspruch und Wirklichkeit im kolonialen Namibia* (Lit Verlag 2001).

Zimmerer J, 'Krieg, KZ und Völkermord in Südwestafrika. Der erste deutsche Genozid' in Joachim Zeller and Jürgen Zimmerer (eds), *Völkermord in Deutsch-Südwestafrika. Der Kolonialkrieg (1904–1908) in Namibia und seine Folgen* (Ch Links 2003).

Zimmerer J, 'Colonialism and the Holocaust. Towards an Archeology of Genocide' in A Dirk Moses (ed), *Genocide and Settler Society. Frontier Violence and Stolen Indigenous Children in Australian History* (Berghahn Books 2004).

Zimmerer J, 'Kolonialer Genozid? Vom Nutzen und Nachteil einer historischen Kategorie für eine Globalgeschichte des Völkermordes' in Vivianne Berg and others (eds), *Enteignet – Vertrieben – Ermordet. Beiträge zur Genozidforschung* (Chronos 2004).

Zimmerer J, 'Colonial Genocide: The Herero and Nama War (1904–8) in German South West Africa and Its Significance' in Dan Stone (ed), *The Historiography of Genocide* (Palgrave Macmillan 2008).

Zimmerer J, 'Der erste Genozid des 20. Jahrhunderts. Der deutsche Vernichtungskrieg in Südwestafrika (1904–1908) und die Globalgeschichte des Genozids' in Jürgen Zimmerer (ed), *Von Windhuk nach Auschwitz? Beiträge zum Verhältnis von Kolonialismus und Holocaust* (Lit Verlag 2011).

Zimmerer J, 'Holocaust und Kolonialismus. Beitrag zu einer Archäologie des genozidalen Gedankens' in Jürgen Zimmerer (ed), *Von Windhuk nach Auschwitz? Beiträge zum Verhältnis von Kolonialismus und Holocaust* (Lit Verlag 2011).

Zimmerer J, 'Nationalsozialismus postkolonial. Plädoyer zur Globalisierung der deutschen Gewaltgeschichte' in Jürgen Zimmerer (ed), *Von Windhuk nach Auschwitz? Beiträge zum Verhältnis von Kolonialismus und Holocaust* (Lit Verlag 2011).

Zimmerer J, *Von Windhuk nach Auschwitz? Beiträge zum Verhältnis von Kolonialismus und Holocaust* (Lit Verlag 2011).

Zlepko D (ed), *Der ukrainische Hunger-Holocaust. Stalins verschwiegener Völkermord 1932/33 an 7 Millionen ukrainischen Bauern im Spiegel geheimgehaltener Akten des deutschen Auswärtigen Amtes* (Verlag Helmut Wild 1988).

Zlepko D, 'Einführung' in Dmytro Zlepko (ed), *Der ukrainische Hunger-Holocaust. Stalins verschwiegener Völkermord 1932/33 an 7 Millionen ukrainischen Bauern im Spiegel geheimgehaltener Akten des deutschen Auswärtigen Amtes* (Verlag Helmut Wild 1988).

Index

Abdul Hamid II 112, 118–19, 122, 124
abolition 16
activism 55, 67
Adamets, Serguei 135
ad hoc tribunals 7, 24, 33, 35
advocacy. *See* activism
Africa 81–2
al-Bashir, Omar 36
Allilujewa, Nadeschda Sergejewna 143
Alvarez, Alex 67
American Society of International Law 63
Andriewsky, Olga 135
annihilation 3
apartheid 93
Arendt, Hannah 97
Argentieri, Federigo 152
Armenian(s) 17, 106–29. *See also* Cilicia; Circassians; Congress of Berlin; Deir ez-Zor; Joint Declaration of 15 May 1915; Pasha, Mehmed Talaat; Sasun; Soghomon Tehlirian; Treaty of Berlin; Treaty of San Stefano; Urfa; Van
  murder of a nation 17
  Patriarchy 111
Armenocide 114–15
Ascherson, Neal 85
Ashirova, Aygul 134–5
Association Internationale de Droit Pénal 19
Association Internationale du Congo. *See* International Association of the Congo
Atatürk 110
atrocity 10
  atrocity labelling 10–12, 49–72
  crime 15
  term 63, 72
Auschwitz 2–3, 52, 87, 89, 105, 126, 155
Austrian Criminal Code 1 n.3
Axis Rule in Occupied Europe 21–3, 32, 75
Azerbaijan 109

Balint, Jennifer 110, 112
barbarity 20
Barcelona Traction 35
Barth, Boris 41, 52, 80, 86, 99, 120, 149
Battle of Waterberg 91, 100–1, 103, 106
Bauer, Yehuda 123
Beachler, Donald 86
Belgium 81
Bennouna, Mohamed 56, 68
Bergdamara. *See* Nama
Bergen-Belsen 149
Berlin Conference 81, 90–1
Berlin Congress 107
Bezwodne 20
Bilinsky, Yaroslav 144
Bismarck, Otto von 81
Bitlis 108
Bley, Helmut 97
Bloxham, Donald 109, 112–14, 116, 118, 121, 123
Boer War 100, 103
Bosnian War 4
Bridgman, Jon 97, 105

Cambodia. *See* Extraordinary Chambers in the Courts of Cambodia
camps 4, 51, 92, 95–7, 101–5, 126, 150, 154–5. *See also* Auschwitz; Shark Island; Trnopolje
Cannae 97
cannibalism 130, 154
Carnegie Endowment of International Peace 21
cattle plague 91
Chalk, Frank 65, 93–4, 96, 105, 126
Charny, Israel 64, 105, 133, 135, 153–4
children 31, 96, 150

Chorbajian, Levon 112–14, 116–17, 122, 126
Churchill, Winston 1 n.7, 21
Cilicia 108, 118
Circassians 106
civilised nations 17
civil society 4
classicide 64
cleansing. *See* ethnic cleansing
Cocker, Mark 83–4, 93–5, 103
Cold War 56
colonialism 73–7, 92, 97
Colonial Studies 74, 77
Comité d'études du Haut-Congo 81
communicative frameworks 50
Communist bloc 32
comparative law 49
concentration camp. *See* camps
Congo 80–90
  colonialism 77–8
  commission of enquiry 82–3
Congo Free State 81–2
Congo Reform Association 82
Congress of Berlin. *See* Berlin Congress
Conquest, Robert 78, 131–2, 134–5, 139–40, 149
Conrad, Joseph 55, 78, 80, 87
Control Council Law No. 10 37
Cooper, John 85–6, 104
Cornevin, Robert 93–4
Count Three (International Military Tribunal) 25, 40–2
crime(s). *See also* genocide
  against Christianity 17
  against civilization 17
  of crimes 2, 12, 47–8, 53, 55
  hierarchy of 54, 71
  against humanity 3, 16–17, 23–5, 37, 54–5, 63, 82, 84
  against humanity (contextual elements) 39–43, 58, 63, 88, 121, 123, 129, 154–5
  against humanity (custom-based crime) 46
  against humanity (nexus requirement) 23–6, 37–8
  against humanity (state or organizational policy) 40–3, 63, 123, 129, 154–5
  Against Humanity Initiative 45
  scale 54
  war (*see* war crimes)
  without a name 1 n.7, 21
Cuba 33
culling 121
customary international law 6–7, 34–5, 38–9, 45

Dadrian, Vahakn 62, 105, 111–12, 122–3, 126
Darfur 46, 54–5
Davies, Robert 148
death toll estimates 84, 94, 112–14, 135
Deir ez-Zor 154
dekulakization 135, 139
democide 64
deportation 23, 24 n.61, 37–40, 54, 109–11, 116–17, 129, 154. *See also* railway
Deutsche Kolonialgesellschaft für Südwestafrika 91
discourse 11, 66, 153
domaine reservé 31
Drechsler, Horst 93–6, 99, 102, 105
Dumoulin, Michel 86–7
Dunant, Henry 15
Durkheim, Émile 10
Dushnyck, Walter 134–5, 137–8

Eastern Question 17, 106
ECCC. *See* Extraordinary Chambers in the Courts of Cambodia
Eckert, Andreas 101
Eichmann, Adolf 15
Ellman, Michael 148
Emerson, Barbara 87
enslavement. *See* slavery
erga omnes 35
ethnic cleansing 3, 10, 12, 15, 42, 48, 54, 68, 70–1, 74, 99, 109, 116, 157
ethnocide 22, 64
eugenics 104
Evans, Gareth 57
extermination 3, 21, 24 n.61, 25, 37–41, 44, 62, 91, 96–7, 100, 103, 116, 123, 138. *See also* Vernichtungsbefehl
extirpation 119
Extraordinary Chambers in the Courts of Cambodia 35, 39

family history 5
famine 96, 109. *See also* Holodomor
Federal Republic of Germany. *See* Germany
Fein, Helen 63, 65, 111, 113–14
Ferguson, Niall 77, 110, 112, 118, 124, 147–8
Final Solution 60, 103, 103 n.214, 126–8
First, Ruth 94–5
First World War 13, 18, 73, 100, 109, 156
Forty Days of Musa Dagh (book) 78, 108
Foucault, Michel 133
France 42–3
free trade 82

gendercide 64
General Assembly Resolution 95 (I) 27
General Assembly Resolution 96 (I) 2, 26–9
genocidalism 52
genocide 21. *See also* Armenian(s); Auschwitz; classicide; Congo; democide; ethnocide; gendercide; Herero; Holocaust; Holodomor; humanicide; linguicide; Nama; Srebrenica; Trnopolje; Ukraine; victims
  accusation 32, 55–6, 67, 124–5
  activism 55, 67
  adjective 54, 62–3, 84–6, 98, 100–2, 131, 137, 139–41, 144, 146, 151, 156
  advocacy (*see* activism)
  blueprint 101, 122–3, 126–7, 155
  canon 60, 118, 125, 140, 151, 155
  colonial 76
  comparative history 6, 55, 153, 156
  conceptual baggage 10, 50, 79
  Convention (criticism) 58–60
  Convention 2, 29, 31–2, 36, 43, 45, 58, 67
  as the crime of crimes 2, 12, 47–8, 53, 55
  and crimes against humanity 37, 39
  as a crime without a name 1 n.7, 21
  cultural 22, 31, 75
  customary international law 34–5, 39
  definition (adaptation) 61–6, 152
  definition (ambiguity) 68
  definition (transplant) 58, 89
  definition (vulgarization) 66–7
  denial 2, 52, 99, 115 n.292, 117–18, 130, 153
  domestic statutes 33–4
  erga omnes 35
  forcibly transferring children 31
  group identity 3
  hierarchy 3, 47, 54, 71
  history 6, 55, 78
  intent 41, 43–4, 58–60, 62, 71, 83, 117, 136, 152
  ius cogens 35
  master plan 60, 127–8
  media 68
  moral gravity 47
  moral judgment 2, 55–6, 156
  Nuremberg 25–6
  pedigree 7
  peremptory norm 35
  phenomenology 73
  plan 60, 117, 127–8, 139, 142
  political groups 29–31, 33, 138, 152
  popular culture 36
  popular use 58
  Studies (literature) 7–8, 8 n.53, 77
  Studies (methodology) 6
  Studies 5–10, 13, 50, 55, 156
  as a subset of crimes against humanity 42
  suspicion 80
  symbolic capital 11, 53–5, 67, 105, 153, 155, 157
  treaty-based crime 46
  trivialization 68
  typology 62
  USA 32–3
  Webster's International Dictionary 32
George Washington University 46
German Democratic Republic 96
German Federal Archive 94–5
German South-West Africa 90–106
  colonialism 77–8
Germany 90, 96
Gewald, Jan-Bart 95, 98
Gilbert, Martin 85, 100, 112–13
Goldblatt, Israel 94–5

Graziosi, Andrea 134–5, 141–3, 145–6, 150
Greek Civil War 31
Grossman, Vasily 150

Hagenbach, Peter von 7
Hague Convention on the Laws and Customs of War (1899/1907) 16
Hague Regulations 22
Hajda, Lubomyr 143, 149
Harvest of Sorrow (book) 78, 131–2, 139–40, 149
Hasian, Marouf 101, 104
Heart of Darkness (book) 78
Herero 90–106
Hesemann, Michael 111–14, 127–8
Hiroshima 97
Hitler, Adolf 88, 103, 125–6, 150–1
Hochschild, Adam 78, 80, 83–5, 87, 99
Hofmann, Tessa 111, 113, 117, 121–2, 128
Holocaust 2–3, 46, 52, 61, 64, 78
- comparisons 87–9, 101–5, 124–8, 149–52, 154–6
- continuity 101–3, 122–3
- hegemony 53
- memory 2–3, 23, 46–7, 53, 57, 153
- Studies 5, 153–4

Holodomor 80, 129–52. *See also* dekulakization; Russia; Ukraine
Hovannisian, Richard 112–14, 119, 124, 127
Howoritz, Irving 126
Hryn, Halyna 143
Hryshko, Wasyl 133–5, 138–9, 150–1
Hull, Isabel 103, 105
humanicide 64
humanitarian inertia 69–71
humanitarian intervention 1, 5, 12, 57, 157
humanitarian law 13, 96
human rights 7, 31, 43
hybrid tribunals 35

IAGS. *See* International Association of Genocide Scholars
ICC. *See* International Criminal Court
ICJ. *See* International Court of Justice
ICTR. *See* International Criminal Tribunal for Rwanda
ICTY. *See* International Criminal Tribunal for the former Yugoslavia
ILA. *See* International Law Association
immolation 128
inertia. *See* humanitarian inertia
INoGS. *See* International Network of Genocide Scholars
insurgency 120
International Association of Genocide Scholars 8
International Association of Penal Law. *See* Association Internationale de Droit Pénal
International Association of the Congo 81
International Commission of Inquiry on Darfur to the United Nations Secretary General 46, 54–5
International Committee of the Red Cross 15–16
International Congo Society. *See* International Association of the Congo
International Court of Justice 11, 31, 36, 45, 56, 68
- Genocide Convention 45

International Criminal Court 7, 36, 39
- Elements of Crimes 33

international criminal law 5, 7, 15, 19, 33, 50, 71
International Criminal Tribunal for Rwanda 7, 24, 33, 35, 39–40, 43–4, 54
International Criminal Tribunal for the former Yugoslavia 7, 24, 33, 35, 38, 42, 54
International Law Association 19
International Law Commission 46
International Military Tribunal 2, 23–5, 40–2. *See also* Count Three (International Military Tribunal)
- indictment of the major war criminals 25, 41

International Military Tribunal for the Far East 24
International Network of Genocide Scholars 8

International Residual Mechanism for Criminal Tribunals 35
Irvin-Erickson, Douglas 134–6
Islam 109, 121
Istanbul 109
ius cogens 35

Jackson, Joe 83–4
Jacobs, Steven 145
Jobst, Kerstin 133, 135, 148, 150
Joint Declaration of 15 May 1915 17, 47, 116
Jokic, Aleksandar 52
Jonassohn, Kurt 65, 93–4, 98, 105, 126
Jones, Adam 77, 134–5

Kaiser, Hilmar 110, 112
Katz, Stephan 64
Khmer Rouge 39
Kiernan, Ben 98
King, Henry 28
King Leopold's Ghost (book) 78, 80, 84, 87, 99
Klid, Bohdan 140–1
Korean War 57
Kremlin. *See* Russia
Kriegsschuldlüge 100
Kulchytskyi, Stanislav 135, 143–4
Kuper, Leo 97–8, 110, 112–14, 116, 118–19, 121–2
Kurds 107–8
Kuromiya, Hiroaki 134–5, 145

labour camp. *See* camps
Lauterpacht, Hersch 15, 23
  and Raphaël Lemkin 43
League of Nations 19
legal definitions 59
legal profession 4, 71
Legal Transplants (book) 49–50
Leipzig trials 18
Lemberg 20
Lemkin, Raphaël 2, 6, 15, 19, 20
  father of Genocide Studies 6
  and Hersch Lauterpacht 43
  history of genocide 6, 78
  image 28–9
  on the move 20–1
  in New York 27
  norm entrepreneur 19, 32
  in Nuremberg 26
  in Paris 26
  in Poland 20
Leopold II 15, 81
Levene, Mark 68–9, 86, 98–9, 111, 113, 120
Lewis, David 83–4, 87
Lindqvist, Sven 93–4
linguicide 64
Luciuk, Lubomyr 135
Lüderitz Bay 90, 92
lynching 63

Mace, James 42, 133, 135, 140, 151–2
Madrid 20
Marathon 97
Marples, David R. 135
Martens, Friedrich Fromhold 15
Martens clause 16
massacre 3–4, 17–19, 63, 79, 100–1, 103, 109–14, 116, 118–28
mass murder. *See* murder
media 16, 66–9, 82
Meds Yeghern 114
Meiches, Benjamin 52, 63, 69
Melson, Robert 126–7
Meslé, France 134
Mesopotamia 111
Midlarsky, Manus 110, 112–13, 122
modernization 74, 127
Morel, Edmund Dene 82, 85
Motyl, Alexander 140–1, 151
murder 1 n.7, 17, 21, 23, 24 n.61, 30, 32, 37–40, 47, 54–5, 58, 60, 68, 76, 84, 86–8, 99, 101, 104, 106, 109, 119, 126–8, 144, 148
Murphy, Sean 46
mutilation 82, 154

Naimark, Norman 78, 94–5, 99, 113–14, 123–4, 145–7
Nama 90–106
Namibia 90
nationalism 73, 121, 126
nation states 73
Nazi perpetrators 15, 97–8
  colonialism 78
Nietzsche, Friedrich 69
Nordbruch, Claus 99–100
Nuhn, Walter 94

nulla poena sine lege 7, 24, 79
nullum crimen sine lege 7, 24, 79
Nuremberg. *See* International Military Tribunal
Nzongola-Ntalaja, Georges 83–4, 87–8

Oermann, Nils 100
Omaheke desert 91, 96–7, 154
Ottoman Empire. *See* Turkey

Pakenham, Thomas 93–4
Paris Peace Conference 18
Pasha, Mehmed Talaat 15, 17
Pella, Vespasian 15
People for the Ethical Treatment of Animals (PETA) 51–2
peremptory norm 35
Poewe, Karla 95, 99
pogrom 3–4, 63, 96, 119–21, 137
Poland 125
political science 5
Power, Samantha 2
Proposed International Convention on the Prevention and Punishment of Crimes Against Humanity 45
punishment 63, 87, 123, 130, 137
Putin, Vladimir 47
Pyrozhkov, Serhiy 134

race war 102
racism 24, 76, 93, 104, 126–7
Radbruch, Gustaf 24
railway 74, 109. *See also* deportation
Rayfield, Donald 144
Red Cross. *See* International Committee of the Red Cross
Reichskolonialamt 93
Renton, David 88
reparations 2, 79 n.41, 90, 106
resistance 91–2, 96, 108, 130
responsibility to protect 12, 57, 71
restitution 2
revisionism 2, 71 n.1, 99–100, 141
rhetoric 57
Rome Statute 46, 54
Rouge, Khmer 39
Rubber Terror 80
Rubinstein, William 83–4, 86, 101, 104, 110–13, 118, 148
Ruhashyankiko Report 36
Russia 11, 17, 20, 47, 56, 68, 74, 78, 109, 120
  colonialism 77
Russo-Turkish War 106
Rwanda 120. *See also* International Criminal Tribunal for Rwanda

Sarkin, Jeremy 94, 99
Sarkissian, Raffi 128
Sartre, Jean-Paul 75
Sasun 108, 111, 113–14
Saunders, David 144–5
scale. *See* victims
Schabas, William 47, 52, 63
Schaller, Dominik 76, 78, 83–4, 94, 102, 106, 111–14, 126
Schnee, Heinrich 99–100
Schrank, Gilbert 93, 96
Second World War 2, 20, 123, 125
Sedan 97
Segesser, Daniel 111–12
semantics 13–14, 50
Serbia and Montenegro 36
Serbyn, Roman 133, 135, 144
Shapoval, Yuri 150
Shark Island 92
Shaw, Martin 62
Sierra Leone 35
slaughter 63, 76, 85, 98, 119
slavery 24 n.61, 101
Smith, Roger 110, 112–14
Snyder, Timothy 30, 134–5, 147, 154
sociology 5
South Africa 93
Soviet Union. *See* Russia
Special Advisor on the Prevention of Genocide 36
Special Court for Sierra Leone 35
Special Rapporteurs on Genocide 36. *See also* Special Advisor on the Prevention of Genocide
Srebrenica 36
Stalin, Josef 15, 76, 131, 136, 139–52
Stalinism 134, 140–52
Stanley, Henry Morton 81
Stapleton, Timothy 93–4, 98, 104
starvation. *See* famine
Sub-Commission on Prevention of Discrimination and Protection of Minorities

of the Commission on Human rights 36
Sudholt, Gert 95, 97
symbolic capital 53

Tehlirian, Soghomon 17, 20
Ternon, Yves 100, 111–14, 122, 125, 145
Thom, Françoise 151
Time magazine 4
totalitarianism 73, 97
Toynbee, Arnold 15, 17, 118
transformation 73, 139
Treaty of Berlin 107
Treaty of Lausanne 19
Treaty of San Stefano 107
Treaty of Sèvres 18
Treaty of Versailles 18, 18 n.20
Trnopolje 4
Trotha, Lothar von 15, 90–106
Truman, Harry S. 57
Turkey 17–19, 74, 104, 106–29
A Typology of Genocide (article) 62

Ukraine 11, 56, 68, 78, 129
  colonialism 77
  émigré community 132
UN. *See* United Nations
UN High Commissioner for Human Rights 63–4
United Nations 12, 27
United Nations War Crimes Commission 16–17
Universal Declaration of Human Rights 31, 43
Un souvenir de Solférino 15
UNWCC. *See* United Nations War Crimes Commission
uprising. *See* resistance
Urfa 128
US Commission into the study of the Ukrainian Famine 42
use of force 1

Vallin, Jacques 134
Van 109
vandalism 20
Vanthemsche, Guy 89
Vatican 88
Vernichtungsbefehl 90–2, 96, 99, 103, 105
victims 4, 41, 53, 62, 67, 154. *See also* death toll estimates
  number 41, 84–5, 87–8, 153
Völkermord 16, 96–7

war crimes 3, 16, 18–19, 48, 54–5, 63
Warsaw 20
Washington University in St. Louis 45
Waterberg. *See* Battle of Waterberg
Watson, Alan 49
Weisbord, Robert 88
Weitz, Eric 106, 110, 112, 119, 154
Wellington, John 85, 97
Werfel, Franz 78, 108
Werth, Nicolas 135, 149–50
Wheatcroft, Stephen 148
Wheaton, Henry 16
Whitaker Report 36, 67, 79
Whitney R. Harris World Law Institute 45
widespread or systematic attack 40
Wilhelm II of Hohenzollern 18, 92
Winter, Jay 110, 112, 120, 125–6
World War I. *See* First World War
World War II. *See* Second World War

Yishu 128
Young Turks 76, 108, 124–5, 152
Yugoslavia. *See* International Criminal Tribunal for the former Yugoslavia; Serbia and Montenegro; Srebrenica; Trnopolje

Zeller, Joachim 98, 101, 104–5
Zimmerer, Jürgen 98, 101–2, 104
Zlepko, Dmytro 151
Zoryan Institute 8

Made in the USA
Las Vegas, NV
19 September 2026

18e7f644-fbd4-4cce-aab4-cae8e2ddd5bcR02